SAINT ELIZABETH ANN SETON

Elizabeth Ann Bayley Seton

An engraving of Mother Seton by Charles B. J. Févret de Saint-
Mémin, ca. 1797, which was used for the portrait painted for
the Filicchi family. The portrait was destroyed by the bombing
of World War II. A reproduction appears on the front cover.

JOSEPH I. DIRVIN, C.M.

Saint Elizabeth Ann Seton

A Spiritual Portrait

Second Edition of *The Soul of Elizabeth Seton*

Edited, annotated, and with a foreword by
Sister Betty Ann McNeil, D.C.

IGNATIUS PRESS   SAN FRANCISCO

Cover art: A reproduction of the portrait painted for the
Filicchi family. An engraving of Mother Seton by Charles
B.J. Févret de Saint-Mémin was used for the face, and
the religious dress based on Italian widow's weeds was
painted around it. *Courtesy, Daughters of Charity, Province of
St. Louise, St. Louis, Missouri.* The Provincial Offices of the
Daughters of Charity, Province of St. Louise, are located
in St. Louis, Missouri, but its historic archives are preserved
on the campus of the National Shrine of Saint Elizabeth
Ann Seton, Emmitsburg, Maryland.

Cover design by Enrique Aguilar

CONTENTS

FOREWORD

Saint Elizabeth Ann Seton: A Spiritual Portrait recounts the spiritual and emotional development of the nineteenth-century woman who became the first native-born canonized saint of the United States. Following the writings of this saint, born in the British colony of New York, Father Joseph I. Dirvin, C.M., relates Elizabeth Ann Bayley Seton's unwavering commitment to seek and fulfill the Will of God on her remarkable journey toward holiness. As the only in-depth treatment of Elizabeth's relationship with God based on archival documents, this text is exceptional. All quotations of the saint are from the definitive publication of the Seton Papers, *Elizabeth Bayley Seton Collected Writings*, edited by Regina Bechtle, S.C., and Judith Metz, S.C.

Catholics do not worship saints but honor them—praying to them as friends in heaven. They honor Elizabeth Ann Seton as a model of virtuous living and as an intercessor with God. Her memory lives on because she was so exemplary in her love of God and neighbor, giving the whole world an example of Christian charity. She now intercedes with God for everyone, not just Catholics or Christians.

Contemporary people of faith can see themselves in Elizabeth's story. By discovering her most significant spiritual themes, they gain a better understanding of how faith shaped Elizabeth as a Christian woman whose responses to human experience make her a model for all ages. Elizabeth is every woman, yet unique. Her story is historic but time-less. Her story is real.

In early childhood, Elizabeth endured the heart-wrenching deaths of her mother and baby sister. Her father remarried, and having grown up with a stepmother, Eliz-abeth would understand the issues of blended families and depressed adolescents. Future research could explore whether conflicts in the extended Bayley family may have contributed to Elizabeth's adolescent depression and suicidal ideation and how she resolved not to do "the horrid deed".[1]

Elizabeth married for love. She bore and nursed infants, fretted over fevers, buried two of her children, and wor-ried about the immaturity of her sons. As a mother, she would empathize with parents in their trials and anxiety for their offspring. As the wife of a man who suffered bankruptcy, disease, and death at a young age, she would identify with the courage of families dealing with marital difficulties, financial struggles, and terminal illness.

An exceptionally literate woman for the nineteenth century, Elizabeth was familiar with French and performed proficiently at the piano. With her charming personality, she mingled with Manhattan society but loved solitude and treasured close friendships. After her conversion to Catholicism, the widowed Elizabeth faced immense chal-lenges due to the prevalence of anti-Catholic bigotry such as opposition and ostracism that caused economic hardship for the Setons. Elizabeth struggled to feed her children, but she overcame adversity with grace.

Saint Elizabeth Ann Seton highlights the circuitous paths in the life of this remarkable woman. It illustrates how her

---

[1] 10.4, *Dear Remembrances*, n.d., in Regina Bechtle, S.C., and Judith Metz, S.C., eds., Ellin M. Kelly, mss. ed., *Elizabeth Bayley Seton Collected Writings*, 3 vols. (New York: New City Press, 2000–2006), 3a:513 (hereafter cited as *CW*).

spiritual and human qualities are a wellspring of inspiration. Her love of God arose not from sentimental piety, claims of apparitions, or religious drama but from seeking God as her center. At a time when some ministers preached about God as stern, punitive, and judgmental, Elizabeth, who was familiar with Sacred Scripture, understood the goodness and mercy of God, whom she knew as her Father and her Friend. Embracing the Person and Model of Jesus Christ became the foundation of her faith and spirituality.

Elizabeth's unwavering faith in Christ enabled her to respond wholeheartedly to His call to a new vocation after the death of her husband. Her commitment to a life of service, concern for female education, and devotion to the religious instruction of her pupils enabled Elizabeth to fulfill her mission. An avid reader, the Widow Seton read the writings of Thomas à Kempis and Francis de Sales and the instructions of Vincent de Paul and Louise de Marillac, which influenced her transformation into Mother Seton—a spiritual leader and formator in apostolic spirituality for a mission-driven community.

Mother Seton modeled her community on the Daughters of Charity of Paris. The mission of the American community was the same: to honor Jesus as the source and model of all charity. The Sisters of Charity continue to serve persons in need, provide religious formation and practical education, and care for the sick compassionately in a spirit of humility, simplicity, and charity.

Throughout her life, Elizabeth believed life on earth to be a journey, a passage that required readiness for spending eternity with God. She also anticipated a never-ending reunion in heaven with her loved ones. Elizabeth would often gaze up toward the sky and pray silently.

Father Dirvin directs the reader to accompany Elizabeth on perilous pathways during her lifelong spiritual trek. Hers is a story of faith in God and of human and divine love. Hers is a story of resilience. Hers is a story of perseverance, resourcefulness, and responsiveness to changing circumstances. Hers is a story of starting over with a vision to make education accessible and to relieve suffering with compassion.

Finally, Elizabeth discovered the pearl of great price and taught others: "Good Will, Simplicity, and Confidence are the Keys of the Sanctuary of DIVINE LOVE."[2] Readers learn the secret embedded in the soul of Elizabeth: "[God] is my *guide*, my *friend* and *Supporter*—with such a *guide* can I fear, with such a friend shall I not *be satisfied*, with such a supporter can I fall?"[3] Anyone desiring closer friendship with God could benefit from reading *Saint Elizabeth Ann Seton*.

Sister Betty Ann McNeil, D.C.
Emmitsburg, Maryland
August 28, 2024

---

[2] 10.1, St. Mary Magdalen de Pazzi Notebook, n.d., "Love with Thy Whole Heart", in *CW*, 3a:450. Since nineteenth-century English grammar was not yet standardized, some quotations in this edition have been slightly modified for the convenience of modern readers.

[3] 8.16, "And do I realize it ...", n.d., in *CW*, 3a:32.

A BRIEF HISTORY OF
SAINT ELIZABETH ANN SETON

By Sister Betty Ann McNeil, D.C.

Elizabeth Ann Bayley was born in New York, probably on Long Island, to Catherine Charlton and Dr. Richard Bayley on August 28, 1774. Her birth occurred when delegates from the British colonies in America were traveling to Philadelphia for the First Continental Congress. Loss punctuated her life. Before Elizabeth was three years old, her mother died, possibly due to complications during childbirth. About sixteen months later, her baby sister, Kitty, also died. Elizabeth remembered looking at the clouds at age four, wishing to join her mother and Kitty in heaven. Amid challenging circumstances as an adult, Elizabeth confided in a close friend that she entrusted all to the mercy of God, who never forsakes those who confide in Him.[1]

The Episcopal Years (1774–1804)

The roots of Saint Elizabeth Ann's sanctity lie in her thirty years of worship in the Protestant Episcopal Church in New York. A devout Christian and a fervent communicant,

---

[1] 1.22, Elizabeth Seton to Julia Scott, July 5, 1798, in *CW*, 1:36.

Elizabeth regularly attended Trinity Church on Broadway, where she found solace. She was wed to William Magee Seton (1768–1803), whom she married for love and with whom she enjoyed much happiness. Elizabeth fully embraced her vocation as a wife and mother of five children.

Elizabeth and Rebecca Mary Seton, a sister-in-law and close friend, were devoted to Holy Communion. Trinity Church had several chapels nearby where Sacrament Sundays were scheduled in rotation. Elizabeth and Rebecca went together to participate in the worship service and receive communion wherever Sacrament Sunday was held. Elizabeth had an affinity for reading the Bible and biblical commentaries, often copying passages and making marginal notes. Psalm 23 was Elizabeth's favorite psalm throughout her life.[2]

Elizabeth favored the preaching of Rev. John Henry Hobart, whose stirring sermons inspired her, particularly during liturgical seasons. Frequently, Elizabeth made notes in her journal from what she had heard on Sunday. Sometimes, she simply recorded her sentiments by jotting remarks on cheerfulness, harmony, benevolence, and so on. Elizabeth and other women in Manhattan collaborated to provide emotional support and practical assistance to struggling families whose breadwinners had died, often due to shipwrecks. Their concern resulted in the establishment of the Society for the Relief of Poor Widows with Small Children (1797), of which Elizabeth was the treasurer.[3]

Little did Elizabeth, a socially prominent mother, realize that the kindness she showered on others would soon revert to her elsewhere. As her husband's tubercular condition advanced, Elizabeth and her oldest daughter sailed

---

[2] 10.4, *Dear Remembrances*, n.d., in *CW*, 3a:510.

[3] 1.17, Elizabeth Seton to Julia Scott, n.d., in *CW*, 1:27n3.

with him to Leghorn (Livorno, Italy) hoping that the warm climate would restore his health.[4] Upon arrival at the port, their hopes were dashed.[5]

Elizabeth describes, in riveting detail, the intensity of the harsh conditions of their month-long quarantine in a stone lazaretto battered by loud waves and howling high winds. When released, the Setons settled temporarily in Pisa. There, William Magee Seton died in Elizabeth's arms on December 27, 1803. Elizabeth trusted that all would be well on their return voyage to New York, but she did not envision the transformation yet to come for herself.[6]

Leghorn was an international port for commercial enterprise. Ethnic, cultural, and religious diversity characterized the population, although most were Catholic. The Filicchi family—friends and business associates of the Setons— embraced the young Episcopalian widow and her daughter, welcoming them to their home with gracious hospitality. Invited to visit cultural and historic sites, the Setons accompanied the Filicchi to church and family visits. Elizabeth was awestruck when she realized that Catholics believe God is present in the Blessed Sacrament.[7] When the visitors entered a dimly lit Catholic church in Florence, Elizabeth shed tears freely, enveloped in obscurity.[8]

Elizabeth visited several ancient churches where she delighted at the exuberance of the religious décor. Her wistful widow's heart echoed Mary's joyous canticle, "My

[4] 2.2, Elizabeth Seton to Eliza Sadler, October 3, 1803, CW, 1:244–45.

[5] 2.6, Journal to Rebecca Seton, November 19, [1803], in CW, 1:249–50. Note that throughout this book, brackets around dates in the Collected Writings indicate approximations.

[6] 2.9, Elizabeth Seton to Rebecca Seton, January 6, 1804, in CW, 1:280–81.

[7] 2.11, Elizabeth Seton to Rebecca Seton, January 28, 1804, entry of February 2, in CW, 1:289–90.

[8] 2.10, Florence Journal to Rebecca Seton, [January 1804], in CW, 1:283.

soul does magnify the Lord."[9] The elaborate beauty she saw contrasted with the plain houses of worship in New York. As Elizabeth viewed the life-size painting of the descent of Jesus from the Cross, she had a profound encounter with grace.[10] As a grieving mother, she identified with Mary, the Sorrowful Mother. Elizabeth described how that image engaged her whole soul and was etched in her mind.[11]

Another experience seared Elizabeth's heart but with shame caused by the rudeness of a man whose shrill sarcasm shattered the sacred silence during the Consecration of the Eucharist.[12] At that moment, Elizabeth perceived the Real Presence of Jesus Christ in the Eucharist, and that filled her with awe. She wondered. She pondered the Divine Mystery and even wrote to her sister-in-law expressing how happy she would be if she (Elizabeth) believed that she could find God in the Catholic Church.[13] Witnessing the Blessed Sacrament carried through the streets in processions and publicly adored by the faithful, Elizabeth longed for that same conviction. The Eucharist drew her deeper into prayer for the light of Divine Truth.

During her stay with the Filicchi, Elizabeth discovered a prayer book in which she saw the Memorare.[14] That prayer to the Blessed Virgin Mary touched Elizabeth deeply, moving her to believe that God would not refuse anything to His Mother. Elizabeth, who had lost her mother as a toddler, felt that she had found a mother in Mary. This realization brought her comfort but prompted questions: Was she in the "True Church" of apostolic

---

[9] Ibid., 286, quoting Lk 1:46–47.

[10] Ibid., 287.

[11] Ibid.

[12] 2.11, Elizabeth Seton to Rebecca Seton, January 28, 1804, entry of February 10, in *CW*, 1:290–91.

[13] Ibid., 292–93.

[14] Ibid., 293.

succession?[15] Why is fasting important during Lent? How and why do Catholics make the Sign of the Cross?

Elizabeth read *An Introduction to the Devout Life* by Saint Francis de Sales and pleaded with God to enlighten her. The more she learned about Catholicism, the more Elizabeth felt drawn to the Catholic Church and understood that "FAITH is a gift of God to be diligently sought and earnestly desired."[16]

The brothers Antonio and Filippo Filicchi not only lived their faith but also were well-versed in Catholic doctrine. They took advantage of teachable moments to respond to Elizabeth's inquiries. For example, half in jest, she asked whether the Filicchi wanted her to become Catholic. Filippo's response challenged her: "Pray, and inquire ..., that is all I ask you."[17] Elizabeth studied religious doctrine and prayed for divine guidance for more than a year while she discerned. During that time, she also encountered personal and family trials.

The Catholic Years (1805–1821)

After Elizabeth made her profession of faith in the Catholic Church in 1805,[18] anti-Catholic bigotry and economic hardship became her lot.[19] However, she dealt with misfortune courageously and persevered amid opposition and

---

[15] 3.6, Elizabeth Seton to Bishop John Carroll, [July 26, 1804], in *CW*, 1:315–16.

[16] 3.31, Journal to Amabilia Filicchi, July 19, 1804, entry of November 1, in *CW*, 1:371–72.

[17] 2.11, Elizabeth Seton to Rebecca Seton, January 28, 1804, entry of February 10, in *CW*, 1:290.

[18] 3.31, Journal to Amabilia Filicchi, July 19, 1804, entry of [March 14, 1805], in *CW*, 1:375.

[19] 3.23, Elizabeth Seton to Antonio Filicchi, April 15, [1805], in *CW*, 1:351–52.

unemployment. The memories of religious expressions she had seen in Tuscany remained with Elizabeth, who revered the sacramental life, dogma, and traditions of the Catholic Church. As an active parishioner of Saint Peter's Church, Barclay Street, Elizabeth appreciated the freedom to worship God according to her conscience. Soon, Divine Providence provided another life-changing encounter.

A priest traveling from Maryland to Boston stopped in New York City. There, Rev. William Dubourg met the Widow Seton by chance.[20] When he learned about her difficult circumstances and interest in teaching, Dubourg invited Elizabeth to move to Baltimore, where he envisioned establishing a small school for girls that she could manage. Dubourg, an opportunist, assured Elizabeth that his community, the Priests of Saint-Sulpice, would support his plan and assist Elizabeth in forming a *plan of life*. At that time her sons, twelve-year-old William and ten-year-old Richard, were pupils at Georgetown College, a boarding school in Washington, D.C.[21]

Relying on her heart of hope, Elizabeth with her daughters, Anna Maria, fourteen, Catherine, eight, and Rebecca, six, passed the shores of New York as they sailed confidently up the Chesapeake on the *Grand Sachem* in June 1808.[22] With neither anxiety nor fear, Elizabeth faced an unknown future while gazing at a breathtaking sunset. The young widow's only desire was to fulfill God's plan.[23]

As they disembarked, a heavy rain was drenching Baltimore. Elizabeth and her daughters took a hackney carriage

[20] 4.27, Elizabeth Seton to Bishop John Carroll, November 26, 1806, in *CW*, 1:420. See also 4.26, Elizabeth Seton to Julia Scott, November 10, 1806, in *CW*, 1:419n4.

[21] 5.4, Elizabeth Seton to Antonio Filicchi, July 8, 1808, in *CW*, 2:19.

[22] 5.1, Elizabeth Seton to Cecilia Seton, June 9, 1808, in *CW*, 2:2–4.

[23] Ibid., 2:4–5.

to Saint Mary's Seminary, Paca Street. The new chapel was being dedicated as they entered. The beautiful blend of chant, organ music, and priests in the sanctuary impressed the Setons. The splendid scene filled Elizabeth's heart with joy and gratitude.[24] After the ceremony, everyone warmly welcomed the Setons to their new home, a small French-style brick dwelling next to the seminary.

From that pivotal moment, the Priests of Saint-Sulpice, called Sulpicians, were key to God's plan for Elizabeth. The Sulpicians had emigrated to America during the French Revolution to establish Catholic seminaries to prepare candidates for the priesthood. They were keen to promote the growth of the Catholic Church in the United States. Some had also hoped to educate Catholic girls to be good wives and mothers who would nurture Catholicism in their families. With the support of the Sulpicians, Elizabeth established her first school, which could accommodate eight to ten Catholic girls as tuition-paying boarding pupils.[25] Located in her home, the elementary-level curriculum was virtue-based with religious instruction.

The founder of the Sulpicians, Jean-Jacques Olier (1608–1657), had been a friend of Vincent de Paul (1581–1660) and was acquainted with Louise de Marillac (1591–1660) in Paris. One could say that Sulpicians and Vincentians are "spiritual cousins". After meeting Elizabeth, the Sulpicians perceived her potential and agreed to support her nascent community.[26] Based on their pastoral experience, they concluded that the Daughters of Charity, cofounded by Vincent de Paul and Louise de Marillac

[24] Ibid., 6–7.
[25] 5.15, Elizabeth Seton to Eliza Sadler, January 20, 1809, in *CW*, 2:48.
[26] Annabelle M. Melville, *Louis William Dubourg*, 2 vols. (Chicago: Loyola University Press, 1986), 1:177.

in Paris in 1633, was the most appropriate model for a community in America.[27] Like Louise, Elizabeth was a widowed mother and would retain responsibility for her young children.

The mission of the American Sisters of Charity was to alleviate suffering among the destitute of society; therefore, they would not be cloistered. Members would fulfill their baptismal consecration by annual vows, renewed each year on the feast of the Annunciation, instead of public, perpetual vows.[28] When Elizabeth pronounced vows privately before Archbishop John Carroll on March 25, 1809, the archbishop gave her the title of Mother Seton.

Mother Seton and her Sisters adopted and adapted the *Common Rules of the Daughters of Charity.*[29] Therefore, she was the first to enculturate the spirit of Vincent de Paul and Louise de Marillac in North America.[30] Cecilia

[27] 6.59 Elizabeth Seton to Archbishop John Carroll, n.d., in *CW*, 2:157n2.

[28] 6.70, Elizabeth Seton to Catherine Dupleix, [February 4, 1811], in *CW*, 2:172n4. See also 7.80, Elizabeth Seton to Rev. Simon Bruté, P.S.S., [March 25,] 1817, in *CW*, 2:470n2.

[29] A-12.3, Rule of 1812, in *CW*, 3b:499–530. See also 6.59 Elizabeth Seton to Archbishop John Carroll, n.d., in *CW*, 2:157n2.

[30] Saints Vincent de Paul and Louise de Marillac addressed social problems of seventeenth-century France by organizing a group of women to provide parish-based service to those suffering from poverty and sickness. The people of Paris saw their kindness and compassion and called them Daughters of Charity.

In 1298, Pope Boniface VIII had issued the papal decree *Periculoso*, which required nuns to live secluded within a cloister. Saint Vincent and Saint Louise knew that the Daughters of Charity would not be able to serve those in need if confined to a cloister. Therefore, they organized the group initially as a confraternity (1633) and later as an apostolic community, which was approved by King Louis XIV (1657) and Pope Clement IX (1668). Care of those in need continues to be the *raison d'être* for the Daughters of Charity. Predating the codification of Canon Law (1917) and its revision (1983), today the Company of the Daughters of Charity is a society of apostolic life.

Elizabeth Ann Seton chose the Daughters of Charity as the model for her Sisters of Charity of St. Joseph's (1809). The Seton foundation was not a religious congregation nor were its members women religious. When its Rule and

O'Conway of Philadelphia was the first candidate who arrived.[31] The Sulpician priests actively recruited women among their directees to join Mother Seton in her emerging religious venture. However, it was she, as their religious formator, who assessed, accepted, and instructed candidates. She taught them how to live community life harmoniously, to develop a spiritual life, and to serve persons in need with compassion.

Mother Seton, age thirty-five, and a group of young women between the ages of eighteen and twenty-six were the founding members of the Sisters of Charity of St. Joseph's, the first Catholic Sisterhood native to the United States. A generous benefactor purchased land for educational and other services but specified northern Frederick County instead of Baltimore.[32] The Sulpicians purchased property near Emmitsburg, Maryland, where Catholic families had been settling since 1728.

Women from diverse backgrounds joined the new community. Mother Seton presented a wealth of wisdom and religious formation to those who consecrated themselves to serve God in the new apostolic community. The Sisters of Charity of St. Joseph's, commonly called the American Sisters of Charity, formally began on July 31, 1809, and elected Mother Seton as its leader. The community adopted a way of life and ministries to address the needs of the Catholic Church in America.

The *Regulations for the Society of Sisters of Charity* made the education of girls an apostolic priority. Mother Seton believed that girls from families without financial means

---

Constitutions were approved by Archbishop John Carroll (1812), the Sisters of Charity of St. Joseph's were the first new society of religious women and the first native apostolic community in the United States.

[31] 5.10, Elizabeth Seton to Cecilia Seton, October 6, 1808, in *CW*, 2:34n7.

[32] 5.20, Elizabeth Seton to Julia Scott, March 2, 1809, in *CW*, 2:59.

deserved access to education, which could transform their lives and society. When Archbishop Carroll approved the *Regulations*, the Sisters began a novitiate, a time of formal study and religious formation. Mother Seton and eighteen Sisters pronounced annual vows for the first time in the chapel of Saint Joseph House (today called the White House) on July 19, 1813.[33]

Mother Seton and her Sisters established Saint Joseph School, Emmitsburg, in February 1810. In addition to providing practical education, their mission included teaching the Catholic faith to children, particularly girls from impoverished families. The students attended for free, but the Sisters soon realized their need to generate income to cover expenses. Elizabeth's natural charm and influential connections attracted parents with financial resources who could enroll their daughters as tuition-paying boarders in May 1810.

Saint Joseph School could be considered a prototype of Catholic schools, but it was not a parochial school since it was sponsored by the Sisters of Charity, not by the parish. Although the Ursulines had been educating girls, including day scholars and boarders, and caring for orphans in New Orleans since 1728, Saint Joseph School was the first Catholic school for girls managed and staffed by Sisters in the eastern United States. The Emmitsburg school flourished and expanded, becoming Saint Joseph's Academy in 1828 and Saint Joseph College in 1902.

Mother Seton continued being a mother to her children, pupils, former students, and spiritual daughters. Sadly, two of her daughters were among the early deaths at Emmitsburg: sixteen-year-old Anna Maria in 1812 and fourteen-year-old

---

[33] A-12.4, Constitutions of the Sisters of Charity in the United States of America, First Vow Formula, in *CW*, 3b:563–64. See also 5.17, Elizabeth Seton to Filippo Filicchi, January 21, 1809, in *CW*, 2:53n1.

Rebecca in 1816. When Mother Seton passed away, Catherine was her only child present; her sons were at sea. Catherine lived with her oldest brother until she entered the Sisters of Mercy of New York in 1846 and dedicated her life to prison ministry until her death at age ninety-one. When sailing as a captain's clerk on the *U.S.S. Cyane*, twenty-five-year-old Richard died of typhus after tending to the sick on the coast of Liberia. Commissioned a lieutenant, William served in the U.S. Navy (1826–1834) and died at age seventy-one, predeceased by his wife, Emily Prime. Seven of their children lived to adulthood, but their last direct descendant died in 1967.

Following the mission of the Sisters of Charity, Mother Seton responded to requests and sent Sisters to serve in Philadelphia (1814), Mount Saint Mary's (1815), and New York City (1817). In a letter to a close friend, she expressed her quintessential mission for the Sisters of Charity: "To speak the joy of my soul at the prospect of being able to assist the poor, visit the sick, comfort the sorrowful, clothe little innocents, and teach them to love God!"[34] The Sisters of Charity Federation continues Elizabeth's legacy around the globe in response to the cries of people oppressed by poverty and disease. Her Seton spirit influences not only direct service but also advocacy for social justice at the United Nations.

Elizabeth's life of faith, love, loss, and resilience illustrates how her heart of hope fueled her perseverance. Her love of the will of God and her submission to God's plan are hallmarks of her path to holiness. As a fervent Episcopalian, Elizabeth sought to put on a "Robe of Righteousness" tailored by her "blessed Redeemer".[35] Reflecting on her remarkable life, Rev. Simon Bruté, a Sulpician priest and

---

[34] 5.21, Elizabeth Seton to Julia Scott, March 23, 1809, in *CW*, 2:62.
[35] 8.10, "My peace I leave with you ...," May 1802, in *CW*, 3a:24.

Elizabeth's spiritual director, recorded that compassion was her most outstanding quality.[36]

A decade or so later, as a Catholic spiritual leader and mentor, Mother Seton instructed the Sisters of Charity: "What was the first rule of our dear Savior's life?... You know it was to do His *Father's Will*. Well, then, the first end I propose in our daily work is to do the *Will of God*; secondly, to do it in the manner He wills it; and thirdly, *to do it because it is His Will*."[37]

This notable Vincentian woman died on January 4, 1821, at the age of forty-six. Saint Paul VI proclaimed her Saint Elizabeth Ann Seton in Saint Peter's Square on September 14, 1975. Her remains rest beneath an altar in her honor in the Basilica of the National Shrine of Saint Elizabeth Ann Seton in Emmitsburg, Maryland.

[36] Rev. Simon Bruté to Antonio Filicchi, May 5, 1851, 1-3-3-12:108(3), Archives, Daughters of Charity, Province of St. Louise, Emmitsburg, Md. (hereafter cited as APSL).

[37] Charles I. White, *Life of Mrs. Eliza A. Seton: Foundress and First Superior of the Sisters or Daughters of Charity in the United States of America*, 3rd edition (Baltimore, Md.: John Murphy & Co., 1859), 322.

AUTHOR'S PREFACE
TO THE FIRST EDITION

This contemplation of a great Christian soul is the result of thirty years of research, study, meditation, writing, and lecturing. Thankfully, it seems an endless process. The depths of Saint Elizabeth Ann Seton's spirituality remain unsounded; the facets of her personality and character continue to reveal themselves; her endless attractiveness is ever drawing new friends and clients. The effect of her life and holiness on the lives and holiness, and indeed the salvation, of generations of religious daughters, intimate devotees, and the whole body, past and present, of American Catholics stands evident and shining before the universal Church and society. I have the personal experience of how benevolently she has changed my life as proof of how she has changed, and continues to change, the lives of countless others.

It is the purpose of this extended reflection on the spirituality of Saint Elizabeth Ann Seton to further still her influence on other souls. We shall never know the glorious reaches of her perfection in God, but we can guess at them, at least, through her own unwitting revelations of heroic virtue. It is to authenticate these revelations that I have allowed her to disclose them in her own words, certified by footnotes and citations, lest they be thought of as wishful fantasies of the author's imagination.

Certain citations appear more than once, usually under different circumstances and for different purposes. Citations have not been edited or tampered with, except for obvious lapses in grammar, slight changes—for the sake of clarity—in punctuation and, in a few instances, spelling and the adoption of a uniform system of capitalization (even awkward or archaic usages have been retained). They have been rigorously checked and rechecked against the originals in the saint's own hand or those of her friends and correspondents.

The rock on which Saint Elizabeth Ann Seton's spirituality was built was that special attention to the Person and Model of Jesus Christ characteristic of the great spiritual masters of the seventeenth century—Saint Francis de Sales, Cardinal de Bérulle, Charles de Condren, Saint Vincent de Paul. This Christocentric approach to perfection was further refined by the personalities and callings of individuals. Thus it came to Saint Elizabeth Ann Seton through the minute attention to Christ and love for those in need and the clergy of Vincent de Paul; the preoccupation with sacred training of his disciple Jean-Jacques Olier, the founder of the Sulpicians, who were her directors; its feminine interpretation by Saint Louise de Marillac, who had also been influenced in her early years by the Capuchins Honoré de Champigny, Ange de Joyeuse, and Bênoit de Canfield; and, of course, the familiar but profound teaching of Francis de Sales and his coworker Baroness de Chantal—it was no accident that Simon Gabriel Bruté likened Elizabeth Seton's soul to that of Saint Jane Frances de Chantal—both of whom were spiritual friends and supporters of Saints Vincent and Louise. (It is for this reason that a generous sprinkling of books available in English concerning Vincent and Louise has been included in the bibliography.)

Mrs. Seton was certainly drawn to the Person of Christ in her Episcopalian worship and, of course without knowing it, to the Vincentian apostolate to women and children in need by her work with the Widows' Society. Thus she took quite naturally to the type of religious life suggested to her by Sulpician Father William Dubourg: "In her frequent conferences with her Director [himself]," he has testified, "Mrs. Seton learned that he had thought for a long time of establishing the Daughters of Charity in America; and as the duties of this institute would be compatible with the cares of her family, this virtuous lady expressed a most ardent desire of seeing it commenced and of being herself admitted into it."[1] When Elizabeth had read the Rule of these same Daughters, she had "not a thought discordant" with it. Among her first gifts to her infant community were her own selected translations of the lives of Saints Vincent and Louise. This innate and committed Christocentrism of Elizabeth Seton should, therefore, be kept constantly in mind while studying her soul in the following pages.

I am grateful to Sister Elizabeth Ann Tonroe, D.C., former assistant and counselor for formation, Emmitsburg Province of the Daughters of Charity, whose invitation to mark the 175th anniversary of Mother Seton's community with a series of lectures on the saint's unique spirituality led to this work; to her and to Father John J. Lawlor, C.M., director of the same province, and Father William J. Casey, C.M., for their wise comments and suggestions; to Sister Aloysia Dugan, D.C., provincial archivist, for her invaluable knowledge of sources and wholehearted assistance; and to all the Sisters of Saint Joseph's Provincial House, as well as my Vincentian confreres of Emmitsburg's Saint Vincent's House, for their hospitality and interest.

May God, our common father Saint Vincent de Paul, and Saint Elizabeth Ann Seton reward them all.

Father Joseph I. Dirvin, C.M.

[1] Joseph I. Dirvin, C.M., "Saint Elizabeth Ann Seton, Mother of the Vincentian Community in America", We Are Vincentians, January 4, 2017, https://vincentians.com/en/saint-elizabeth-ann-seton-mother-of-the-vincentian-community-in-america/.

"She Is a Saint"

The announcement by Pope Saint Paul VI (1897–1978) on December 12, 1974, that Elizabeth Ann Seton would be canonized during the Holy Year of 1975 brought, besides the satisfaction and joy of millions of American Catholics, some curious responses. A priest asked whether she was being canonized because some called her a foundress of the American parochial school.[1] One of her own religious daughters expressed her distaste for the pomp and circumstance of the approaching event as "unnecessary, since we already know she is a saint".[2] A syndicated columnist in Catholic newspapers, who dismissed canonization as "just [recognizing] that some person had demonstrated exceptional qualities in life ... worthy of imitation", thought that the local episcopal conference could handle it without going "to Rome", wondered whether the "now generation" might not think a 150-year-old saint "just a little quaint", and was disappointed that "one more religious" was being canonized.[3]

---

[1] In a conversation with the author [date not known]. Saint John Neumann organized the first diocesan school system in Philadelphia in 1852 and is recognized for establishing the Catholic parochial school system in the United States. Saint Elizabeth Ann Seton founded St. Joseph's School (1810, Emmitsburg, Maryland) and pioneered free Catholic education for females.

[2] An unidentified sister on a television panel with Rev. Joseph I. Dirvin, C.M.

[3] Mary Carson, "Let's Speed Up Canonization", *The Catholic Standard and Times*, January 30, 1975.

All three displayed various degrees of ignorance concerning the nature of canonization. The priest should have known that people are canonized not for what they do but for what they are, not for the greatest and most enduring of accomplishments but for extraordinary personal holiness. The Sister should have known that, despite the grace given her and her colleagues to know the appealing sanctity of Mother Seton, millions of their fellow Catholics in the nation and the world did not know what they knew and the Church was most anxious that they should, for their own spiritual benefit. The columnist was the least informed of all. Canonization is profoundly related to the dogma that saints are to be venerated and invoked as models and intercessors. It is the theologically certain teaching of the Church that the canonization of a saint is an infallible and irrevocable decision of the supreme pontiff by which he also imposes a precept on the faithful of the Universal Church to venerate the person canonized with all the saints.[4] The infallible intention of the act is plain in the formula used to proclaim it, which is essentially the same as the formula for *ex cathedra* definitions of Catholic dogma. The Vatican Council II developed the Church's teaching on sanctity as a universal call to holiness rooted in the Sacrament of Baptism.

> New citizens of human society are born, who by the grace of the Holy Spirit received in baptism are made children of God....
>
> The followers of Christ are called by God, not because of their works, but according to His own purpose and grace....

---

[4] Adolphe Tanquerey, *Synopsis theologiae dogmaticae fundamentalis: ad mentem S. Thomae Aquinatis, hodiernis moribus accommodata: de vera religione, de ecclesia, de fontibus theologicis*, v. 1 of 3, Editio sexta, Stereotypa. (Paris: Typis Societatis Sancti Joannis Evangelistæ, Desclée et Socii, 1937), no. 931.

Thus . . . , all the faithful of Christ of whatever rank or status, are called to the fullness of the Christian life and to the perfection of charity. . . .

The classes and duties of life are many, but holiness is one—that sanctity which is cultivated by all who are moved by the Spirit of God, and who obey the voice of the Father and worship God the Father in spirit and in truth. . . . Every person must walk unhesitatingly according to his own personal gifts and duties in the path of living faith, which arouses hope and works through charity.[5]

Thus, on Sunday, September 14, 1975, Pope Paul VI proclaimed:

For the honor of the Most Holy Trinity, for the exaltation of the Catholic Faith and the increase of the Christian life, by the authority of Our Lord Jesus Christ, of the holy Apostles Peter and Paul and by Our authority, after mature deliberation and most frequent prayer for divine assistance, having obtained the counsel of many of our brother bishops, we declare and we define that Blessed Elizabeth Ann Bayley Seton is a saint, and we inscribe her name in the calendar of saints, and mandate that she should be devoutly honored among the saints in the universal Church.[6]

The Holy Father then expounded the theology of canonization with great precision in the first paragraphs of his homily. "Yes, Venerable Brothers and beloved sons and daughters," he began, "Elizabeth Ann Seton is a Saint! We rejoice and we are deeply moved that our apostolic

---

[5] Vatican Council II, Dogmatic Constitution on the Church *Lumen Gentium* (November 21, 1964), nos. 11, 40, 41, https://www.vatican.va/archive/hist _councils/ii_vatican_council/documents/vat-ii_const_19641121_lumen -gentium_en.html (hereafter cited as *LG*).

[6] Paul VI, *Officium Caeremoniarum Pontificalium*, September 14, 1975, Saint Elizabeth Ann Seton, 1-3-5-5 (4), APSL.

ministry authorizes us to make this solemn declaration before all of you here present, before the holy Catholic Church, ... before the entire American people, and before all humanity. Elizabeth Ann Bayley Seton is a Saint!"[7] It is the pope's apostolic office as successor of Saint Peter that gives him the authority to canonize; his pronouncement is universal, to the whole Church and to all the world, and it is now part of the Church's Magisterium, or teaching. "The Church", he continued, "has made this study of the life, that is, the interior and exterior history, of Elizabeth Ann Seton. And the Church has exulted with admiration and joy, and has today heard her own charism of truth poured out in the exclamation that we send up to God and announce to the world: She is a Saint!"[8]

Having thus established the authenticity of the teaching, the pope then set it in the context of the transcendent doctrines of the Church as Christ's Mystical Body and the communion of saints: "This will be one of the most valuable fruits of the Canonization of the new Saint: to know her, in order to admire in her an outstanding human figure; in order to praise God who is wonderful in his saints; to imitate her example which this ceremony places in a light that will give perennial edification; to invoke her protection"—Elizabeth Seton now has awesome power: to influence her fellow creatures to salvation by the power of her example and to speak for them before God's throne by the power of intercession—"now that we have the certitude of her participation in the exchange of heavenly life in the Mystical Body of Christ, which we

---

[7] Ibid., 1-3-5-5 (7), APSL. See also Paul VI, homily, Canonization of Elizabeth Ann Seton, September 14, 1975, *Acta Apostolicae Sedis—Commentarium Officiale*, https://www.vatican.va/content/paul-vi/en/homilies/1975/documents/hf_p-vi_hom_19750914.html (hereafter cited as Paul VI, *AASCO*).

[8] Paul VI, *AASCO*.

call the Communion of Saints and in which we also share, although still belonging to life on earth."[9]

The "now generation" may very well be unimpressed by many things because no one ever took the trouble to teach them what they have a right to know. Men and women dead for centuries have enormous influence on today's world. Rousseau's wrong-headed doctrine of hedonism is still widely accepted and practiced. A great saint like Vincent de Paul still inspires millions of people—priests, religious, and other laity—who perpetuate his abundant charity, to say nothing of his impact on social work and workers who may never have heard of him. He had a decided influence on Elizabeth Seton. As for saints of bygone days bursting on the modern world, it is a fact of history that God gives the Church and the world the saints they need at a particular time. It is true that many of the saints provided for various crises were alive during them; that God gives these critical days a saint dead for more than 150 years is significant in itself. Many of the Jews of Jesus' day failed to recognize Him because they were looking for a different kind of Messiah than the One who came.

Elizabeth Seton had the kind of simple, serene faith, unfaltering hope, and practical love of God and man that the modern world needs desperately. She had total dedication to God, Church, family, and country; to those suffering from poverty, illness, and neglect; to the priesthood and those in consecrated life; to the Christian education of the young—to so many things that continue in crisis today. She was, indeed, a spiritual leader, the foundress of the first American apostolic community, but for only twelve of her forty-six years. A laywoman for thirty-four years, she was a Protestant laywoman for thirty of them.

[9] Ibid.

Even her calling to consecrated life was for the laity, as she told her young pupils, not "to teach you how to be good nuns or Sisters of Charity; but ... to fit you for that world in which you are destined to live; to teach you how to be good ... mothers of families".[10]

Cardinal Joseph Bernardin (1928–1996), as president of the American National Conference of Catholic Bishops, chose to address this very timeliness of Mother Seton's canonization. In thanking the Holy Father "on behalf of the bishops, clergy, religious and Catholic people of the United States" for his gift of the new saint, the archbishop insisted that she

> did not live long ago and far away. She died a little over 150 years ago. New York, Baltimore and the Maryland countryside were the setting for her work and growth in holiness. She was a wife and mother, a religious sister and educator, a woman who faced crises and setbacks which she surmounted by love, devotion and openness to the grace of God. In proclaiming her a saint, the Church invites each of us to respond like her to the challenges in our own life.
>
> She was an American religious and foundress of a religious community, and she remains a model for religious today. She was the "mother" of the Catholic school system in the United States, whose efforts underline the importance of the educational apostolate. She was a Roman Catholic whose spiritual life was nourished by long membership in the Episcopal Church. The coming-together in her of two great Christian traditions is an inspiration to contemporary work for Christian unity.[11]

[10] Charles I. White, *Life of Mrs. Eliza A. Seton: Foundress and First Superior of the Sisters or Daughters of Charity in the United States of America*, 3rd edition (Baltimore, Md.: John Murphy & Co., 1859), 344.

[11] Joseph Bernardin, *Statement on Canonization of St. Elizabeth Ann Seton*, document location unknown. Elizabeth Ann Seton chose the Daughters of

Cardinal John Wright (1909–1979), prefect of the Sacred Congregation of the Clergy, discussed the significance of Saint Elizabeth Ann's canonization as it related to her native land. "Why do we Americans rejoice in the canonization of this particular saint," he asked,

> even while insisting, if our theology is straight, that while there may be a saintly American, there is no such thing as an *American* saint and while there may be and assuredly are many Americans who are saints, there are no *saints* who depend on their *Americanism* or *Gallicanism* or *Italianism* or *Orientalism* for their sanctity? It merely means—*but this means very much*—that while her nationality may or may not contribute to the essence of her sanctity, her sanctity does very much for her nationality and if we had enough citizens like her, her nation would become indeed a holy place as well as the beautiful and admirable place we know it to be.

The Cardinal then proceeded to expand on the true and wondrous universality now attained by this little woman who had ended her days in the isolated woods and mountains of Maryland—a universality extending itself first to her fellow citizens and then to all the world. "Our mass media ... headlines the news that now the Church has an *American* saint, whereas the fact is that America has a canonized saint who is the symbol of the millions of uncanonized saints who go to work or tend their homes or suffer in their hospitals or do their good works or beg the help of their neighbors all over the United States."

Charity of St. Vincent de Paul, founded in Paris (1633), as the model for her Sisters of Charity of St. Joseph's (1809) and thus her foundation was an apostolic community. It was not a religious congregation nor were its members women religious. The Sisters served those in need, made private, annual vows, and lived in community according to the Rule and Constitutions approved by the Sulpician superior Rev. Jean Tessier and Archbishop John Carroll (1812).

"It does not mean", the Cardinal reiterated, "that the Church recognizes that a Catholic convert has 'made good' by American standards; it means that an American wife, mother, educator, religious, convert to Catholicism and heroic woman has 'made good' by God's much more exacting standards. It is ample reason for *American* rejoicing but it is a cause for universal joy in the Church throughout the world and in heaven itself."[12]

No matter what Elizabeth Seton did, however, or how well, or in what land, she attained sainthood only by complete union with God. "Being a Saint means being perfect," Paul VI reminded us, "with a perfection that attains the highest level that a human being can reach." But this perfection is attained only because

a Saint is a human creature fully conformed to the will of God. A saint is a person in whom all sin—the principle of death—is cancelled out and replaced by the living splendor of divine grace. The analysis of the concept of sanctity brings us to recognize in a soul the mingling of two elements that are entirely different but which come together to produce a single effect: sanctity. One of these elements is the human and moral element, raised to the degree of heroism: heroic virtues are always required by the Church for the recognition of a person's sanctity. The second element is the mystical element, which express[es] the measure and form of divine action in the person chosen by God to realize in herself—always in an original way—the image of Christ.[13]

These elements are surely recognizable in the pains Elizabeth took to do all things well, whether attendance at Mass

[12] John Cardinal Wright, North America's Tribute to Mother Seton, Reflections on Mother Elizabeth Ann Seton, Catacomb of San Callisto, September 15, 1975, 1-3-5-5(14), APSL.
[13] Paul VI, *AASCO*. Cf. Rom 8:29.

or the daily running of her school, despite the steady downward pull of illness, as well as in the ecstatic, sometimes nearly wild and incoherent love poured out in her private spiritual jottings and notes to her director.

It is indeed true, as Paul VI has remarked, that "the science of sanctity is ... the most interesting, the most varied, the most surprising and the most fascinating of all the studies of that ever mysterious being which is man."[14] It is the very humanity of saints that makes it so, for shared as humanity is by all, its manifestations are as varied as are men and women. Conversely, it is also true that the humanity in the people of God seeks out the humanity in the saints and is consequently attracted to, indifferent to, or repelled by them. Thus, there are very few modern Christians who are drawn to the austerity of the Desert Fathers, but there are myriads drawn to the delightful personality of Elizabeth Ann Seton. She was pleasant, loving, wise, witty, and even mischievous; however, she was also long-suffering, brave, disciplined, and relentless for the truth in herself and others. She cannot be wholly embraced, she cannot be truly loved or effectively admired—indeed, she can do little good—unless souls drawn to her accept the elements of her sanctity: the human, moral, and mystical.

Fortunately, Elizabeth herself commingled these elements so that they were the warp and the woof of her daily life. They appear in startling juxtapositions—family events with holy indignation, the divine and the trivial—but without jostling or jarring. Elizabeth's letters are filled with examples of this saintly dexterity. Thus she wrote to her dear Filicchi in sympathy and reminder, "When thought goes to you, Antonio, and imagines you in the promiscuous company you must meet, without any solid gratification—fatigued by your excursions, wandering in

[14] Paul VI, *AASCO*.

your fancy, etc.—Oh how I pray that the Holy Spirit may not leave you and that your dear Angel may even pinch you at the hour of Prayers rather than suffer you to neglect them."[15] To this same Antonio, whom she could tease mercilessly, she could also be frank in affection because her affection was fastened in God. "I could cry out now, as my poor Seton used to: 'Antonio, Antonio, Antonio'", she wrote in the same letter, "but call back the thought and my Soul cries out: 'Jesus, Jesus, Jesus!'—there it finds rest and heavenly Peace, and is hushed by that dear sound as my little babe is quieted by my cradle song." Is there any more beautiful expression of earthly and divine love, any more profound sublimation of the one to the other, nay, holy merging of the two? "Jonathan loved David as his own Soul," she continued in the same poignant vein, "and if I was your Brother, Antonio, I would never leave you for one hour—but, as it is, I try rather to turn every affection to God, well knowing that there alone their utmost exercise cannot be misapplied and most ardent hopes can never be disappointed."[16] This letter is not only sublime but also most important, for it goes to the heart of Elizabeth Seton, which was wholly affectionate and loving. She loved her family and friends with a passionate intensity that could easily have obscured and usurped her love of God. This letter confirms that it did not, and why. She knew the joys of love and friendship, but she also knew the priorities of salvation and perfection, and she managed both carefully and well. This balance extended to every sphere of life. For example, the following lines, written to Amabilia Filicchi on the day of Elizabeth's reception into the Catholic Church, are a delightful

[15] 3.9, Elizabeth Seton to Antonio Filicchi, September 27, [1804], in CW, 1:324.
[16] Ibid., 324–25.

mélange of good-humored exasperation, profound adoration and union, and maternal happiness:

> For as to going a walking any more about what all the
> different people believe, I cannot, being quite tired out.
> And I came up light at heart and cool of head the first
> time these many long months, but not without begging
> Our Lord to wrap my heart deep in that opened side so
> well described in the beautiful Crucifixion, or lock it up in
> His little tabernacle where I shall now rest forever—Oh,
> Amabilia, the endearments of this day with the Children
> and the play of the heart with God while keeping up their
> little farces with them.[17]

One of the happy by-products of Elizabeth's grasp of
the complex interweaving of the earthly and heavenly, the
human and divine, was the way she could talk about the
profoundly spiritual in the homeliest of terms, thus putting
it in the reach of all, as God intended. As her strength
ebbed away in her last years, she once wrote to a young
priest she had befriended from the day he entered the seminary, "I ... cannot die one way, it seems, so I try to die
the other, and keep the straight path to *GOD ALONE*.
The little daily lesson: to keep soberly and quietly in His
Presence, trying to turn every little action on His Will;
and to praise and love through cloud or sun shine, is all
my care and study—*Sam* offers his battles from time to
time"—Sam was her own nickname for the devil—"but
our beloved stands behind the wall and keeps the wretch
at his distance. So much for your Mother's little nothing
part—but oh," she urged, "mind your own, so great and

---

[17] 3.31, Journal to Amabilia Filicchi, July 19, 1804, entry of [March 14,
1805], in *CW*, 1:375–76. A painting of the Crucifixion by Mexican artist José
Vallejo, given by Archbishop Nunez de Haro of Mexico City in 1789, hangs
above the main altar of St. Peter's Church, Barclay Street, New York City.

glorious, for whether in action or at rest you are forever
his PRIEST."[18]

No one knows a soul better than a spiritual director.
In a sense, he knows the soul of his penitent better than
his own, because he has a more objective view of it. After
Elizabeth Seton's death, her spiritual director, Father
Simon Gabriel Bruté, had this to say of her: "I will say as
the result of my long and intimate acquaintance with her,
that I believe her to have been one of those truly chosen
souls ... who, if placed in circumstances similar to those
of St. Theresa [of Avila] or St. [Jane] Frances de Chantal,
would be equally remarkable in the scale of sanctity. For it
seems to me impossible that there could be a greater elevation, purity, and love for God, for heaven, and for supernatural and eternal things than were to be found in her."[19]

This is an authoritative and uncompromising testimo-
nial to Elizabeth Seton's sanctity, but one perhaps more
authentic, because more personal, more moving. Bruté
confided to his private journal (in the broken and awkward
English that gave Elizabeth such mischievous delight) on
May 19, 1821:

> O my Mother! be blessed in Heaven, I hope already! Many
> times pressed to write of you this morning, at least this line
> of my conviction, how sincere, holy, elevated, humble,
> kind, merciful, eager to do good, attached to faith, loving
> your Jesus, ardent for His divine presence in the Eucharist
> you were!—What a mind, a heart, a soul I have known
> and enjoyed, and lost. O! my whole life to remember you,

[18] 7.214, Elizabeth Seton to Rev. John Hickey, P.S.S., [June 14, 1819], in
CW, 2:614.
[19] [Sister Loyola Law, D.C., ed.], *Mother Seton: Notes by Rev. Simon Gabriel
Bruté*, entry of July 5, 1821, (Emmitsburg, Md.: Daughters of Charity, 1884),
81–82.

and to cherish the remembrance! How much of grace I have received by you!

You said you did by me, but, alas! how do I regret the many pains, many acts of indiscreet zeal, reproof, request, trouble, I have been guilty towards you! One good, perhaps was from it, our good, good God was to keep you the better attached to Him alone, and, indeed, to Him alone I wanted to give you, with the same horror of self you yourself had....

Mother! how pleased I feel to have written some lines,—Alas! foolish, if not to feed my heart and renew impressions which drew me so forcibly to my God! My God! my God! Thou alone![20]

---

[20] Ibid., entry of May 19, 1821, 66–67.

Reflections on eternal life by Elizabeth Ann Seton[21]

Courtesy, Sisters of Charity of Seton Hill, Greensburg, Pennsylvania

[21] 11.52, The Following of Christ, in *CW*, 3b:79.

2

And Then Eternity

Entering eternal life and acting according to God's plan became motivating factors of Elizabeth Seton's life and sanctification. It was an all-embracing focus for her. It meant more than the next world's lasting forever. It meant God, happiness, and reunion with loved ones.

Even when Elizabeth was a small child, eternity was never far from her thoughts. Granted, it was not the encompassing vision of her later years, but the elements were there in the simple, uncomplicated turning to God and longing for her mother, who had died when Elizabeth was only three.

Elizabeth recalled when she was only four, "sitting alone on a step of the door, looking at the clouds, while my little sister Catherine, two years old, lay in her coffin; they asked me: Did I not cry when little Kitty was dead? No, because Kitty is [sic] gone up to heaven. I wish I could go, too, with Mama."[1]

She recalled a year or so later carrying her half sister, Emma, up to the topmost window of the house to watch the sunset and telling the infant very solemnly that "God lived up in heaven, and good children would go up there."[2] At her uncle William Bayley's country seashore

[1] 10.4, *Dear Remembrances*, n.d., in *CW*, 3a:510.
[2] Ibid.

home in New Rochelle, where she spent much of her childhood because of the absence of her father, who was studying medicine in England, and indifferent stepmother, "every little leaf and flower or animal, insect, shades of clouds, or waving trees" became "objects of vacant unconnected thoughts of God and heaven" to the little eight-year-old, who also found it a "delight to sit alone by the waterside—wandering hours on the shore, humming and gathering shells".[3]

It is obvious that even in these tenderest years, Elizabeth had grasped the basic truth that "here we have no lasting city, but we seek the city which is to come."[4] She had undoubtedly learned it in a child's unquestioning way from her grandfather, the Reverend Richard Charlton, who was an Episcopal minister, and his daughter Catherine, Elizabeth's mother. Looking back, it's clear there was more to the story. The fact that this truth resonated with her on a deeper level than just memorizing a lesson, and that it brought her pleasure and direction, is evidence of God's plan and providential care watching over the young girl. This focus on eternity was an integral part of a burgeoning spirituality, unusual in one so young. She has testified that she had "pleasure in learning anything pious".[5] It is significant that Elizabeth's childhood recollection of her stepmother was that she "learnt me the 22nd [23rd] Psalm: 'The Lord is my Shepherd, the Lord ruleth me'—and all life through it has been the favorite Psalm 'though I walk in the midst of the shadow of Death, I will fear no evil, for thou art with me.' "[6] This is

[3] Ibid., 511.
[4] Heb 13:14.
[5] 10.4, *Dear Remembrances*, n.d., in *CW*, 3a:511.
[6] Ibid., 510. In contemporary editions of the Catholic Bible, this psalm appears as Psalm 23.

quite understandable because the psalm's teaching was the compass of her whole spirituality.

This early awareness of the things of God gave rise to memorable adolescent religious experiences, the first of which has all the earmarks of contemplation when Elizabeth was not yet fifteen.

> In the year 1789 when my Father was in England, I jumped in the wagon that was driving to the woods for brush about a mile from Home. The Boy who drove it began to cut and I set off in the woods—soon found an outlet in a Meadow, and a chestnut tree with several young one[s] growing round it, attracted my attention as a seat, but when I came to it, [I] found rich moss under it and a warm sun—here then was a sweet bed. The air still a clear blue vault above, the numberless sounds of Spring melody and joy—the sweet clovers and wild flowers I had got by the way, and a heart as innocent as a human heart could be, filled with even enthusiastic love to God and admiration of his works.[7]

A quarter of a century later, when Elizabeth recorded the event, it was still so vivid that she could see and delight in, as it were, every blade of grass. What is so extraordinary is her unaffected and mature judgment at the age of fifteen, when a young girl is awakening to the world and the vapors of romance are distorting reality. Hers was "a heart as innocent as a human heart could be"; and it was not an innocuous innocence, an empty naiveté; no, that heart was "filled with even enthusiastic love to God and admiration of his works".[8]

---

[7] 2.7, Journal to Rebecca Seton, November 19, 1803, entry of December 1, in *CW*, 1:264, first brackets in published version.
[8] Ibid.

Elizabeth continued: "God was my Father, my All. I prayed, sang hymns, cried, laughed, talking to myself of how far He could place me above all Sorrow. Then [I] laid still to enjoy the Heavenly Peace that came over my Soul; and I am sure, in the two hours so enjoyed, grew ten years in the spiritual life."[9] This considered judgment seems extraordinary. Quite calmly, Elizabeth was recognizing genuine union with God with all its "signs and wonders", the *silent* prayer, after all the hymns and crying and babbling, however well meant, the mutual gazing of God and creature, the all-pervading peace, the permanent spiritual growth. It is possible to trace the ultimate source of this awesome spiritual event to Elizabeth's affinity for spiritual reading, especially the Holy Bible. Among her voluminous writings preserved at Emmitsburg, there are page after page of favorite psalms meticulously and lovingly copied in her youthful Protestant years. Surely "the heart as innocent as a human heart could be", the "enthusiastic love to God" and the "admiration of his works" are authentic echoes of the threads of praise binding these psalms together. To the Bible Elizabeth added the religious poetry of authors such as John Milton and James Thomson, whose *Seasons* Haydn has set to glorious music, but it was the Bible that rooted her mind, her life, and her teaching.

Elizabeth's second unforgettable experience occurred about two years later and was a complete contrast to her first. It appears to have been the ultimate temptation toward self-destruction. This may have been triggered by perceptions and feelings surrounding family circumstances and possibly related to her previous euphoric encounter with God, during which she was enamored with enthusiasm for God and admiration of creation.

[9] Ibid.

Far too many young people, especially in our desperate times, are tempted to suicide, and indeed an alarming number succumb. Depression is no stranger to the emotional fluctuations of adolescence. Elizabeth's fascination with God and the things of the Spirit, however, bids us to look deeper into the nature of her perilous temptation. There are no sure indications of what precipitated it; perhaps on the threshold of adulthood she began to feel truly the malevolence of her lack of family life and love, and there were the usual feverish absurdities to complicate growing up. She recorded in her *Dear Remembrances*: "16 years of age—family disagreement—could not guess why when I spoke kindly to relations they did not speak to me—could not even guess how anyone could be an enemy to another. Folly—sorrows—romance—miserable friendships ..."[10] It is all very unsatisfactory, but also endlessly suggestive. At any rate, when darkness enveloped her, it may have been some form that God reserves for privileged souls who seek to know and please Him. When the dark night came, its threat of eternal darkness was very real: "Alas, alas, *alas! Tears of blood*—" she recalled with stark vividness, "My God!—horrid subversion of every good promise of God in the boldest presumption—God had created me—I was very miserable. He was too good to condemn so poor a creature made of dust, driven by misery, this the wretched reasoning—Laudanum—the praise and thanks of excessive joy not to have done the horrid deed, the thousand promises of ETERNAL GRATITUDE."[11] That she had definitely considered death as a surcease of sorrow is borne out in a letter written years later to her brother-in-law Henry Seton, who had asked whether it was wrong of

---

[10] 10.4, *Dear Remembrances*, n.d., in *CW*, 3a:512.

[11] Ibid., 512–13.

him to wish he had not survived a shipwreck; she recalled in answer "the moment twenty years ago in which I asked [myself] the same question, dictated by that anguish of Soul which can find no relief".[12] Other dark nights were to descend upon her, but none evoked the same panic, which was the natural lot of a young heart. Even so, the conquering faith and love were also there to rout the horror, to spare her the sad fate of so many troubled young hearts in today's empty world.

Elizabeth's third teenage "experience" was really her awakening to a truth that many good-intentioned people have encountered before and since: that the world apart from God and the spiritual life do not mix very well. Elizabeth was a lively, outgoing young woman, loving all the good things of life: dancing, horseback riding, skating parties on the frozen Long Island Sound and Hudson and East Rivers, and attending the theater; but, at eighteen, she puzzled over a new awareness—"after being at public places, why I could not say my prayers and have good thoughts as if I had been at home".[13] It was her first taste of the distracting power of even the most innocent diversions. It was really not a problem for her because she was already "astonished at people's care in dress, in the world, etc.", thought "how silly" it was "to love anything in this world", and "preferred going to my room to any amusement out of it".[14] Nevertheless, despite her best intentions, it would be a long time before Elizabeth would attain the maturity to live a virtuous life *in the world* but not *of the world*. Wisdom develops gradually.

With the settling influence of her marriage to William Magee Seton and her first pregnancy, Elizabeth's

---

[12] 6.71, Elizabeth Seton to Henry Seton, February 19, 1811, in *CW*, 2:175.

[13] 10.4, *Dear Remembrances*, n.d., in *CW*, 3a:512.

[14] Ibid.

motivation of eternity returned in full force. It had not
yet the purity of later years, dwelling instead on the natural human fear of eternal punishment—as she herself
was aware in later memories, in which could still recall
the bewildered amazement of the new young wife: "My
own home at 20—the world—that and heaven too, quite
impossible! So every moment clouded with that fear: 'My
God, if I enjoy this, I lose You'—yet no thought of who
[*sic*] I would lose, rather fear of hell and shut out from
heaven."[15] It was the uncomprehending cry of the soul in
Francis Thompson's *Hound of Heaven*, "Lest having Him,
I should have naught beside", and it would terrorize her
until she understood the meaning of God in everything
and everything in God.[16] It was love, but imperfect love;
the fear of loss surely bespoke love, but the wary, half-
given love, the love that elicits imperfect sorrow rooted
in fear of a judgmental God rather than the perfect contrition for having freely and willingly offended a loving God,
who is all good and deserving of all our love.

After Elizabeth had gone through the trial of her husband's last illness and death, had experienced her own
conversion to the Catholic faith, and had begun living a
consecrated life in an apostolic community, she was able
to lift the clouding fear and recognize the unassailable love
beneath it. "For my part, I find so much contentment in
this love [of God]", she then told her dear, lifelong confidante and friend Julia Sitgreaves Scott,

> that I am obliged to put on my consideration cap to find
> out how anyone can raise their eyes to the light of heaven
> and be insensible to it. I remember when Anna was six
> months old and everything smiled around me—venerating

[15] Ibid., 513.
[16] Francis Thompson, *The Hound of Heaven and Other Poems* (Westwood,
N.J.: Fleming H. Revell Company, 1965), 11–18.

the virtues of my Seton and sincerely attached to him, accustomed to the daily visits and devoted love of my father, [and] possessed of all I estimated as essential to happiness—alone with this Babe in the see-saw of Motherly love, frequently the tears used to start and often overflow, and I would say to myself while retrospecting the favors of heaven: All these and heaven too?[17]

There is no mistaking the true love of God of this young wife and mother. The only things lacking are the peace and calm that drive out fear, the peace and calm that recognize the certainty of love, indeed, are that love's ultimate reward, the peace and calm that see no use for the desperate proofs to which Elizabeth still drove herself.

"Sometimes falling on my knees with the sleeping suckling in my arms, I would offer her and all my dear possessions—Husband, Father, Home—and entreat the bountiful giver to separate me from all, if indeed I could not possess my portion here, and with Him too."[18] The offer was as honest as it was habitual: "Nor do I remember any part of my life, after being settled in it, that I have not constantly been in the same sentiment, always looking beyond the bounds of time and desiring to quit the gift for the giver."[19] It was just that, like anything good and desirable, it took practice to acquire in all its purity.

It is not surprising that, in those earlier days of her life, "after being settled in it", her attraction to eternity itself should still at times take a bumbling expression. It could, for instance, be cavalier, as when she told Julia: "[I] am jogging on Old style, trying to accomplish every duty,

[17] 6.30, Elizabeth Seton to Julia Scott, March 26, 1810, in *CW*, 2:116.
[18] Ibid., 116–17.
[19] Ibid., 117.

and *Hoping* for the reward; without *that* in View, heaven knows this life would be a scene of confusion and vexation *to me*, who neither values it nor desires it. I always thought, and ever shall, that *Husbands* can be consoled, Children sometimes prosper as well without, as with Parents; and, at all events, Life has such varieties of disappointments that they may as well proceed from one cause as another."[20] The best that can be said for such high-handed sentiments is that they are amazing. Elizabeth must have been feeling a bit giddy and feckless the day she wrote them. That she, sober and earnest to the nth degree, was truly serious can be immediately rejected.

Her enthusiasm could be clumsy, as when she wished her friend Eliza Craig Sadler "Happy Birthday" by sending her some prayers of preparation for death! Mrs. Sadler was predictably upset, and Elizabeth wrote in apology: "My own dear Eliza, I fear you did not understand sufficiently my meaning in the use of those little prayers I gave you—which was to impress on your mind the necessity of preparing for a Blessed Death.... I have observed, dear, that any good resolutions or exercises begun on the period of our Birth are more seriously impressed, and chose this for you at this time, as reflecting on a Birth day on Earth more easily transfers our thoughts to the Birth day of our future existence."[21]

Elizabeth could be just a bit straitlaced, even unwittingly harsh, as evidenced by her answer to a bewildered Julia, who had long had no letters from her: "How many reproaches my heart makes me when I think of you. So many years I have called you dear friend, and shall your dear friend be insincere to you? Dear Julia, then I will tell you the plain

[20] 1.33, Elizabeth Seton to Julia Scott, November 25, 1798, in *CW*, 1:54–55.
[21] 4.121, Elizabeth Seton to Eliza Sadler, n.d., in *CW*, 1:545.

truth, that my habits both of Soul and Body are changed—
that I feel all the habits of society and connections of *this* life
have taken a new form and are only interesting or endearing
as they point the view to the next."[22]

Both of these letters demonstrate the very human reaction to the discovery of something new and enchanting.
Having glimpsed the inviting depths of the spiritual life,
Elizabeth had, like a child with a new toy, to show them
off to others who had no comprehension of them. Yet
awkward as these spiritual yearnings were, they were nonetheless true and deeply felt, the very reason that her love
for husband and children grew ever more solicitous, that
Eliza was pacified, that Julia and Elizabeth corresponded
faithfully until the latter's death.

Elizabeth was always a quick learner, and in her *Leghorn
Journal*, written sometime after her unconscious rebuff to
Julia, there emerges for the first time *eternity* not only as
the never-ending love of God but also as the reunion with
loved ones—the first faint glimmer of the fruitful and constant communion of saints. Far from home or any knowledge of it, nursing a dying husband in the dank quarantine
horror of Livorno's (Leghorn's) San Jacopo Lazaretto, she
wrote: "Dear Home, dearest Sisters, my little ONES—
WELL—either protected by God in this World—or in
Heaven. It is a sweet thought to dwell on, that all those I
most tenderly love, love God; and if we do not meet again
here—there we shall be separated no more. If I have lost
them now, their gain is infinite and eternal."[23]

The doctrine of the communion of saints has not only
the general and objective aspects of interaction among

---

[22] 1.165, Elizabeth Seton to Julia Scott, November 16, 1802, in *CW*, 1:212.
[23] 2.7, Journal to Rebecca Seton, November 19, 1803, entry of [Novem-
ber 24], in *CW*, 1:258.

God's people in heaven, in purgatory, and on earth but also the intimate union of family and friends, living and deceased, at any desired moment of prayer. All are ever one, ever near, in the realm of the spirit. It was only a matter of time before Elizabeth's heart for family and friends should discover so satisfying a reality. In the lazaretto, she had not grasped it completely, dwelling only on future reunion, not yet fully aware of the communion of the living, except for God's mutual protection.

Years later, when Elizabeth had indeed lost her first-born, Anna Maria, who had been with her throughout that ordeal in the lazaretto, the calm truths she had adverted to and invoked there were useless to prevent deep, deep anguish of soul and body. She was torn apart. As she told a friend, "For three months after Nina was taken, I was so often expecting to lose my senses, and my head was so disordered, that unless for the daily duties always before me, I did not know much what I did or what I left undone."[24]

The fact of eternity had its part in purifying the souls of mother and child for the reunion it promised. "Poor, poor Mother, let her talk to you, Eliza", Elizabeth cried out to Mrs. Sadler when the floodgates of her grief had broken.

If you could have seen at the moment when kneeling at the foot of her bed to rub her cold, cold feet a day or two before [her death]—she saw the tears, and without being able to hide her own, though smiling at the same time, she repeated the so-often asked question: "*Can it be for Me? Should you not rejoice—It will be but a moment and reunited for Eternity—a happy eternity with my Mother!—what a thought!*"[25] These were her very words. And when in

[24] 6.114, Elizabeth Seton to George Weis, July 30, 1812, in *CW*, 2:224–25.
[25] 6.104, Elizabeth Seton to Eliza Sadler, May 3, [1812], in *CW*, 2:217.

death's agony her quivering lips could with difficulty utter one word, feeling a tear fall on her face, she smiled, and said with great effort: *"Laugh, Mother, Jesus!"*—at intervals, as she could not put two words together—... Poor Mother must say no more now—only pray, Eliza, that she may be strengthened....

You believe me when I say with my whole soul, "His Will be done forever!" *Eternity* was Anna's darling word. I find it written in everything that belonged to her: music, books, copies, the walls of her little chamber, everywhere that word.[26]

Who had taught her that word?

In the teaching, Elizabeth herself had learned the hard lesson that eternal reunion with loved ones is often only won by separation from them here. That sting was in a letter to Julia Scott, nearly a year later: "I sit writing by the Windows, opposite my darling darling's little *Wood*—the white palings appear through the trees. Oh, Julia, my Julia, if we may but pass our dear Eternity together! Are you good? Do you try to be good? I try with my whole heart. I long so to get above this blue Horizon. Oh, my Anna, the child of my soul—all, all [my] dear ones so many years gone before ETERNAL REUNION!"[27]

How well Elizabeth had learned the lesson is evident in contrasting even her human reaction to the death of her youngest, Rebecca, four years later: "The Mother is a miracle of divine favor", noted Father John Dubois, third Sulpician superior of the Sisters of Charity. "Night and day by the child, her health has not appeared to suffer. She held the child in her arms without dropping a tear all the

[26] Ibid.
[27] 6.126, Elizabeth Seton to Julia Scott, January 25, 1813, in *CW*, 2:239.

time of her agony and even eight minutes after she had died. *Mulierem fortem* [a strong woman]."[28]

When she herself slipped sharply toward eternity, two years after Bec, she wrote joyfully to a friend: "Bec's birthday. She would be *16*, but counts time no more, Sweet darling—what a thought to go to *her* and our *Nina*, to go to *God*."[29]

The sacrifice of separation to win everlasting reunion had already taken firm root in Elizabeth's soul with her son William's departure for Italy to train for commerce with the Filicchi in 1815. She would see very little of him in the remaining five years of her life. On his eighteenth birthday, a month before he left, she first sounded the theme she would worry until the day she died: letting go of him here to be with him forever. "My darling Child—[your] Mother's heart can say no more", she wrote in her birthday note.[30] His mother had a dear commission for him: "Our Eternity, my William!"[31] She continued, "Be blessed a thousand, thousand times—take a few little moments in the church to say in union with your Mother's heart, to place yourself again and again in the hands of God. Do, my dearest one."[32] She had not abandoned her strategy of using earthly birthdays as reminders of heavenly ones; she had only refined it.

Elizabeth's reminders to William became a gradual crescendo in the ensuing years, gathering in intensity as her fears increased. The intensity and her anxiety had their

[28] Annabelle M. Melville, *Elizabeth Bayley Seton 1774–1821*, ed. Betty Ann McNeil, D.C. (Hanover, Pa.: The Sheridan Press, 2009), 329.

[29] 7.176, Elizabeth Seton to Ellen Wiseman, August 20, 1818, in *CW*, 2:574.

[30] 6.182, Elizabeth Seton to William Seton, [January 1815], in *CW*, 2:298.

[31] 6.174, Elizabeth Seton to William Seton, November 25, 1814, in *CW*, 2:285.

[32] Ibid.

source in Elizabeth's tendency to favor her firstborn son. She owned it quite frankly. She wrote him in an unusually intimate vein as he awaited naval assignment in Boston in 1818: "Last night I had you close where you used to lie so snug and warm when you drew the *life stream* twenty years ago, and where the heart still beats to love you dearly, dearly till its last sigh, *which even then loved you best of all.*"[33] And again: "I often ask, but what is this dear Rover to me so much more than all the world? Why do my heart strings all wind around him so? *That I cannot tell.* Let it pass, for it depends not on me."[34]

Elizabeth confided this primacy of love and her bewilderment over it to Antonio Filicchi in a letter that at the same time absolved her of all foolish maternal bias: "I cannot hide from Our God, though from everyone else I must conceal the perpetual tears and affections of boundless gratitude which overflow my heart, when I think of him secure in his *Faith* and your protection. Why I love him so much I cannot account, but own to you, my Antonio, all my weakness. Pity and pray for a mother attached to her children through such peculiar motives as I am to mine. I purify it as much as I can, and Our God knows it is their Souls alone I look at."[35] She confirmed the purity of her maternal love in her very last letter to Antonio: "For many years I have had no prayer for my children but that our blessed God would do everything to them and in them in the way of affliction and adversity, if only He will save their soul[s]."[36]

---

[33] 7.144, Elizabeth Seton to William Seton, [February 25, 1818], in *CW*, 2:532.

[34] 7.153, Elizabeth Seton to William Seton, [April 6, 1818], in *CW*, 2:544.

[35] 6.214, Elizabeth Seton to Antonio Filicchi, November 20, 1815, in *CW*, 2:356.

[36] 7.265, Elizabeth Seton to Antonio Filicchi, October 19, 1820, in *CW*, 2:670.

In light of future events—William may have faltered for a time in the practice of his faith—Elizabeth's partiality may well have been, all unknown to her, the partiality of the Good Shepherd for the strayed and lost of His flock. In any event, there can be no discounting the anguish of her separation from her older son or the terror with which she urged her own "dear eternity" upon him, with a mother's love as her means of persuasion.

"Be sure, as I told you, to remain faithful to your exterior duties", was Elizabeth's advice to William regarding his stay with the Filicchi in Livorno.[37]

> Child of my Soul, *be good* and *be happy*! The only thought that frightens me when I feel weak and faint is that I will see you no more in this World, but that is Nothing—*if only in the next*. Write me how often you have been to the tribunal since you left me....
>
> O my William, tears will overpower and my Soul cries for our Eternity! My dear, dear one, if the world should draw you from Our God, and we not meet there, that thought I cannot stand—I will *hope, do hope*—my God who knows a mother's Soul sees, and he will [have] pity.[38]

When William's restless nature showed signs of dissatisfaction with the world of trade, Elizabeth's foreboding that he might leave the spiritual haven of her pious friends in Tuscany—which he had indeed already resolved to do—prompted her to write in panic:

> My Soul's own William: The bitter, freezing North wind is now always rattling, and they write me on every

[37] 6.187, Elizabeth Seton to William Seton, [February 1815], in *CW*, 2:304.
[38] 6.199, Elizabeth Seton to William Seton, August 4, 1815, in *CW*, 2:336–37; 6.192, Elizabeth Seton to William Seton, May 18, 1815, in *CW*, 2:309. When inquiring how frequently her son has gone to Confession since he left Maryland, Elizabeth refers to the Sacrament of Reconciliation as the *tribunal*.

side—New York and Baltimore—that the ice will let no Vessel go to you. Yet, my head and heart is so full of you, that though letters for you are waiting at both ports, I must write. If I wake in the night, I think it is your Angel wakes me to pray for you. And last night I found myself actually dropping asleep, repeating your name over and over, and appealing to Our Lord with the Agony of a Mother's love for our long and dear and everlasting reunion.[39]

Three years later, that agony reached an almost unbearable peak as she lay dying:

William, William, William, is it possible the cry of my heart doesn't reach yours? I carry your beloved name before the tabernacle and repeat it there as my prayer, in torrents of tears which Our God alone understands.

Childish weakness, fond partiality, you would say half-pained, if you could see from *your present scene* the agonized heart of your Mother. But its agony is not for our *present* separation, my beloved one; it is our long, eternal years which press on it beyond all expression—To lose you here a few years of so embittered a life is but the common lot; but to love as I love you, and lose you *forever*—oh, unutterable anguish!

A whole Eternity miserable, a whole Eternity the enemy of God, and such a God as He is to us![40]

The wild outburst of pain, which she no longer cared to conceal, pierced the silence in her distress: "Dreading so much your Faith is quite lost, having everything to extinguish and nothing to nourish it. My William, William,

[39] 7.75, Elizabeth Seton to William Seton, February 14, 1817, in *CW*, 2:465.
[40] 7.255 Elizabeth Seton to William Seton, July 23, 1820, in *CW*, 2:662.

William, if I did not see your doting Bec and Nina above, what would save my heart from breaking?"[41]

This maternal pain, constant over the years and never assuaged, should be seen against the daily round of Elizabeth's community life with the Sisters of Charity. The heartache she shared with all mothers was not visited on her Sisters; she let no part of its burden fall on them. She led the prayers, presided over meals and recreation, and directed the schoolwork like any other local leader and principal. Only in the night, when all were in bed and the house still and her physical pain and hacking cough would not let her sleep, would she "draw our little basket of chips [for the fire] you so well remember", she told William, "[and] make up a small blaze in your stove", and in so many nights put on paper the fear that haunted her soul. For one so holy, the fear and consequent pain of the sword in the heart must have been truly exquisite.[42]

Elizabeth Ann Seton focused on Eternity. It was the star she steered by. It motivated everything—love of God and neighbor, every action spiritual and temporal. It was the refrain of her teaching, the silent watchdog of her conscience. It was the spur to every good action, the barrier to every omission.

"Eternity, oh how near it often seems to me. Think of it when you are hard pushed", Elizabeth urged a friend, bowed under trials.[43] "How long will be that day without a night, or that night without a day. Pray and praise and bless and adore forever."[44] There was an essential rightness, therefore, in her dear Eternity being the Amen to her sojourn on earth. Father Simon Bruté recorded that during

[41] Ibid.
[42] 7.150, Elizabeth Seton to William Seton, [March 1818], in *CW*, 2:539.
[43] 6.78, Elizabeth Seton to George Weis, June 24, 1811, in *CW*, 2:187.
[44] Ibid.

her final hours, toward midnight, one of the nurses, Sister Susan Clossey, offered Elizabeth a drink, which "she refused a moment in hope, she said, that on the morning she might be granted one communion more.... 'Eternity' ".[45]

Rev. Simon Gabriel Bruté, P.S.S.

Spiritual director of Elizabeth Ann Seton and first bishop of the Diocese of Vincennes, Indiana. *Courtesy, Daughters of Charity, Province of St. Louise, St. Louis, Missouri.*

[45] A-7.268, Account by Rev. Simon Bruté, P.S.S., of Elizabeth Seton's Last Days, January 2, 1821, entry of January 4, in *CW*, 2:768–69.

3

His Blessed Will

While saints are one in their heroicity of holiness, each has a hallmark, some quality of virtue or apostolate. With Francis of Assisi, it is his love of poverty; with Francis de Sales, his gentleness and affability; with Thérèse of Lisieux, her simple "little way" of loving God; with Vincent de Paul and Louise de Marillac, their devotion to serving those suffering from poverty.

A hallmark of Saint Elizabeth Ann Seton is her love of the Will of God—not only her *submission* to that holy Will but also her *love* of it. She defined it simply and uncompromisingly as early as 1804: "God has given me a great deal to do," she confided to Julia Sitgreaves Scott, "and I have always, and hope always, to prefer His Will to every wish of my own."[1] Her choice of the word *prefer* is a sure indication of committed love.

Even to submit to God's Will demands faith, but when faith is nourished to the point of taking over one's whole existence and governing one's every act, mere submission is transformed to an eager acceptance that can only be born of love. Saint Elizabeth Ann quickly progressed even beyond such acceptance to a *reaching out* for what God offered.

[1] 3.5, Elizabeth Seton to Julia Scott, July 15, 1804, in *CW*, 1:313.

Faith and love then become so intertwined that they can scarcely be distinguished, and it may be asked why they should be. Even on a purely human plane, trust must be at the root of all true love. Elizabeth Seton expressed it with shining clarity: "Faith lifts the staggering soul on one side, Hope supports it on the other. Experience says it must be—and love says, let it be."[2] Let it be. Without these words, all is a submission; with them, all is love—not a grudging "well, if I have to" but a glad, wholehearted "yes". Elizabeth's practical perception, "Experience says it must be"—nothing can really be done about most of life's happenings—echoes Jesus' injunction to Saul on the road to Damascus, "It hurts you to kick against the goads", but "Let it be" is also an echo, the sublime echo of Saul's humble answer, "What shall I do, Lord?"[3]

Elizabeth's faith was the faith of Abraham, who left his own country at God's word, who believed on the same word that his aging and barren wife would conceive and bear the father of a numberless people, yet who was willing to sacrifice his son of the promise at the same word. Elizabeth's love was the love of Job, who cried to the Lord, "Behold, he will slay me; I have no hope; yet I will defend my ways to his face."[4] Elizabeth gave tongue to this same fathomless faith, this same limitless love, as her last, long decline began: "Oh, if all goes well for me, what will I not do for you!" she promised her director, Father Simon Bruté. "You will see. But, alas, yet if I am not one of His Elect, it is I only to be blamed, and when *going down* I must still lift the hands to the very last look in praise and gratitude for what He has done to

---

[2] 6.30, Elizabeth Seton to Julia Scott, March 26, 1810, in *CW*, 2:117.
[3] Acts 26:14; 22:10.
[4] Job 13:15.

save me. What more could He have done? That thought stops all."[5]

Elizabeth early sealed her love in the Lord's own way with a covenant. At twenty-eight she was a deeply pious Episcopalian, but until that time her piety had been eclectic and random for want of someone to put it in order. However, Rev. John Henry Hobart, the young Protestant Episcopal curate of Trinity Church, had recently come into her life and become her spiritual guide. What before she had only sensed, she now comprehended. As sure knowledge grew in the structure of an ordered spirituality, she made the indispensable and irrevocable choice, setting it down thus:

> This Blessed day—Sunday 23d May 1802—my Soul was first sensibly convinced of the blessing and practicability of an entire surrender of itself and all its faculties to God. It has been the *Lord's day* indeed to me—though many, many temptations to forget my heavenly possession in his constant presence have pressed upon me—but blessed be my precious shepherd in this last hour of *his day*. I am at rest within his fold sweetly refreshed with the waters of comfort which have flowed through the Soul of his Ministering Servant, our Blessed Teacher and faithful Friend. Glory to my God for this unspeakable blessing— Glory to my God for the means of grace and the hopes of glory w[h]ich he so mercifully bestows on his unworthy Servant.
>
> O Lord, before Thee I must ever be unworthy, till covered with the Robe of Righteousness by my blessed Redeemer, He shall fit me to behold the vision of Thy glory.[6]

---

[5] 7.208, Elizabeth Seton to Rev. Simon Bruté, P.S.S., [Spring 1819], in *CW*, 2:606.

[6] 8.10, "My peace I leave with you …", May 1802, in *CW*, 3a:23–24, brackets in published version.

The language is lushly biblical, even pompous. Indeed, Elizabeth's proclivity for such "Protestant expressions" embarrassed her in later years. At the time, however, it was the only spiritual language she knew, and there can be no mistaking the sincerity of her feeling and devotion.

Father Bruté has characterized faith as "Mother's eminent disposition"—"FAITH"—he wrote the word in large letters—"and whole trust in God for herself, [her] children", the "only desire, *Salvation*".[7] He then went on to prove the rightness of his judgment by quoting Elizabeth's own words: "One thing I have asked of the Lord, one thing only, and will persist in asking, and will hang upon him for, trust in him for, and for which I think I have his promise, even the life of their and my Soul."[8] The words are simple and scriptural, the faith simple too, but, oh, how immense and unyielding! In another place, Bruté has described Elizabeth's faith in those things she especially loved: her God, the Catholic Church, the Divine Presence in the Eucharist, her children and friends, the Blessed Virgin, and the priesthood.[9]

In Elizabeth's retrospective memoir, *Dear Remembrances*, she records her sentiments in preparing for the voyage to Italy with her seriously ill husband, and the emotions are wholly prophetic: "At 29—Faith in our Leghorn Voyage, reliance that *all* would turn to good"[10]—she was not so naïve as to think that Will could recover, but she spoke of the greater ambit of the future, her own and her children's, and yes, hidden from her then, her country's and the world's—"delight in packing up all our Valuables to

[7] Rev. Simon Bruté, *Memoir on Elizabeth Seton*, May 19, 1821, 1-3-3-12(13), Saint Elizabeth Ann Seton, APSL.

[8] Ibid.

[9] Cf. ibid.

[10] 10.4, *Dear Remembrances*, n.d., in *CW*, 3a:514.

be sold, enjoying the *adieu* to each article to be mine no more"—then the strangest and most specifically prophetic of all—"thousand secret hopes in God of Separation from the world".[11]

When Elizabeth had put her covenant in writing, she felt immediately the reward of surrendering all, the heavenly peace not of the world: "My Peace I leave with you, my Peace I give unto you, not as the World gives give I unto you. Let not your hearts be troubled, neither be afraid." She savored the sweetness of the words of giving and promise: "This gift of our blessed Lord is the testimony of His love, the earnest[ness] of His continued affection, and the perfection of future blessedness to His faithful and obedient Servants, *which* is for the consummation of this Peace in the vision of His celestial presence and glory. From Him *it* proceeds, to Him it tends, and in Him it concentrates."[12] She understood so well that Christ was all, and everything in Him. The understanding enlightened and directed her prayer, as we shall see, making it forthright and fruitful.

Four months later, "Sunday, 12th September, three weeks and two days after the birth of *my Rebecca*, I renewed my covenant that I would strive with myself and use every earnest endeavor to serve my dear Redeemer and to give myself wholly unto Him."[13] The lengthening weeks of perseverance and quiet determination are unwavering proof that Elizabeth's total giving of herself was no passing whim or fancy. The next day's entry in her journal was even more important, for it actualized what she had promised: "Began a new life—resumed the occupations and duties which fill

---

[11] Ibid. The Setons declared bankruptcy and vacated their rented dwelling at 8 State Street in Lower Manhattan.

[12] 8.10, "My peace I leave with you ...", May 1802, in *CW*, 3a:23.

[13] 8.25, Notebook of Psalm 23 and Rev. John Henry Hobart's Sermons, entry of September 13, 1802, in *CW*, 3a:171.

up the part He has assigned me."[14] She meant that she began life anew. How well she understood, even then, that perfection was not pursued in high-flown phrases but by fidelity to the duties and drudgeries of everyday life. How well she grasped the spiritual truth that, while the "occupations and duties" were the same, she had indeed begun life anew focused on helping neighbors in need. A short time later, Elizabeth prepared the bedside table of a dying parishioner of Trinity Church for the reception of communion to hail the sacrament as "the Seal of that covenant which I trust will not be broken in life nor in death, in time nor in Eternity"[15]—a true, anticipated Catholic perception of the Eucharist as "the pledge of future glory".

Elizabeth Seton had entered into her covenant, which was to rule the rest of her life, with eyes wide open. She knew from bitter experience what it would demand of her. Behind her was the loneliness of a neglected childhood spent as an uncertain guest of relatives (her father was immersed in medicine; he had separated from her stepmother and their seven children). Elizabeth's married life, though happy, had had its fill of loved ones' illnesses and deaths. Even as she wrote the precious promise to her Lord, she was living in greatly reduced circumstances because of the financial failure of her husband's business and his precarious health due to tuberculosis. She was soon to suffer even more acutely through his last illness and death in the dank horror of Livorno's San Jacopo Lazaretto, or quarantine, and the subsequent long, drawn-out anguish of conversion to the Catholic faith.[16] Her conversion would

---

[14] Ibid.

[15] Ibid., 172.

[16] William Magee Seton died at Pisa, Italy, December 27, 1803, scarcely a week after release from a month's confinement in the San Jacopo Lazaretto. Rev. Matthew O'Brien received Elizabeth Seton's profession of faith in the Catholic Church on March 14, 1805, at St. Peter's Church in Lower Manhattan.

bring fresh trials in the ostracism of family and friends and
her frustrated efforts to earn bread for her children.

None of these moved Elizabeth from her committed
path. She "renewed the entire sacrifice fervently", she
wrote in the summer of 1807, and "yielded all and offered
every nerve, fiber, and power of Soul and Body to sickness, Death, or any and every appointment of His blessed
Will".[17] And she assured Antonio Filicchi:

> I repeat to you, Antonio (as you may be anxious on the
> subject), these are my happiest days. Sometimes the harassed
> mind, wearied with continual contradiction to all it would
> most covet—solitude! silence! peace!—sighs for a change;
> but five minutes' recollection procures an immediate Act of
> Resignation, convinced that this is the day of Salvation for
> me. And if, like a coward, I should run away from the field
> of battle, I am sure the very Peace I seek would fly from
> me, and the state of Penance sanctified by the Will of God
> would be again wished for as the safest and surest road.[18]

Elizabeth had indeed learned the hard way how to love
God, to do what *He* wanted, not what *she* wanted, however good and holy it seemed, and to wait for Him to
reveal what He wanted by circumstances. Thus far, circumstances of persons, illness, death, and revelation had
changed her life radically at every turning. A wife at nineteen, she was a widow at twenty-nine. She had chosen
marriage as her vocation but was led inexorably to consecrated life. She had lived fervently in the Episcopal Communion as few before or since yet was harried by grace to
a Church despised by all the world she knew, a circumstance that finally drove her from her beloved native city.

---

[17] 4.55, Spiritual Journal to Cecilia Seton, August 10–October 16, 1807, in
CW, 1:469.

[18] 4.39, Elizabeth Seton to Antonio Filicchi, June 22, 1807, in *CW*, 1:444.

Yet the pain of exile forced from her only an affirmation of the divine Will she had come to love with her whole being. She wrote of the parting to Eliza Craig Sadler:

> I saw once more the windows of State Street, passed the quarantine, and so near the shore as to see every part of it. Oh, my Lord—in that hour! Can a heart swell so high and not burst? ... My Eliza, think of me when you pass it again, battering the waves of my changeable life. Yet would I change one shade or trial of it—that would be madness, and working in the dark. Oh, no—the dear, dear, dear Adored Will be done through every moment of it! May it control, regulate, and perfect us; and when all is over, how we will rejoice that it was done![19]

The affirmation was repeated as she sat writing far into the night on board the *Grand Sachem* in Baltimore Harbor, June 15, 1808, waiting to land the next day: "Tomorrow, do I go among strangers?" she asked in a letter to her youngest sister-in-law, Cecilia Seton. "No. Has an anxious thought or fear passed my mind? No. Can I be disappointed? No. One sweet Sacrifice will unite Soul with all who offer it. Doubt and fear fly from the breast inhabited by Him. There can be no disappointment where the Soul's only desire and expectation is to meet *his* Adored Will and fulfill it."[20]

Here was a total commitment to an unknown future, a serene commitment, gladly accepting whatever trials that future might hold. And this deeply personal commitment is wrapped with theological surety in the Mystical Body of Christ and its common offering of the holy Sacrifice of the Mass. From hindsight it can be stated that the loving docility that had brought Elizabeth Ann Seton, against all odds, to Baltimore, and its fruition in Emmitsburg, was

---

[19] 5.15, Elizabeth Seton to Eliza Sadler, January 20, 1809, in *CW*, 2:50.
[20] 5.1, Elizabeth Seton to Cecilia Seton, June 9, 1808, in *CW*, 2:5.

one of God's great gifts to the Church in the new republic, the United States of America.

The haven of Baltimore, where Catholics were accepted, and the security of support for her children in the little school provided there might have led a soul less seasoned than Elizabeth to look for a halt in the roll of events or circumstances and their opposition. She knew better. She was satisfied that her own good was "always best advanced in poverty and in tears".[21]

Elizabeth's germinating apostolate of Catholic education planted in Baltimore was the initial fruition of pleasurable experiences of teaching her youngest Seton in-laws at home and an incipient inclination for consecrated life and service. She hinted at the latter in a letter to Antonio Filicchi in 1805: "I have a little secret to communicate to you when we meet (a sweet dream of imagination)";[22] and in another, the following year: "If you were now here, my dear Brother, I think you would exert your Friendship for us and obtain the so long desired refuge of a place in the Order of St. Francis for your converts."[23] At Baltimore, the desire flowered into reality as "my, or rather *the scheme* of these reverend gentlemen [the Sulpician priests]".[24] Less than a month after her arrival, Elizabeth

[21] 5.7, Elizabeth Seton to Antonio Filicchi, August 20, 1808, in *CW*, 2:28.

[22] 4.7, Elizabeth Seton to Antonio Filicchi, [October 11, 1805], in *CW*, 1:391.

[23] 4.24, Elizabeth Seton to Antonio Filicchi, August 10, 1806, in *CW*, 1:415.

[24] 5.7, Elizabeth Seton to Antonio Filicchi, August 20, 1808, in *CW*, 2:28. The scheme "refers to the establishment of a girls' school and ultimately the genesis of the American Sisters of Charity at the initiation of the Sulpicians in Baltimore, primarily Rev. William Dubourg. Ever since he had been unable to engage Ursulines from France for Baltimore, Dubourg entertained the idea of establishing a native sisterhood. Before Elizabeth left New York, Dubourg had written May 27, 1818, that if all went well for her school, he wished to 'secure permanency to the Institution ... perpetuating it by the association of some other pious ladies who may be animated with the same spirit.'" (ibid., n3). Cf. Annabelle M. Melville, *Elizabeth Bayley Seton 1774–1821*, ed. Betty Ann McNeil, D.C. (Hanover, Pa.: The Sheridan Press, 2009), 169–72.

wrote Antonio Filicchi, "It is proposed ... to begin on a small plan admitting of enlargement if necessary, in the hope and expectation that there will not be wanting ladies to join in forming a permanent institution."[25] Three months later she was calling herself "your poor little nun"[26] in a letter to Julia Scott and assuring Cecilia Seton, "It is expected I shall be the Mother of many daughters."[27]

An unforeseen obstacle reared momentarily amid this euphoria when Elizabeth was introduced to Samuel Sutherland Cooper, a wealthy Philadelphia convert who was about to enter Saint Mary's Seminary, Baltimore. They were attracted to each other—and marriage would have solved handsomely the problem of support for Elizabeth's children. She admitted quite candidly to Cecilia Seton that "if we had not devoted ourselves to the heavenly spouse before we met, I do not know how the attraction would have terminated";[28] but, she assured Julia Scott, "the only result of this partiality has been the encouragement of each other to persevere in the path which each has chosen."[29] The seeming obstacle was in reality an integral part of the unfolding of God's Will, for Cooper was to be the necessary benefactor of property for the proposed Sisterhood and school.

It is important to note that, despite Elizabeth's quickly corrected remark ("my"), the proposal and its development originated with and were implemented by the Sulpician priests of Baltimore. She wanted it that way in her usual waiting on God's Will and fearing to force it. Her only wish, far from being a foundress, was to live

---

[25] 5.4, Elizabeth Seton to Antonio Filicchi, July 8, 1808, in *CW*, 2:19.

[26] 5.11, Elizabeth Seton to Julia Scott, October 10, [1808], in *CW*, 2:37.

[27] 5.10, Elizabeth Seton to Cecilia Seton, October 6, 1808, in *CW*, 2:34.

[28] 5.8, Elizabeth Seton to Cecilia Seton, August 26, 1808, in *CW*, 2:30.

[29] 5.21, Elizabeth Seton to Julia Scott, March 23, 1809, in *CW*, 2:61.

a devout life of service by making herself "useful as an assistant in Teaching".[30] Her only activity in the matter was to attempt to interest the Filicchi in supporting the plan financially, for it seemed natural to her to look for God's Will in that direction while at the same time leaving things wide open to Divine Providence. "In every daily Mass and at Communion, I beg Him to prepare your heart, and our dear Antonio's, to dispose of me and mine in any way which may please Him", she wrote Filippo Filicchi. "You are our Father in Him; through your hands we received that new and precious being which is indeed true life."[31] But Elizabeth's basic stance was plain: "All is in His hands. If I had a choice, and my will should decide in a moment, I would remain silent in His hands. Oh, how sweet it is, there to rest in perfect confidence."[32] And again, the humble and wise recognition of what was good for her: "For my part, I so naturally look for disappointments and have always found them so conducive to the soul's advancement, that if we succeed in forming the proposed establishment, I shall look upon it as a mark that Almighty God intends an extensive benefit, without calculating my particular interest, which is always best advanced in poverty and in tears."[33]

Of course, Elizabeth was right to expect disappointments, to expect her directors' plans to be contradicted. Experience had taught her so, and so it was.

The Sisters were to staff "an institution for the advancement of Catholic female children in habits of religion".[34]

[30] 4.27, Elizabeth Seton to Bishop John Carroll, November 26, 1806, in CW, 1:420.

[31] 5.18, Elizabeth Seton to Filippo Filicchi, February 8, 1809, in CW, 2:55.

[32] Ibid.

[33] 5.7, Elizabeth Seton to Antonio Filicchi, August 20, 1808, in CW, 2:28.

[34] 5.18, Elizabeth Seton to Filippo Filicchi, February 8, 1809, in CW, 2:54.

Specifically, Elizabeth later told Antonio Filicchi, it was Cooper's "meaning and my hopes" that it "was to have been a nursery only for Our Savior's poor country children", but after a few months, Elizabeth soon realized that providing free education for day scholars deprived the Sisters of Charity of income necessary to buy school supplies and provisions to feed the community.[35] Therefore, she wisely acceded to her advisors and admitted tuition-paying boarding pupils to Saint Joseph School in May 1810. That decision was driven by financial considerations but resulted in a vibrant, mission-driven educational institution. The student body included day scholars, boarding pupils, and orphans. Seven years later, Elizabeth admitted, "it seems it is to be the means of forming *city* girls to Faith and piety as wives and mothers."[36] And these city girls were from comfortable families who could afford to pay for their schooling—they had formed the nucleus of the Baltimore school, and it soon became evident that the Emmitsburg establishment could not succeed without regular income.

Besides, she told Filippo Filicchi, Mr. Cooper "desires extremely to extend the plan to the reception of the aged, and also uneducated persons, who may be employed in spinning, knitting, etc., so as to found a manufactory on a small scale which may be very beneficial to the poor".[37] Cooper's idea of establishing a "manufactory" did not become a reality.

Archbishop Carroll and the Sulpicians desired that the establishment be in Baltimore. According to Cooper's

[35] 7.87, Elizabeth Seton to Antonio Filicchi, June 1, 1817, in *CW*, 2:479. Saint Joseph School began on February 22, 1810, to educate girls from impoverished families in the area.

[36] Ibid.

[37] 5.18, Elizabeth Seton to Filippo Filicchi, February 8, 1809, in *CW*, 2:54.

stipulation, it was made at Emmitsburg, "contrary to all the former convictions of this ecclesiastic [Dubourg] and those of the founders"—according to Dubourg himself— "and what is still more astonishing, in spite of the strongest opposition of the venerable Archbishop Carroll, who yielded at last to the force of circumstances".[38] Circumstances and contradictions again—and they were not to cease. The Sisterhood an established fact, Elizabeth's first and lasting contradiction was intensely personal. She simply did not like being a superior, a distaste with which many religious superiors can surely empathize. Certainly her heart was high at the realization of her "sweet dream of imagination" and the life of charity it offered, when she wrote to Julia Scott two days before pronouncing private vows of chastity and obedience: "To speak the joy of my soul at the prospect of being able to assist the Poor, visit the sick, comfort the sorrowful, clothe little innocents, and teach them to love God!—there I must stop!"[39] When she and the first little band of candidates were discussing the future of the community with Archbishop Carroll and her Sulpician advisors, the full force of the responsibility for what she had undertaken bore down suddenly on her. Whether from suppressed emotions, feelings of inadequacy, or cumulative stress of life transitions, Elizabeth wept silently for some minutes; then, falling to her knees, she confessed before them all her faults and failures since childhood and, with hands and eyes raised to heaven, cried out: "My gracious God! You know my unfitness for this task. I, who by my sins have so often crucified you, I blush with shame

---

[38] Rev. William Dubourg to Abbé Henri Élévès, July 15, 1828, Saint Elizabeth Ann Seton, 1-3-3-2 (102), APSL.

[39] 5.21, Elizabeth Seton to Julia Scott, March 23, 1809, in *CW*, 2:62.

and confusion. How can I teach others, who know so little myself, and am so miserable and imperfect?"[40]

Elizabeth accepted her mission with humility and fulfilled it nobly. When the Rule was formally ratified in 1812, Mother Seton wrote in her journal: "Eternity! Mother! What a celestial commission intrusted [sic]! Mother of the [Sisters and] Daughters of Charity, by whom so much is to do also for God through their short life!"[41]

In a strictly human sense, Elizabeth was quite right about her scarce preparation to be not only a superior but also a foundress. A convert of only four years, she knew as little as her artless Sisters about living a consecrated life in community. When she and they began a spiritual retreat at Emmitsburg on August 10, 1809, it was the first any of them had made. It was understandable, therefore, that this further solemn step in the community's development—when she dwelt upon its fresh call to duty and candidly recognized her own lack of experience—should reawaken the uneasiness of her soul.

Sister Cecilia O'Conway, Elizabeth's first candidate, countered it with fond, wise advice: "My beloved Mother, how [you] surprise me by your alarm on the duties of a Superior", the young woman wrote.

Precious soul, what is the difference between it and those of a Christian parent? . . .

Spiritual parent[s] must be both attentive to soul and body, attentive to keep the proud and self-willed under obedience, the same restrained as a spoiled child, yielding with parental indulgence where neither sin, fault, nor breach of rules are in danger. . . .

[40] Charles I. White, *Life of Mrs. Eliza A. Seton: Foundress and First Superior of the Sisters or Daughters of Charity in the United States of America* (Baltimore, Md., John Murphy & Co., 1859), 240.

[41] 11.15, "Suffer patiently . . .", n.d., in *CW*, 3b:31.

Be a mild, patient but firm MAMMA, and you need not tremble under the burden of superiority. Jesus can never give you a task above your courage, strength, or ability. Come, precious darling, don't let uneasiness and fear appear so plain to the weak. You must at least be the MOON, if the sun is too bright and too dignified a character. The more gentle and modest light will suit our valley in the growing fervor of your little Company.[42]

Gratefully, Elizabeth wrote on the back of the letter: "One of Cecilia's admirable lessons to me—do read it and pray for her."[43]

Father Simon Bruté, Elizabeth's spiritual companion and dear friend, attested to her reticence in the role, noting that she was "little inclined to preach to others ... to have, as Superior, to instruct, direct, reprove ... so impressed that she did poorly, badly, neglectfully, and to the injury of souls".[44] This was a cross, indeed, to be obliged to "instruct, direct, reprove" her Sisters—all good and trusting souls!! Elizabeth herself described her pain humbly but graphically. "Conscience reproaches aloud—how little charity and delicacy of love I practice in that vile habit of speaking of the faults of others", she acknowledged to Bruté, "of the *short, cold, repulsive conduct* to my betters, as all certainly are, and for much of my behavior to you, my VISIBLE SAVIOR, I would put it out (especially some words of reproach and disappointment the other day). I would put them and it out with my blood!... I am in one

---

[42] 7.199, Memorandum, Christmas 1818, in *CW*, 2:597n1, brackets in published version.

[43] Ibid., 597.

[44] [Sister Loyola Law, D.C., ed.], *Mother Seton: Notes by Rev. Simon Gabriel Bruté*, "Her Humility", entry of August 24, 1820 (Emmitsburg, Md.: Daughters of Charity, 1884), 94.

continual watch to keep down my eyebrows and wear a ready smile, if even it sometimes be 'ghastly!' "[45]

Basically, her humility sometimes led Elizabeth to excessive self-scrutiny. All her tasks as superior were not harsh and displeasing, but the pleasant ones prompted her examination most of all, as she admitted to Bruté, "This part of *sitting at the pen smiling at the people* young and old, it is too dangerously pleasing"—yet even here—"His dear Will is *All*, though."[46] Like all holy persons, she had a keen understanding of her imperfections and a purity of love that made awareness of them painful for her. Ordinary men and women are inclined to smile at the apprehensions of guilt of holy persons as exaggerations. They are nothing of the kind. Holy men and women abhor sin and understand its consequences. The smallest imperfection stands out in stark contrast to the clarity of their souls. Vincent de Paul demonstrated this clear-eyed vision when admonishing a brother who had expressed his shame for "profiting so little from the good example" of Vincent and the "marvelous thing he saw" in him. The saint replied later: "Brother, it's a practice among us never to praise anyone in his presence" and added that "he was truly a wonder, but a wonder of malice, more wicked than the devil . . . that he wasn't exaggerating."[47]

Bruté understood the supreme standards of the saints and, therefore, even during the last retreat of Elizabeth's

---

[45] 7.257, Elizabeth Seton to Rev. Simon Bruté, P.S.S., [August 1820], in *CW*, 2:663–64; 6.169, Elizabeth Seton to Rev. Simon Bruté, P.S.S. [August 6, 1814], in *CW*, 2:281.

[46] 7.283, Elizabeth Seton to Rev. Simon Bruté, P.S.S. [January 24], in *CW*, 2:683.

[47] Document 93, Reflections from Repetition of Prayer, June 26, 1642, *Vincent de Paul: Correspondence, Conferences, Documents*, ed., trans., Marie Poole, D.C. et al., 14 vols. (New York: New City Press, 1983–2014), 11:108.

life, did not hesitate to admonish her "to watch constantly over your exterior—your words, above all. This increasing authority tempered by a certain modesty and goodness will inspire confidence and respect without diminishing affection. God gives it to you so naturally."[48] Yet his judgment of the minuteness of guilt in Elizabeth is evident in her honest acknowledgment: "As to *private* concerns, I have none, unless it be my trials occasionally at the conduct of different Sisters, and that you have forbid me speaking of; and since you think proper, and I am acquitted before God, I am too happy it is so."[49] Bruté made his judgment public after Elizabeth's death: she was, he attested, "a true pattern to her Sisters: their Mother for love, their Servant for humility, their true Superior for prudent guidance, their friend in Every pain" they felt.[50]

Striking examples that Elizabeth was indeed "their friend in every pain" were her vigorous defenses of the Sisters' rights. The first occurred at the very outset of their community life. For reasons best known to himself, Father William Dubourg, their first Sulpician superior, forbade them to go to Confession to his confrere Father Pierre Babade, whom the Sisters considered their first spiritual father, and to cease all correspondence with him. The second was even more serious for the community's durability. Father John Baptist David, who despite Mother Seton's expressed misgivings had been appointed second superior of the Sisterhood when Dubourg had resigned in a huff over the Babade affair and Elizabeth's forthright reaction to it, took over the community as his private fief, usurped the Mother's office, and even determined to replace her

[48] [Law], *Mother Seton: Notes*, 91.
[49] 7.191, Elizabeth Seton to Rev. Simon Bruté, P.S.S., [November 1818], in *CW*, 2:591.
[50] Bruté, *Memoir*, Saint Elizabeth Ann Seton, 1-3-3-12(9), APSL.

with his protégé, Sister Rose Landry White. His actions came close to destroying the Sisterhood before it was firmly established.

Both these crises, by exacerbating Elizabeth's innate distaste for governing, were serious tests of her commitment to God's Will and her religious obedience. She was candid about the anguish they caused her and intrepid in suffering it. "I have had a great many very hard trials, my Father, since you were here," she acknowledged to Archbishop Carroll,

> but you, of course, will congratulate me on them, as this fire of tribulation is no doubt meant to consume the many imperfections and bad dispositions Our Lord finds in me. Indeed, it has at times burnt so deep that the anguish could not be concealed; but by degrees custom reconciles pain itself, and I determine, dry and hard as my daily bread is, to take it with as good a grace as possible. When I carry it before Our Lord, sometimes He makes me laugh at myself and asks me what other kind I would choose in the Valley of tears than that which Himself and all His followers made use of.[51]

And to her friend Matthias O'Conway she made a truly startling admission: "You will laugh at me when I tell you I have seen more real affliction and sorrow here in the ten months since our removal [from Baltimore] than in all the thirty-five years of my past life, which was all marked by affliction", she wrote. "You will laugh, I repeat, because you will know that the fruit will not be lost—at least, I hope not; though, indeed, sometimes I tremble."[52]

---

[51] 6.12, Elizabeth Seton to Archbishop John Carroll, December 14, 1809, in *CW*, 2:92.

[52] 6.46, Elizabeth Seton to Matthias O'Conway, June 5, 1811, in *CW*, 2:140.

The deaths of her young sisters-in-law, Harriet and Cecilia Seton, and the constant illness in the house were, to be sure, part of the affliction and sorrow, but it cannot be doubted that the assaults on the peace and future of her community were uppermost.

Elizabeth continued to do what she had to do, much as she disliked it, because "the Dearest says, 'You shall, you must, only because I will it.' "[53] She believed that He spoke to her through her archbishop, who wrote of her community and her office, "It is not to flatter or nourish pride ... that I declare an opinion and belief, that its ultimate success under God depends on your sacrificing yourself, notwithstanding all the uneasiness and disgust you may experience, and continuing in your place of Superior."[54] And again: "If you should ever be permitted to resign your maternal charge over your Community, I would rejoice on your own individual account, but my hope for the continuance of the establishment would be very much weakened."[55] It was not the first time Elizabeth waited for the revelation of the Will of God on the nod of a superior, no matter for how long, or the first time she waited for Carroll's approval. When Cecilia Seton was detained in New York at the insistence of her pastor, Elizabeth had laid the matter before Carroll. "Whatever he decided," she told Cecilia, "I shall conclude to be the Will of God, and will never say one word more about your joining me until it pleases him to show us it is right."[56]

[53] 7.326, Elizabeth Seton to a Clergyman, [after 1810], in *CW*, 2:708.

[54] Archbishop John Carroll to Elizabeth Seton, March 11, 1810, Saint Elizabeth Ann Seton, 1-3-3-1(42), APSL.

[55] Ibid.

[56] Archbishop John Carroll to Elizabeth Seton, [March 24, 1809], formerly in Archives, Sisters of Charity of New York, 100-115-1-45; transferred 2022-EAS-2-73 to APSL.

Elizabeth was not yet spiritually adept, but her heart was right—lowly and obedient. When Dubourg, to her dismay, had resigned—an action she had neither intended nor wanted—she admitted humbly to Carroll: "In my place, my dear Father, you would have experienced my trial, but you would at once have offered it up to God. I am late in seeing the necessity of this measure, but not too late, I hope, since it is never too late with our good Lord.... You will see how good a child I am going to be. Quite a little child. And perhaps you will have often to give me the food of little children yet, but I will do my best as I have promised you in every case."[57]

It would never be too late for Elizabeth Seton for, however she might stumble, her eyes were fixed on God and her "dear eternity", and she knew and accepted the rough road ahead. "His adorable Will be done during the few remaining days of my tiresome journey," she wrote with finality to her friend George Weis, "which, being made with so many tears and sown so thick with crosses, will certainly be concluded with joy and crowned with eternal rest."[58]

How many testimonies there are to Elizabeth's clear-sighted—and farsighted—vision and hard-won accep-tance! When the archbishop and the Sulpician priests, Elizabeth's "Reverend Gentlemen", were pondering the feasibility of having a mother with five children as head of the Sisterhood, she stated her own position simply to Weis: "Here I stand with hands and eyes both lifted to wait the adorable Will. The only word I have to say to every question is: *I am a Mother*. Whatever providence

[57] 6.9, Elizabeth Seton to Archbishop John Carroll, November 2, 1809, in *CW*, 2:88.

[58] 6.57, Elizabeth Seton to George Weis, August 9, 1809 or 1810, in *CW*, 2:156.

awaits me consistent with that plea, I say Amen to it."[59] Indeed, she reminded the archbishop that "surely, an Individual is not to be considered where a public good is in question; and you know I would gladly make every sacrifice you think consistent with my first and inseparable obligations as a Mother."[60] It was on the occasion of one or another of the succession of decisions made by her superiors, decisions that affected her deeply, that she wrote calmly: "At this very time the question must be in motion, and the *Adored's Vote* will decide."[61] Such a surety that God would always prevail made life tranquil underneath the storms of contradictions and pain. God did not wait for eternity to reward Elizabeth's steadfastness. When the long, drawn-out turmoil of clerical interference was ended with Carroll's first approval of the Rule, he assured her that the future would free her "from a state in which it was difficult to walk straight, as you had no certain way in which to proceed".[62] Nothing like the Babade-Dubourg controversy would ever again be allowed to disturb peace of soul, for "every allowance shall be made not only to the Sisters generally, but to each one in particular."[63] As for usurpation of authority, like David's, not only would no Sulpician "but your immediate Superior, residing near you ... have any share in the government or concerns of the Sisters",[64] but also even his role was generally to be restricted. The archbishop

[59] 6.74, Elizabeth Seton to George Weis, [April 27, 1811], in *CW*, 2:181.

[60] 6.83, Elizabeth Seton to Archbishop John Carroll, September 5, 1811, in *CW*, 2:196.

[61] 6.88, Elizabeth Seton to George Weis, [December 11 or 12, 1811], in *CW*, 2:200.

[62] A-6.83a, Archbishop John Carroll to Elizabeth Seton, September 11, 1811, in *CW*, 2:746.

[63] Ibid., 745–46.

[64] Ibid., 746.

made plain his will "to confine the administration of your own affairs, and the internal and domestic government, as much as possible, to your own institutions once adopted, and within your own walls. Your Superior or Confessor need be informed or consulted in matters where the Mother and her Council need his advice."[65] The wisdom of the Father of the Church in America never shone more brightly than in these determinations.

The peace and reward that had come to her community did not, of course, exempt Elizabeth from the personal testing that she had long recognized as "the safest and surest" way to sanctity and heaven. When death claimed Anna Maria, called Annina, at age sixteen, Elizabeth freely confessed the depths of her grief: "The Separation from my Angel has left so new and deep an impression on my mind, that if I was not obliged to live in these dear ones, I should unconsciously die in her"—but, lest she be misunderstood—"unconsciously," she repeated, "for never by a free act of the mind will I ever regret *His Will*".[66] Four years later, the untimely death of fourteen-year-old Rebecca, her youngest, was still to be endured, as well as the separations from her restless sons, to say nothing of the constant heartbreaks from their thoughtlessness and her anxiety for their souls. Her unswerving attitude of soul in it all would ever be, nonetheless, an echo of her cry to Julia Scott in the midst of the sickness and death of that first awful Christmas at Emmitsburg: "Here I go like iron or rock, day after day, *as He pleases and how He pleases*; but, to be sure, when my turn comes

[65] Ibid.

[66] 6.116, Elizabeth Seton to Eliza Sadler, September 14, 1812, in *CW*, 2:227. During Anna Maria's stay in Livorno, the Filicchi family affectionately referred to her as Annina (little Anna), an endearing name she used for the rest of her life.

I shall be very glad."[67] Even the unending string of personal trials were, however, softened with extraordinary graces, of which the gift of Father Simon Bruté as spiritual companion and friend was the chief. Rejoicing in his understanding of her eager, bursting soul, Elizabeth exulted: "Blessed G., I am so in love now with the rules that I see the bit of the bridle all gold, and the reins all of silk. You know my sincerity, since, with the little attraction to your Brother's [Dubois] government, I ever eagerly seek the grace [of the] cords he entangles me with."[68]

Elizabeth's greatest reward was the divine, contemplative peace of her last months. "I once told you how I wished to do as you have done," she finished a letter of advice to a priest friend, "and I will tell you *in return*, that all the illusioning and spider web of *earthly weaving* is broken, and nothing now more bright and steady than the *divine lamp* He feeds and trims Himself, *because, as I suppose, I stayed in Obedience*. Oh, this Master and *Father* we serve! ... How can we be happy enough in His service?"[69] She did not mean obedience to any particular hierarchical supervisor, priest, or director but to the Will of God, which she loved with her whole soul and which she had sought *through* her superiors and in the events and contradictions of a constantly shifting life.

Elizabeth's final denouement was hardly surprising. When she began the long, final decline to death in September, Bruté tried to cheer her: "Well, they think you a little better—a hard fight—they here below praying their best to keep you with us—they, above calling, I suppose to

[67] 6.14, Elizabeth Seton to Julia Scott, December 27, 1809, in *CW*, 2:95.

[68] 6.146, Elizabeth Seton to Rev. Simon Bruté, P.S.S., n.d., in *CW*, 2:259.

[69] 7.147, Elizabeth Seton to Rev. John Hickey, P.S.S., [before March 19, 1818], in *CW*, 2:536.

have you happy with them!" She cut through it all: "You, Will—only the Will." "I hope ..." Elizabeth responded. And again: "Only the Will."[70]

As Mother and foundress, Elizabeth Seton was careful to transmit to her Sisters the spiritual principle of following the Will of God in which she was now indeed adept. "What was the first rule of our dear Savior's life?" she asked in a conference.

> You know it was to do His *Father's Will*. Well, then, the first end I propose in our daily work is to do the *Will of God*; secondly, to do it in the manner He wills it; and thirdly, *to do it because it is His Will*. I know what His Will is by those who direct me; whatever they bid me do, if it is ever so small in itself, is the Will of God for me. Then do it in the *manner* He wills it—not sewing an old thing as if it were new, or a new thing as if it were old; not fretting because the oven is too hot, or in a fuss because it is too cold, etc., etc. You understand—not flying and driving because you are hurried, nor creeping like a snail because no one pushes you. Our dear Savior was never in extremes. And the third object is *to do this Will because God wills it*, that is, to be ready to quit at any moment, and do anything else we may be called to do.[71]

The Church has selected this blueprint for perfection to be read in the Office of Readings on her feast. Another Vincentian woman, her sister in religion, Saint Catherine Labouré, the Daughter of Charity in France whom the Blessed Virgin instructed to have the Miraculous Medal made in 1830, echoed it in her own formula for sanctity:

---

[70] [Law], *Mother Seton: Notes*, 15.
[71] 9.9, Mother Seton's Last Writings, n.d., in *CW*, 3a:254–55.

to do what she was given to do by her superiors, as well as she could, and for God.

Elizabeth Ann Seton held to her firm commitment to God's Will, as an Episcopalian and a Catholic, in an age that laughed at such folly and even before she was fully instructed and guided by orderly spiritual direction. The age was one of change and confusion, much like the present. Spawn of the Enlightenment, Voltaire's rationalism, skepticism, and rejection of the supernatural, and Rousseau's doctrines of the natural goodness of man—and man, the sole judge of his own actions—held powerful sway (Elizabeth herself had been fascinated by the latter's works, especially *Emile*, which "once", she admitted ruefully, "composed my Sunday devotion").[72] Like these two protagonists of the Enlightenment, Elizabeth's father, seemingly, and a fair number of her friends were Deists, believing vaguely in God but denying His interest in or influence over His creatures. The freedom and individuality of man were very much in the air in the wake of the American and French Revolutions. Yet, to her everlasting glory, Elizabeth refused to go with the tide, binding herself fast to the God of Revelation and His designs, tightening the bonds, as she knew Him better as a loving God.

Elizabeth was confident she had chosen wisely, as she assured Julia Scott: "If you knew half the really good your friend possesses, while the world thinks she is deprived of everything worth having, you would ... allow that she has truly and really the best of it."[73] And she wrote in happy awe to Antonio Filicchi: "Oh Antonio, my Brother dear,

[72] 4.55, Spiritual Journal to Cecilia Seton, August 10 to October 16, 1807, entry of September 16, in *CW*, 1:475.
[73] 6.7, Elizabeth Seton to Julia Scott, September 20, 1809, in *CW*, 2:85.

the ways of Our God how wonderful! See my good ...
sister [Mary Bayley] Post and excellent Mrs. [Julia] Scott
wrapped in their blindness, and *I* in the milk and honey of
Canaan already, beside the heavenly perspective."[74]

[74] 6.214, Elizabeth Seton to Antonio Filicchi,. November 20, 1815, in *CW*,
2:357, brackets in published version.

4

Prayer of the Heart

Every saint, indeed, must be committed to prayer. The prayer of the saints, their lifeline to God, communicates their vulnerabilities and their needs to Him, receiving back the warmth and strength of God's love. In prayer a person seeks light and finds enlightenment, longs for love and experiences Divine Love.

Prayer experiences of Elizabeth Seton, even in childhood and adolescence, have already been noted. As she settled into maturity, prayer became truly her way of life and influenced everything she did as a wife, mother, and society matron. Following Saint Paul with wholehearted earnestness, whether she ate or drank or whatever else she did, she did all for the glory of God. Her life of devotion and prayer developed progressively because of her reading and reflection on Sacred Scripture and hearing well-prepared sermons by Rev. John Henry Hobart at Trinity Church. Guided by the Holy Spirit, Elizabeth intuited God's presence and relied on Divine Providence throughout her life.

As an Episcopalian woman of faith, Elizabeth's prayer was unerringly built on the Presence of God, a practice that for centuries the Church has enjoined on eager young novices who are in religious formation for living a consecrated life. "Do I realize it", she asked herself, "*the protecting presence, the consoling grace of my Redeemer and God*? He raises me from the Dust to feel that I am near Him; He drives away all sorrow to fill me with His consolations. He is my *guide, my friend*, and *Supporter*—with such a *guide*, can I fear? With such a friend, shall I not *be satisfied*? With such a supporter, can I fall?"[1] It was the wide-eyed discovery of the beginner: she would not use the word *feel* to express the nearness of God in later years, nor would she then wish sorrow driven away or be filled with or even expect consolations—but it was authentic and typical of God's early tenderness toward the willing disciple.

Even more, while worshipping at Trinity Church, Elizabeth's pious soul, already tried with sorrow, quickly responded to the starker realities beneath God's tenderness. In an entry in a notebook of reflections in 1802, Elizabeth wrote this about human life and Divine Love: "It is true the Journey is long, the burden is heavy, but the Lord delivers His faithful servants from all their troubles—and sometimes, even here, allows them some hours of sweetest Peace as the earnest of eternal blessedness—Is it nothing to sleep serene under His guardian wing, to awake to the brightness of the glorious sun with renewed strength and renewed blessings?"[2] She was beginning to feel the sting anew; it had not gone away, and she was counting her blessings almost defensively, but in the next breath there is a burst of insight that pierces to the heart of prayer and the spiritual life: "To be blessed with the power of instant communion with the Father of our Spirits, the sense of His presence—the influences of His love".[3] How much that one word *instant* reveals of her progress! How close already her communion with her only Beloved! How wholly her life is already influenced, molded, and guided by His love

[1] 8.16, "And do I realize it . . .", n.d., in *CW*, 3a:32.
[2] 8.10, "My peace I leave with you . . .", May 1802, in *CW*, 3a:24.
[3] Ibid.

is in the understanding and acceptance of what follows: "To be assured of that love is enough to tie us faithfully to Him, and while we have fidelity to Him, all the surrounding cares and contradictions of this Life are but Cords of mercy to send us faster to Him who will hereafter make even their remembrances to vanish in the reality of our eternal felicity."[4] Her perception of the purpose and effectiveness of trials and tribulations would not be more unerring on her deathbed.

Elizabeth wrote these words on the eve of the Ascension, and her entry for the feast itself has the impulsiveness of love and the humility of patience: "Oh that my Soul could go up with my blessed Lord—that it might be *where He is also*—Thy will be done—my time is in Thy hands. . . . raise us up by a life of faith with Thee."[5]

Although far from as common among creatures as it should be, the mystery of divine union (the sense of God's presence) is simple and uncomplicated, even easy. The problem is the complexity of fallen human nature, which sees difficulties everywhere and insists upon doing things its own way, thus posing the greatest difficulty of all. "How pitiful is it", Elizabeth lamented to her spiritual daughters, "to put our devotion in a multitude of prayers too often repeated, without attention to what we say, and scarcely thinking to whom we speak—without listening to God, who would receive so much more glory from even the shortest adorations proceeding from the heart. The least sentence—'I adore you, my God; I love you, my God; I submit wholly to Your adorable Will'—would be so much more agreeable to Him."[6]

---

[4] Ibid.

[5] Ibid., 24–25.

[6] 9.20, Exercise of the *Presence of God*, n.d., "In What Does the Exercise of the Presence of God Consist", in *CW*, 3a:398.

Elizabeth's own uncomplicated docility saw this wondrous mystery of divine union as simply "instant communion" and as "the simple look of the heart to God". In her later years of spiritual wisdom, little had changed. Even her urging it upon her Sisters was gentle: This "simple look of the heart to God", she assured them, "draws and unites it to Him in a sentiment of peace and confidence, the fruit of His goodness to those who love Him".[7] It was common practice, one with which they were familiar in varying degrees, she insinuated encouragingly: "Those less practiced in this heavenly exercise must humbly beg Him to advance them in it, that *the look of their Soul* may be continually toward Him, and when they find it has been sometime diverted from this adorable object, it must say to itself: 'What have we been doing; where were we so long without thinking of Our God?'"[8]

Elizabeth herself had become truly proficient by now, as she once artlessly revealed to her director: "I have not done as much community work of hearing, seeing, and speaking in the last month as this day, with a heart as 'still as a calm at sea'.... Now *sleep* with *Him* from whom I think I have not parted a minute since I saw you."[9] Easy as this unbroken union seemed, she knew it was not and instructed the Sisters of Charity "that God does not grant to all the facility of thinking of Him *continually*, though all can *frequently* do it if they will".[10]

As always, Elizabeth did not demand of her Sisters "six impossible things before breakfast" but patiently showed them how to master what may have seemed impossible

---

[7] Ibid., 397.

[8] Ibid. ·

[9] 7.62, Elizabeth Seton to Rev. Simon Bruté, P.S.S., [November], in *CW*, 2:449.

[10] 9.20, Exercise of the *Presence of God*, n.d., "In What Does the Exercise of the Presence of God Consist", in *CW*, 3a:403.

to them at first.[11] "A simple remembrance of the Presence of God *in us*" was a starting point.[12] It was "particularly recommended", she said, "not to exclude the view of His presence everywhere, but to call our attention to our own interior, and help us the more easily to be recollected". The "trial ... of much exterior occupation" could be an obstacle, she conceded, but such occupation did not include the work they had embraced consecrated life to do: "It must be repeated there is no greater error", she insisted, "than to imagine that the very employments which God Himself gives us shall force us to forget Him while we are engaged in them"; to forestall objection, she resorted to practical experience: "In the most hurried time, we speak to those who are round us, talk of the work we are doing, and yet cannot remember *HIM* who is so powerful and ready to help us through it."[13]

"*The love of talk*", Elizabeth reminded as well, "distracts all the powers of our Soul from God, and fills them with earthly objects and impressions, like a vessel of water which cannot be clear and settled while you are continually stirring the earthy particles from the bottom."[14] And, "*self-love* is directly opposed to charity and an insuperable obstacle to our union with God."[15] Above all, she implored, "be not like those who are before Him like a slave and wait the end of their duty of obligation to find their liberty and pleasure in leaving Him."[16]

---

[11] Rev. Charles L. Dodgson (Lewis Carroll) in Chapter 5, "Wool and Water", *Through the Looking Glass* (London: Macmillan and Co., 1871), 42. Cf. http://www.literaturepage.com/read/throughthelookingglass-42.html#google_vignette.

[12] 9.20, Exercise of the *Presence of God*, n.d., "In What Does the Exercise of the Presence of God Consist", in *CW*, 3a:397.

[13] Ibid., 406.

[14] Ibid., 405.

[15] Ibid., 404–5.

[16] Ibid., 405.

Nonetheless, they were to be proud of their calling to the active apostolate: "If the contemplative Magdalenes enjoy more sweetness, they do not possess more merit", Elizabeth stated bluntly.[17] "One who runs over a whole city carrying God in their thoughts is much more pleasing in His sight than another who lets their thoughts run about while they are kneeling in an oratory."[18]

After all explanation and warning, however, Elizabeth returned to what she had learned as a young Protestant matron: "The best means to increase the *love* of God in our heart, which would make the practice of the Presence of God so easy to us, is to consider Him as our *tender Father. . . . Our look of love at Him draws back a look of love on us*, and His divine look enkindles that fire of love in us which makes us remember Him continually."[19]

"Fire of love" is an expression used routinely but seldom experienced.[20] Elizabeth Seton knew what it meant when she used it. "Nothing in our state of clouds and Veils I can see so plainly as how the saints died of love and joy," she once penned to Bruté, "since I, so wretched and truly miserable, can only read word after word of the blessed 83rd and 41st Psalms in unutterable feelings even to Our God through the thousand pressings and overflowings—God—God—God, that the Supreme delight, that He is God, and to open the mouth and heart wide that He may fill it."[21] She understood the necessity of letting go of oneself, of giving

[17] Ibid., 407.

[18] Ibid.

[19] Ibid., 401.

[20] The fire of God's love embraces everyone: "I came to cast fire upon the earth; and would that it were already kindled!" (Lk 12:49). "The Living Flame of Love", a poem by St. John of the Cross, reflects this theme.

[21] 7.286, Elizabeth Seton to Rev. Simon Bruté, P.S.S., n.d., in *CW*, 2:684. Psalms 83 and 41 (Ps 84 and 42 in the contemporary Catholic Bible) are prayers of longing for God.

way completely to God, of immersing oneself in Him, as she expressed it, as the blessed reward of His love and peace flooded every recess of her soul. "God is so infinitely present to us that He is in every part of our life and being—nothing can separate us from Him. He is more intimately present to us than we are to ourselves, and whatever we do is done in Him."[22]

Elizabeth expressed it even more fully in a supreme definition of the Presence of God that is also as supreme a definition of prayer: "A respectful *Silence* before the Divine Majesty, a silence which the Great Saint Denis calls the *highest praise*."[23] (Saint John Paul II has called this silence "the greatest prayer".) Such silence, Elizabeth continues, "when proceeding from our impressions of His perfections and greatness, is the most suitable homage we can offer Him, losing ourselves in His Divine Presence, in our deep abasement having no desire or wish but to be conformed to His Will and wholly sacrificed to Him."[24]

It is not surprising that she who was the most devoted of mothers, wives, relatives, and friends should especially seek the ones she loved in God and share the discovery, so comforting to weak humanity, with others. "The accidents of life separate us from our dearest friends, but let us not despond", Elizabeth cautioned her Sisters. "God is like a looking-glass in which souls see each other."[25] It was a bold but penetrating grasp of God's simplicity and omniscience thus to see in them the communion of saints, for it is evident that it was friends of God she meant. "The more we are united to Him by love, the nearer we are to those who belong to Him. Jesus Christ encompasses all

[22] 9.20, Exercise of the *Presence of God*, n.d., in *CW*, 3a:392.
[23] Ibid., "In What Does the Exercise of the Presence of God Consist", 398.
[24] Ibid.
[25] 11.29, "Union in God," n.d., in *CW*, 3b:42.

places, and all His members center in Him; we need but prostrate at His feet to find them. They may be hidden from the eyes of our body, but not from the eyes of our soul and of Faith."[26]

Elizabeth's prayer, quite naturally, grew, intertwining itself with her daily life and its every action and event. It would be impossible to search out every thread, but it can be rewarding to trace the pattern of prayer in major crises of her life to perceive its luminous power.

Throughout the terrifying ordeal of her husband's last illness in the San Jacopo Lazaretto, prayer was Elizabeth's only resource. From the very first day, it was her "trust that God ... will carry us on. He is our all indeed. My eyes smart so much with crying, wind, and fatigue, that I must close them and lift up my heart."[27] When, on the second day, "the Matin Bells awakened my Soul to its most painful regrets", she regretted that her "agony of Sorrow ... could not at first find relief even in prayer"; but "I ... came to my senses and reflected that I was offending my only Friend and Resource in my misery and voluntarily shutting out from my Soul the only consolation it could receive. Pleading for Mercy and Strength brought Peace."[28] This first taste of peace in a forlorn situation quickly communicated itself to Elizabeth's frightened little daughter Anna Maria: "Ann with a flood of tears prayed a blessing and soon forgot her sorrows; and it seemed", the mother recognized anew, "as if opening my Prayer Book and bending my knees was the Signal for my Soul to find rest".[29] This blessed tranquility reached almost an ecstasy of divine union as the horrible hours and days dragged on

---

[26] Ibid.
[27] 2.7, Journal to Rebecca Seton, November 19, 1803, in *CW*, 1:253.
[28] Ibid., 254.
[29] Ibid., 255.

and on. Asked whether she would not want another person with her during the ordeal—"Oh, no! What had I to fear? And what had I to fear? I laid down as if to rest, that he [William Magee Seton] might not be uneasy. Listened all night: sometimes by the fire, sometimes lying down, sometimes thought the breathing stopped—and kissed his poor face to feel if it was cold—and sometimes [I was] alarmed by its heaviness. Well, was I alone? Dear, indulgent Father! Could I be alone while clinging fast to Thee in continued Prayer or Thanksgiving?"[30]

Prayer—her own and her Catholic friends'—effected Elizabeth's conversion, brought her, she acknowledged, "to the light of Thy truth, notwithstanding every affection of my heart and power of my will was opposed to it".[31]

Prayer undergirded Elizabeth's apostolic community and her school. "[Father Babade] applies to me the Psalms in our Vespers: 'The Barren Woman shall be the joyful Mother of children', and tells me to repeat it Continually," she wrote Cecilia Seton, "which you must do with me, my darling."[32] And she informed Antonio Filicchi, "Every morning at the Divine Sacrifice, I offer (as I know they [the Sulpician Fathers] do also) the whole success to Him whose blessed Will alone can sanctify and make it fruitful."[33] Father William Dubourg gave the most startling testimony about the manifestation of the power of prayer at work:

An insurmountable obstacle impeded any plans, which was the complete lack of financial means to lay the foundations of this new Society. They [Dubourg and Elizabeth]

[30] Ibid., 268.
[31] 2.14, Journal to Rebecca Seton continued, April 18, [1804], in *CW*, 1:299.
[32] 5.10, Elizabeth Seton to Cecilia Seton, October 6, 1808, in *CW*, 2:34–35.
[33] 5.7, Elizabeth Seton to Antonio Filicchi, August 20, 1808, in *CW*, 2:28.

decided to pray God together to remove the obstacle. One morning in 1808, Mrs. E[lizabeth] Seton went to see her director [Dubourg] and said to him, even if she might seem a visionary to him, she felt obliged to put forward to him what Our Lord had just ordered her in a clear and intelligible voice after communion. "Go," He had told her, "speak to Mr. Cooper; he will give all that is necessary to begin the establishment."[34]

That evening Samuel Cooper, independently and knowing nothing of the project, asked Dubourg why nothing was done for the education of women. Apprised of Elizabeth's intentions and the obstacle in their way, he replied, "I have ten thousand dollars which I can give you for this purpose."[35]

Elizabeth, now called Mother Seton, and her first band of Sisters, destined for consecrated life, began to live together as a community of apostolic women in the tiny Stone House in Saint Joseph's Valley near Emmitsburg, Maryland, on July 31, 1809. They did so in the spirit of profound prayer. The previous day, seeking God's blessing together, they solemnized their intent by participating in the Liturgy of the Eucharist at the earliest Mass at Saint Joseph's Church in the village of Emmitsburg, all going to Confession and receiving their Lord in Holy Communion. They were responding to their Baptism and God's call to consecrate their lives to God for the service of poor persons and the education of young women.

Dubourg drafted *Provisional Regulations* in accord with that "order of regularity" that Mother Seton insisted on from the

[34] Rev. William Dubourg to Abbé Henri Elévès, July 15, 1828, Saint Elizabeth Ann Seton, 1-3-3-2 (102), APSL.
[35] Ibid.

first and that "cannot be skipped over here".[36] The *Regulations* included rising at five o'clock, morning prayers and meditation before (in the earliest months), walking to Mass at Saint Joseph's Church in town or Saint Mary's Church on the mountain, and reciting the Rosary on the way back; the day went on with Sacred Scripture and *The Spiritual Combat* read at meals, examens of conscience, visits to the Blessed Sacrament, spiritual reading, work, and recreation.[37] Soon Elizabeth sent a letter to update Archbishop Carroll:

> Now I am going straight on by Faith but, if I were to indulge myself, instead of rejoicing in the delightful prospect of serving and honoring God in a situation I have so long earnestly desired, death and the Grave would be my only anticipation. But you know your child too well to believe any such indulgence is allowed. On the contrary, I abandon myself to God continually and invite all my dear companions to do the same.[38]

Saint Elizabeth Ann's personal approach to prayer was, as one would expect, in accord with theological traditions of the Church and the masters of the spiritual life. She believed, first of all, in God's Divine Providence and tender solicitude for the creatures of His love. "God is with us—and if sufferings abound in us, His Consolations also greatly abound, and far exceed all utterance", she wrote staunchly amid the sufferings of the lazaretto.[39] "If the

[36] 6.54, Elizabeth Seton to Eliza Sadler, [August 3, 1810], in *CW*, 2:153.

[37] Charles I. White, *Life of Mrs. Eliza A. Seton: Foundress and First Superior of the Sisters or Daughters of Charity in the United States of America* (Baltimore, Md.: John Murphy & Co., 1859), 249.

[38] 6.4, Elizabeth Seton to Archbishop John Carroll, [August 6, 1809], in *CW*, 2:78.

[39] 2.7, Journal to Rebecca Seton, November 19, 1803, in *CW*, 1:253.

wind that now almost puts out my light and blows on my William through every crevice, and over our chimney like loud Thunder, could come from any but His command; or if the circumstances that have placed us in so forlorn a situation were not guided by His hand—miserable indeed would be our case."[40] And again: "If I could forget my God one moment at these times, I should go mad."[41]

The next step, to trust in God's power and willingness to intervene in human concerns, was easy, and Elizabeth's belief as firm. "God will not forsake me, Antonio", she assured her "dear Filicchi" in the agony of her conversion to the Catholic faith.[42] "I know that He will unite me to His flock; and, although now my faith is unsettled, I am assured that He will not disappoint my hope, which is fixed on His own word that He will not despise the humble, contrite heart."[43]

This same confidence was still fresh and firm a dozen years later in a letter of promise to Bruté, who had just been named president of Saint Mary's in Baltimore: "Yes, our dear President, you will, you shall have prayers plenty of these most innocent hearts [her daughters and the Sisters], and I say so often *I have a Jesus to offer*— and look up *confidently*—He will not leave you who have left all for Him, nor leave you in weakness while loading yourself for His sake. No, no, no, G—*He will not*. So we press the Crucifix close on the heart, and trust All."[44] What a bold assertion: "*I have a Jesus to offer*"! Yet, she was quite right. Jesus has given Himself to those

---

[40] Ibid., 254.
[41] Ibid., 258.
[42] 3.7, Elizabeth Seton to Antonio Filicchi, August 30, 1804, in *CW*, 1:318.
[43] Ibid.
[44] 7.1, Elizabeth Seton to Rev. Simon Bruté, P.S.S. [January 1816], in *CW*, 2:366.

He redeemed that they might offer Him continuously to the Father. It takes a holy person, an intimate, to say it so bluntly. Elizabeth acknowledged that acquaintances found her "unsettled about the great object of a true Faith",[45] and with her "humble, contrite heart",[46] she put her finger on what can weaken or even obstruct the efficacy of prayer: the dispositions of the one who prays. Her own dispositions, at the time, may indeed have been imperfect, for Bishop Carroll worried whether "the tears she sheds and the prayers she offers to heaven are purely for God's sake and arise solely from compunction for Sin, and are unmixed with any alloy of worldly respects or inordinate Solicitude for the attainment of Some worldly purpose".[47] In later years, Mother Seton herself added to the list of bad dispositions "useless thoughts, inconsiderate words, expressions of natural feelings, and changes of temper", which she saw as stopping "the operations of grace, too often, indeed, even to grieving the Divine Spirit and sending him away".[48]

Elizabeth insisted upon purity of intention and relied upon it to cleanse and clothe those daily actions that were themselves prayers, "going as you know to meet everybody in the grace of the moment, which we never can know till we find the humor and temper of the one we are to meet with—the many mistakes all swallowed and comforted by intention, intention, intention—Our true peace and Security with our beloved".[49]

[45] 3.31, Journal to Amabilia Filicchi, July 19, 1804, in CW, 1:368.

[46] 3.7, Elizabeth Seton to Antonio Filicchi, August 30, 1804, in CW, 1:318.

[47] Rev. William Dubourg to Abbé Henri Elévès, July 15, 1828, Saint Elizabeth Ann Seton, 1-3-3-2 (102), APSL.

[48] White, Mrs. Eliza A. Seton, 326.

[49] 7.31, Elizabeth Seton to Rev. Simon Bruté, P.S.S. [June 1816], in CW, 2:402.

Another delightful quality of prayer and good living Elizabeth urged was *cheerfulness*—a surprising quality at first glance, but not for someone like her, endowed with spirited enthusiasm. "Cheerfulness", she was not afraid to say, "prepares a generous mind for all the noblest acts of Religion—love, adoration, praise, and every union with Our God, as also for duties, charity, happy zeal, useful concern for our neighbor, and all those acts of Piety which should improve cheerfulness and dispose the poor Soul to joyful serenity—resting All upon infinite goodness!, thrice infinite goodness of our adored and beloved."[50] Would that all who love God reflected His good humor as well! Elizabeth Seton exhorted her community that their vocation included both diligence in fulfilling *duties* and the satisfaction of spiritual consolations. This wisdom offered a framework for her companions in their life of service.

Elizabeth herself was the apostle of cheerfulness, as in this note to her friend George Weis concerning the use of holy water, which she used "every day and night ... in the morning to defend from danger—at night to efface the errors of the day. You must allow that Enthusiasts have a region of happiness where the *wise ones* do not enter; [or] if they did, they would find a sort of Greek they could not understand."[51] To poke fun, thus, at the pompous is the best way to deflate them, like the ludicrous plight of the liberated young student of the Sorbonne who discovered that the old man he was baiting for saying the Rosary was Louis Pasteur. The world needs the spirit of fun of an Elizabeth Seton to rout the sober "intellectuals" who find sacramentals highly suspect and seem to have banished the Miraculous Medal and the Christian

[50] 11.15, "Suffer patiently ...", n.d., in *CW*, 3b:31.
[51] 6.38, Elizabeth Seton to George Weis, May 13, 1810, in *CW*, 2:125–26.

mothers who guarded their households from the threat of lightning with a blessed candle and holy water or soothed the bumps and cuts of childhood with a kiss and the Sign of the Cross on the wounds.

God's interests and desire always had priority in Elizabeth's prayers. When her son William and friend Bruté were on the high seas in constant danger from storms, pirates, and ships of warring nations, she asked, "What is the worst and the worst that can happen to the *dearest*, Death? And what of that? But the poor 'pupil' who may make shipwreck of his dear eternal interest, or the one hand less to hold the chalice—*there the point*—and the *immense interests!*"[52] This zeal for the Kingdom embraced the whole world, as she confided to her older son on the cessation of hostilities with Britain in 1815: "Your poor mother looks only at Souls. I see neither American nor English, but souls redeemed and lost."[53]

The final dogged quality of Mother Seton's prayer was perseverance. She had learned it from Filippo Filicchi during the frustrations of her struggle to believe. " 'What must I do, my dear Filicchi?' I hear you say"—so he had written—"Pray, pray incessantly, pray with fervor and confidence.... You cannot ask without something being given you; you cannot knock and find the door always shut; you cannot seek never to find. Sincerity, confidence and perseverance in prayer; calmness and tranquility of mind; courage and resolution in heart; a perfect resignation to Providence—you cannot fail to succeed."[54] Elizabeth applied the lesson unflaggingly until she had reached

[52] 6.195, Elizabeth Seton to Rev. Simon Bruté, P.S.S., Journal 1815, entry of [May 8], in *CW*, 2:323.

[53] 6.189, Elizabeth Seton to William Seton, February 16, 1815, in *CW*, 2:306.

[54] Philip Filicchi to Elizabeth Seton, October 22, 1804, Saint Elizabeth Ann Seton, 1-3-3-10 (14), APSL.

the haven of sure faith, and she continued to apply it afterward under the abuse of false-hearted family and friends, by prayer and action buoyed up by Antonio Filicchi— "Courage and perseverance!"[55]—by Bishop Carroll urging the same, by Father Francis Matignon of Boston, one of her spiritual advisors, who promised that "your perseverance and the help of grace will finish in you the work which God has commenced."[56] And Bishop John Cheverus, in the travail of establishing the community, expressed the same serene confidence in the outcome of her persevering will.

It is obvious from these and other examples of Elizabeth Seton's combined prayer and holy action that she was certainly not so naïve as to expect prayer to effect everything or anything without human effort. She once reported to Bruté:

Gave our Reverend J[ohn] Hickey a scolding he will remember. The congregation so crowded yesterday, and so many strangers—to whom he gave a sermon so evidently lazy; and answered this morning: "I did not trouble myself much about it, Ma'am."

"Oh, sir, that awakens my anger. Do you remember a priest holds the honor of God on his lips. Do you not trouble ... to spread His fire He wishes so much enkindled? If you will not study and prepare while young, what when you are old? There is a Mother's lesson."

"But prayer ..."

"Yes, prayer—and *preparation, too.*"[57]

[55] Antonio Filicchi to Elizabeth Seton, November 3, 1806, Saint Elizabeth Ann Seton, 1-3-3-10 (33), APSL.

[56] Rev. Francis Matignon to Elizabeth Seton, September 22, 1806, Saint Elizabeth Ann Seton, 1-3-3-1, 34b(2), APSL.

[57] 6.195, Elizabeth Seton to Rev. Simon Bruté, P.S.S., Journal 1815, entry of [May 8], in *CW*, 2:323, brackets in published version.

This indefatigable Mother once jotted down for her Sisters what really amounts to a guarantee of prayer's efficacy; there is nothing magical about the formula, but, if followed faithfully and lovingly, it cannot fail with God. "There *are three* particular points on which God will always listen to us with most pleasure," she wrote with calm certainty, "the declarations of our *Sorrow for Sin*; our *Faith, love, and hope* on the mysteries of Redemption; *our gratitude* for His deliverance from the many dangers of our *past* life, and *present* desires of better service and *fidelity.*"[58] Here, indeed, is the way, the path of a soul who truly loves God and to whom God listens.

Elizabeth's overall grasp of the nature of prayer and its function as a never-failing lifeline between God and the soul is beautifully expressed in an instruction written for fifteen-year-old Cecilia Seton, drawn by Elizabeth's example to the Catholic Church when Elizabeth was but a few months in that faith. "We must pray literally without ceasing—without ceasing, in every occurrence and employment of our lives", she exhorted the young woman.

> You know I mean that prayer of the heart which is independent of place or situation, or which is, rather, a habit of lifting up the heart to God, as in a constant communication with Him. As, for instance, when you go to your Studies, you look up to Him with sweet complacency and think: O Lord, how worthless is this knowledge, if it were not for the enlightening [of] my mind and improving it to thy Service; or for being more useful to my fellow creatures, and enabled to fill the part thy Providence may appoint me. When going into society or mixing with Company, appeal to Him who sees your heart and knows

[58] 9.20, Exercise of the *Presence of God*, n.d., "In What Does the Exercise of the Presence of God Consist", in *CW*, 3a:409.

how much rather you would devote every hour to Him; but say: "Dear Lord! You have placed me here, and I must yield to them whom You have placed me in subjection to—Oh keep my heart from all that would separate me from Thee." When you are excited to impatience, think for a moment how much more reason God has to be angry with you than you can have for anger against any human being; and yet how constant is His patience and forbearance.

And in every disappointment, great or small, let your dear heart fly direct to Him, your dear Savior, throwing yourself in His arms for refuge against every pain and sorrow. "He will never leave you nor forsake you."[59]

[59] 4.6, Elizabeth Seton to Cecilia Seton, October 7, 1805, in *CW*, 1:389.

5

Our Lord and Our Lady

Two devotions especially captured Elizabeth Seton's soul. The first was devotion to the celebration of Mass and to the reception of Holy Communion; the second was devotion to Mary, Mother of God. Both have a preeminence in the Catholic Church. The first, the Eucharist, is at the very heart of the Church's faith and mission, and the second recognizes the essential role of Mary in both. Surprisingly, as an Episcopalian, Elizabeth had an ardent devotion to "the sacrament", in other words, to the reception of communion, which played a strong part in her being drawn to the Catholic faith. She did not initially have devotion to Mary, for the Protestant Episcopal Church in New York promoted none, but she drew close to Mary as she drew close to the Catholic Church. Although a convert, Elizabeth is called the mother of the Catholic Church in the United States, and she cherished liturgical worship and Marian devotion as much as, if not more than, the American Catholics of her day.

Our Lord

Elizabeth relished the spiritual presence of Christ in the Episcopal sacrament of communion. She and Rebecca

Seton attended Sacrament Sundays regularly in order to participate in the service, which was scheduled about six times a year and included the words of Christ at the Last Supper, prayed over bread and wine, and followed by distribution of communion.

During the emotional and spiritual turmoil of her discernment about religious conversion, one terrible Sunday a trial broke the dam of Elizabeth's doubts and swept her into Catholicism. She described for Amabilia Filicchi how she went "trembling to communion, half dead with the inward struggle, when they said the Body and Blood of Christ...—and I remember in my old Prayer book of former edition when I was a child; it was not as now—said to be Spiritually taken and received".[1] She was quite right. When the newly formed Protestant Episcopal Church in the United States held its first General Convention in Philadelphia in 1789, delegates revised the sentence in the Anglican Book of Common Prayer "the Body and Blood of Christ ... are verily and indeed taken and received by the faithful in the Lord's Supper" to read "spiritually taken and received".[2]

Elizabeth treasured receiving communion on Sacrament Sundays. Her deep and abiding devotion to communion was a prelude to learning about the Roman Catholic belief in the Real Presence during her stay in Italy. It has been noted that she seized upon it as "the Seal of that covenant which I trust will not be broken in life nor in death, in time nor in Eternity".[3] The first Seton biographer, Rev.

[1] 3.31, Journal to Amabilia Filicchi, July 19, 1804, entry of January 1805, in CW, 1:373. Elizabeth Seton used the Book of Common Prayer adopted by the Church of England and later its revised edition (1789) for the Protestant Episcopal Church in New York.

[2] John A. Hardon, The Protestant Churches of America (Westminster, Md.: Newman Press, 1956), 39.

[3] 8.25, Notebook of Psalm 23 and Rev. John Henry Hobart's Sermons, entry of September 13, 1802, in CW, 3a:172.

Charles Ignatius White, wrote: "It is related of Mrs. Seton, that such was the profound awe awakened in her by the communion, that in receiving it, her teeth clattered against the cup which contained the elements. Her whole mind was intently riveted upon the act she was performing."[4] Endeavoring to think of the Divine Presence when she received communion as an Episcopalian, possibly from frigid winter temperatures, Elizabeth admitted that she was sometimes shaky. Her sister-in-law Rebecca Seton and friend Catherine Mann Dupleix used to join her in asking the sexton for the remnants of the sacramental wine that they might receive again. Elizabeth reminded Rebecca Seton of their rather extravagant devotion in describing the Catholic practice she witnessed in Livorno, which evidently delighted her:

How often you and I used to give the sigh, and you would press your arm in mine of a Sunday evening and say, "*No more until next Sunday*", as we turned from the Church door, which closed on us (unless a prayer day was given out in the week). Well, here [in Italy] they go to church at 4 every morning, if they please. And you know how we were laughed at for running from one church to the other *Sacrament Sundays*, that we might receive as often as we could. Well, here people that love God and live a good, regular life can go (though many do not do it), yet they can go *every day*.[5]

The doling out of the Eucharist was a real deprivation for Elizabeth in Manhattan, and she turned to devotional extravagance as compensation. "Poor fool, no Sacrament Sunday," she noted in her *Dear Remembrances*, "most

[4] Charles I. White, *Life of Mrs. Eliza A. Seton: Foundress and First Superior of the Sisters or Daughters of Charity in the United States of America* (Baltimore, Md.: John Murphy & Co., 1859), 37.

[5] 2.14, Journal to Rebecca Seton continued, April 18, [1804], in *CW*, 1:297.

reverently drank on my knees behind the library door the little cup of wine and tears to represent what I so much desired."[6] God surely did not laugh at the symbolic remembrance lashed with the tears of yearning love in another attempt to conjure up the sacrament, in a time of dire need.

There can be no doubt that Elizabeth's constant yearning for sacramental union with Jesus as an Episcopalian prepared the way for the eagerness, despite a tentative reticence, with which she reached out to the Catholic doctrine of the Eucharist. With her first known entrance into a Catholic church—La Santissima Annunziata in Florence—there is a sense of homecoming: "Forgetting Mrs. F[ilicchi], companions, and all the surrounding scene," she told Rebecca, "I sunk to my knees in the first place I found vacant and shed a torrent of tears at the recollection of how long I had been a stranger in the house of my God, and the accumulated sorrow that had separated me from it. I need not tell you that I said our dear service with my whole soul, as far as in its agitation I could recollect."[7] However unconsciously, grace and a sense of a Presence was stealing into her soul, for she felt "delight in seeing old men and women, young women, and all sorts of people kneeling promiscuously about the Altar, as inattentive to us or any other passengers as if we were not there.... Everyone is so intent on their prayers and Rosary that it is very immaterial what a stranger does."[8] The "stranger" she then was turned wistful in the church of San Firenze as she "saw a young Priest unlock his little Chapel, with that composed and equal eye as if his Soul had entered before him". She wrote,

[6] 10.4, *Dear Remembrances*, n.d., in *CW*, 3a:514.
[7] 2.10, Florence Journal to Rebecca Seton, [January 1804], in *CW*, 1:283.
[8] Ibid., 283–84.

"My heart would willingly have followed after."[9] That heart was itself unlocked by the exuberance of San Lorenzo, unlike anything she had known in the plain places of worship in early nineteenth-century Manhattan. The natural exuberance of her soul—the "wildness", as she called it—so long suppressed by accustomed forms of staid worship, responded: "A sensation of delight struck me so forcibly that as I approached the great Altar, formed of all the most precious stones, marbles, etc., that could be produced, 'My Soul does magnify the Lord, my spirit rejoices in God my Savior' came in my mind with a fervor which absorbed every other feeling."[10]

The real moment of truth came in the Shrine of Our Lady of Grace of Montenero, patron of Tuscany, high above Livorno, overlooking the harbor and the Ligurian Sea. At the very moment of the elevation of the Host, a young Englishman leaned toward Elizabeth and explained in a loud, rude whisper, "This is what they call their real *PRESENCE*."[11] The words were a shock of grace: "My very heart trembled with shame and sorrow for his unfeeling interruption of their sacred adoration"[12] was her first, well-bred, and at the same time sense-of-religious-outrage reaction. But then: "Involuntarily I bent from him to the pavement, and thought secretly on the words of St. Paul, with starting tears, 'They discern not the Lord's Body.'"[13] It was an instinctive, unwitting

[9] Ibid., 284.

[10] Ibid., 285–86.

[11] 2.11 Elizabeth Seton to Rebecca Seton, January 28, 1804, entry of February 10, in *CW*, 1:291. Elizabeth gives another account of this pivotal moment. See 10.4, *Dear Remembrances*, n.d., in *CW*, 3a:516.

[12] 2.11 Elizabeth Seton to Rebecca Seton, January 28, 1804, entry of February 10, in *CW*, 1:291.

[13] Ibid.

gesture of faith-filled adoration. The moment passed, but it triggered a spate of confused questions: "The next thought was, how should they eat and drink their very damnation for not *discerning* it, if indeed it is not *there*? Yet how should it be *there*? And how did He breathe my Soul in me? And how, and how a hundred other things I know nothing about? I am a *Mother*, so the Mother's thought came also. How was my GOD a little babe in the first stage of His mortal existence *in Mary*? But I lost these thoughts in my babes at home, which I daily long for more and more."[14]

No matter, the iron had struck deep into Elizabeth's soul. Weeks later she was writing her "soul's sister", Rebecca:

> How happy would we be if we believed what these dear Souls believe: that they *possess God* in the Sacrament and that He remains in their churches and is carried to them when they are sick! Oh, my! When they carry the B[lesse]d Sacrament under my Window, while I feel the full loneliness and sadness of my case, I cannot stop the tears at the thought: My God, how happy would I be, even so far away from all so dear, if I could find You in the church as they do (for there is a chapel in the very house of Mr. F[ilicchi]). How many things I would say to You of the sorrows of my heart and the sins of my life![15]

The sacramental Lord she had always loved was drawing her to His fullness, and finally: "The other day, in a moment of excessive distress, I fell on my knees without thinking when the Blessed Sacrament passed by and cried in an agony to God *to bless me*, if He was *there*—that my whole *Soul* desired only Him."[16]

[14] Ibid.
[15] Ibid., entry of February 24, 292, brackets in published version.
[16] Ibid., 292–93.

The ache is even more poignant in Elizabeth's *Dear Remembrances*: "The anguish of heart when the Blessed Sacrament would be passing the street, at the thought, was I the only one *He* did not bless?"[17] It must have been anguish indeed for one so committed to Jesus, to wonder whether she was outcast, ignored by Him. The pain was nearly unbearable "the day he passed my window when, prostrate on the floor, I looked up to the blessed Virgin, appealing to her that, as the Mother of God, she *must* pity me".[18] She desperately wanted more than pity. She had come to the point where her prayer to Mary was to "obtain from him that blessed Faith of these happy Souls around me—rising after many sighs and tears—the little prayer book Mrs. Amabilia [Filicchi] had given Annina was under my eye ... how many thoughts [of] the happiness of those who possessed this the blessed Faith of Jesus still on earth with them".[19] *That* is what drew her, what fascinated her: the thought of having this Lord whom she loved so dearly actually *with* her at all times—if she could only believe that! She had already worked out what it would mean to her: "How I should enjoy to encounter every misery of life with the heavenly consolation of speaking heart to heart with Him in His Tabernacles, and the security of finding Him in His churches."[20] It was why she had special "reverence and love [for] Mrs. Amabilia Filicchi when she came home from COMMUNION".[21]

These Filicchi, every one of them, were her God-appointed saviors. A double family wedding celebrated by Amabilia's brother Nicóla Barigazzi brought "impressions

[17] 10.4, *Dear Remembrances*, n.d., in *CW*, 3a:516.
[18] Ibid.
[19] Ibid., brackets in published version.
[20] Ibid.
[21] Ibid.

of awful reverence ... and full continuance of it when he visited our chamber (Annina sick) in his robe of ceremony after the marriage of his Brother and Sister".[22] Like the splendor of the churches, the liturgical vestments were doing their work of teaching, of drawing the eye of the beholder to the Creator of all.

Later yet, on the eve of Elizabeth's departure for her home in New York, her mind had settled and her soul lay open awaiting the gift of faith with a poignant hunger for Eucharistic union. "Oh, my soul, how solemn was that offering!"[23] she wrote of her last Mass in Livorno. "For a blessing on our voyage—for my dear ones, my sisters, and all so dear to me—and, more than all, for the souls of my dear husband and father"—all one in the communion of saints—"earnestly our desires ascended with the blessed sacrifice, that they might find acceptance through Him who gave Himself for us." How well she understood the divine ladder of sacrificial praise and grace ascending and descending. "Earnestly we desired to be united with Him, and would gladly encounter all the sorrows before us, to be partakers of that blessed body and blood. Oh, my God, spare and pity me."[24] The hunger was stark in a line scribbled to Rebecca Seton: "MY SAVIOR—MY GOD—Antonio and his wife—their separation in God and Communion—poor I, not. But did I not beg him to give me their Faith and promise him all in return for such a gift? Little Ann and I had only strange tears of Joy and grief."[25]

Back in New York, Elizabeth's quest for the ultimate gift became a real struggle to the death, unnerved and

[22] Ibid. "Robe of ceremony" refers to the liturgical vestments worn by the priest who presided at the Filicchi wedding.
[23] 2.14, Journal to Rebecca Seton continued, April 18, [1804], in *CW*, 1:298.
[24] Ibid., 298–99.
[25] Ibid., 298.

unraveled as she now became with the polemic treatises
forced on her by well-meaning relatives and friends on
both sides; however, the cry of her heart still rang clear.
When Bishop Carroll wrote to sustain her, she assured
Antonio Filicchi: "The Bishop's letter has been held to
my heart, on my knees beseeching God to enlighten me
to see the truth, unmixed with doubts and hesitations. I
read the promises given to St. Peter and the 6th Chapter
[of] John"—the explicit promise of the Eucharist—"every
day, and then ask God, can I offend Him by believing
those express words?"[26] And she told his wife, Amabilia,
that she had gone to her old trysting place Saint Paul's
Chapel for reasons of "peace and persuasion about pro-
prieties, etc.... Yet I got in a side pew which turned my
face toward the Catholic Church in the next street and
found myself twenty times speaking to the Blessed Sacrament there, instead of looking at the naked altar where I
was or minding the routine of prayers."[27] Drawn by the
"supreme desire of [her] Soul to know the Truth", she
lingered outside Saint Peter's Catholic Church on Barclay
Street "every day to visit my Savior there and pour out my
Soul before Him".[28]

How happy the Ash Wednesday of 1805, when at last
Elizabeth could write exultantly to Mrs. Filicchi:

A day of days for me, Amabilia. I have been—where?—to
the Church of St. Peter with a CROSS on the top instead
of a weathercock! That is mischievous—but I mean I have

[26] 3.7, Elizabeth Seton to Antonio Filicchi, August 30, 1804, in *CW*,
1:317–18.
[27] 3.31, Journal to Amabilia Filicchi, July 19, 1804, entry of September, in
CW, 1:369–70.
[28] 3.6. Elizabeth Seton to Bishop John Carroll, [July 26, 1804], in *CW*, 1:316;
3.10, Elizabeth Seton to Antonio Filicchi, October 9, 1804, in *CW*, 1:327.

been to what is called here among so many churches the
Catholic Church. When I turned the corner of the street
it is in, "Here, my God, I go," said I, "heart all to you."
Entering it, how that heart died away as it were in silence
before the little tabernacle and the great Crucifixion over
it. "Ah, My God, here let me rest," said I—and down the
head on the bosom and the knees on the bench.[29]

If there were any doubt that Elizabeth Seton's instinctive
turning to the Sacrament of the Eucharist from her earliest
days as an Episcopalian, her grasp of it even then as the
heart of the Church, her eager opening to the full-blown
Eucharistic doctrine of the Catholic Church had exerted the
strongest pull of all to that true Faith, the ecstasy of her first
Communion dispels it in an instant. "ANNUNCIATION
DAY", she informed Amabilia. "I shall be made one with
Him who said, 'Unless you eat my flesh and drink my blood
you can have no part with ME.' "[30] She had accepted the
sixth chapter of John with simple, grateful belief. "I count
the days and hours. Yet a few more of hope and expectation, and then—how bright the Sun, these morning walks
of preparation. Deep snow or smooth ice, all to me the
same. I see nothing but the little bright cross on St. Peter's
steeple."[31] And finally, the long-awaited day:

At last, Amabilia, at last GOD IS MINE and I AM HIS!
Now, let all go its round—I HAVE RECEIVED HIM.
The awful impressions of the evening before, fears of not

[29] 3.31, Journal to Amabilia Filicchi, July 19, 1804, entry of February 27,
1805, in *CW*, 1:375. Elizabeth refers to the painting by José Vallejo depicting
the Crucifixion that hangs above the main altar at St. Peter's Church, Barclay
St., Manhattan.
[30] Ibid., entry of [March 20, 1805], 376. Cf. Jn 6:53–54.
[31] Ibid.

having done all to prepare, and yet even then, transports of confidence and hope in His GOODNESS.

MY GOD! To the last breath of life will I not remember this night of watching for morning dawn; the fearful, beating heart so pressing to be gone; the long walk to town; but every step counted, nearer that street, then nearer that tabernacle, then nearer the moment He would enter the poor, poor little dwelling so all His own.

And when He did, the first thought I remember was: "Let God arise, let His enemies be scattered!"—for it seemed to me my King had come to take His throne, and instead of the humble, tender welcome I had expected to give Him, it was but a triumph of joy and gladness that the deliverer was come, and my defense and shield and strength and Salvation made mine for this World and the next.[32]

Another contradiction, but a glorious one: not what she had carefully and prayerfully planned, but what He wished. He knew well, after all she had been through, what favor to bestow. It had the victory and exaltation of Easter—Resurrection—in it, not only for the spent, humble soul of His beloved and elected one but also for His people whom she would inflame with His love.

And, tuned now as Elizabeth was to *her* Beloved, she knew how to respond: "Now then, all the excesses of my heart found their play, and it danced with more fervor—no, must not say that—but perhaps almost with as much as the royal Prophets before his Ark. For I was far richer than he, and more honored than he could ever be. Now, the point is for the fruits."[33] She was not so lost in heavenly enjoyment that she could not discern its purpose. Nor did she fail to perceive that this first Eucharistic encounter

[32] Ibid., entry of March 25, 376–77.
[33] Ibid., 377.

had worked an irreversible change in her soul that was both the promise and the wellspring of constant future spiritual growth: "So far, truly I feel all the powers of my soul held fast by Him who came with so much Majesty to take possession of this little poor kingdom."[34] And she began to prepare for "an Easter COMMUNION ... in my green pastures, amidst the refreshing waters for which I thirsted truly"—chief of which was "the Divine Sacrifice, so commanding and yet already so familiar for all my wants and necessities. That speaks for itself, and I am All at home in it."[35]

Years later, the exquisite wonder of Elizabeth's "first Communion in the Church of God" was still a fresh delight in her soul as she jotted down her *Dear Remembrances* because "it would be such INGRATITUDE to die without noting them".[36] "Hours counted, the watch of the heart, panting for the Supreme happiness it had so long desired—the Secret"—there was, then, as might be expected between two such ardent lovers, a communication no one will ever know, nor should. "The mystery of Benediction—heavenly delight, bliss—inconceivable to angels, no word for that—Faith burning."[37] The words themselves seem to gasp and pant in an effort to express the inexpressible. "The lively hope that since He had done so much He would at last admit so poor a creature to HIMSELF *forever*"[38]—she had not forgotten what she had learned with the self-abandonment of the covenant in 1802, that this true Eucharist now fully attained was the pledge of everlasting life. "The two miles walk back with the Treasure of my Soul—first kiss and blessing

[34] Ibid.
[35] Ibid., entry of April 14, 377.
[36] 10.4, *Dear Remembrances*, n.d., in *CW*, 3a:510.
[37] Ibid., 519.
[38] Ibid.

on my 5 Darlings, bringing *such a Master* to our little dwelling."[39] As she had known enough instinctively to regard the person of Amabilia Filicchi when she returned home after Communion, Elizabeth, now the bearer, rejoiced in sharing her blessed burden with her children and, through the attentive practice of charity, with the neighbor: "Now the quiet, satisfied heart in the thousand encounters of the CROSS embraced so cordially, but so watchful to preserve peace with *all*."[40]

Once safe in God's green pastures, Elizabeth's impish nature reasserted itself with the freedom of the children of God, even in something so awesomely sacred. "'FAITH for all defects supplies, and SENSE is lost in MYSTERY'—'Here the Faithful rest secure, while God can Vouch, and Faith insure.' But you would sometimes enjoy, through mischief," she wrote cheerily to Amabilia, "if you could just know the foolish things that pass my brain after so much Wonderful Knowledge as I have been taking in it, about idol worshipping, etc., etc.,—even in the sacred Moments of the elevation, my heart will say, half-serious, 'Dare I worship you, Adored Savior?' But he has proved well enough to me there, what he is, and I can say with even more transports than St. Thomas, 'MY LORD and MY GOD!' "[41] Then the impatience of the convert, forgetting for the moment what she had had to suffer to believe, burst forth:

> Truly, it is a greater Mystery how Souls for whom He had done such incomprehensible things should shut themselves out by incredulity from His best of all Gifts, this Divine Sacrifice and Holy Eucharist—refusing to believe

[39] Ibid.
[40] Ibid.
[41] 3.31, Journal to Amabilia Filicchi, July 19, 1804, entry of [April 14, 1805], in *CW*, 1:377–78.

in [the] spiritual and heavenly order of things that WORD
which spake and created the Whole Natural Order, re-
creating through succession of ages for the body, and yet
He cannot be believed to recreate for the soul. I see more
mystery in this blindness of redeemed souls than in any of
the mysteries proposed in His Church. With what grateful and unspeakable joy and reverence I adore the daily
renewed virtue of THAT WORD by which we possess
Him in our blessed MASS and Communion![42]

That He was Elizabeth's possession, indeed, her bulwark, in His glorious Sacrament was evident in her gentle
turning aside of Antonio's insistence on her settling with
her family in Italy for the peace of their religion: "Since
I hope always to find the morning MASS in America, it
matters little what can happen through the few successive
days I may have to live, for my health is pitiful."[43] She was
already leaning wholly on this sacramental strength. "From
circumstances of particular impressions on my mind," she
told Antonio, "I have been obliged to watch it so carefully
and keep so near the fountain head, that I have been three
times to Communion since you left me, not to influence
my Faith, but to keep Peace in my Soul, which without
this heavenly resource would be agitated and discomposed
by the frequent assaults which, in my immediate situation,
are naturally made on my feelings."[44]

Elizabeth knew interior assaults as well, and the remedy: "The heart down—discouraged at the constant failure
in good resolutions; so soon disturbed by trifles; so little Interior Recollection and forgetfulness of His constant

[42] Ibid., 378, brackets in published version.
[43] Ibid.
[44] 3.25, Elizabeth Seton to Antonio Filicchi, April 22, 1805, in *CW*, 1:356.
"Fountain head" refers to the Eucharist and the Roman Catholic Church.

Presence. The reproaches of disobedience to the little ones
much more applicable to myself. So many Communions
and Confessions with so little fruit often suggest the idea of
lessening them—to fly from the fountain while in danger
of dying from thirst, but in a moment, He lifts up the Soul
from the dust."[45] It was the constant struggle for perfection
with its relapses and gains.

Elizabeth's comparison of her "disobedience" to that of
the children was not a passing thought. She combined the
intuitions of mother and saint-in-the-making to strive for
holiness. "Beloved Kate, I will take you, then, for my pattern", she confided in her *Spiritual Journal*,

> and try to please Him as you to please me. To grieve with
> the like tenderness when I displease Him, to obey and
> mind His voice as you do mine. To do my work as neatly
> and exactly as you do yours, grieve to lose sight of Him
> for a moment, fly with joy to meet Him, fear He should
> go and leave me even when I sleep—this is the lesson of
> love you set me. And when I have seemed to be angry,
> without petulance or obstinacy you silently and steadily
> try to accomplish my wish, I will say: "Dearest Lord,
> give me grace to copy well this lovely image of my duty
> to Thee."[46]

Through her children, too, she deepened her understanding of and participation in the communion of saints:
"Received the Longing Desire of my soul", she recorded,
"and my dearest Anna, too. The bonds of Nature and
Grace all twined together. The Parent offers the Child,
the Child the Parent, and both are United in the source

---

[45] 4.55, Spiritual Journal to Cecilia Seton, August 10 to October 16, 1807,
entry of September 14, in *CW*, 1:474.

[46] Ibid., entry of August 20, 472.

of their Being, and rest together on Redeeming Love."⁴⁷
This unseen but constant communion of souls in the Sacrament was, again, her rebuttal of the fear to "go among
strangers" as she created her life anew in Baltimore—
"One sweet sacrifice will reunite [my] Soul with all who
offer it."⁴⁸ It indeed reunited her with the very roots of
her faith! "Imagine", she conjured up for Cecilia Seton,
"twenty Priests all with the devotion of Saints, clothed
in white, accompanied by the whole troop of the young
Seminarians in surplices also, all in order surrounding the
blessed Sacrament exposed, singing the hymn of the Resurrection. When they come to the words, 'Peace be to all
here', it seems as if Our Lord is again acting over the scene
that passed with the Assembled disciples."⁴⁹

As might be expected, Elizabeth's intense love for
the Holy Eucharist, so carefully nurtured and joyously
indulged, could only deepen with the years. Father Bruté
wrote with a kind of sacred envy after her death: "May
my heart, my soul know the grace—improve the grace
of the holy sacraments of my Jesus as Mother did!"⁵⁰ As
might be expected, too, her love generated extraordinary insights reserved for chosen souls. Thus, she communicated to Bruté a new understanding of the beatitude
"Blessed are the poor in spirit" and God's predilection
for the lowly: "Most precious Communion, preceded by
alarm and thoughts of fear—but all settled in one thought:
how he loves and welcomes the poor and desolate."⁵¹ Nor was

---

⁴⁷ Ibid., entry of August 23, 473.
⁴⁸ 5.1, Elizabeth Seton to Cecilia Seton, June 9, 1808, in *CW*, 2:5.
⁴⁹ 5.22, Elizabeth Seton to Cecilia Seton, April 3, [1809], in *CW*, 2:65.
⁵⁰ [Sister Loyola Law, D.C., ed.], *Mother Seton: Notes by Rev. Simon Gabriel Bruté*, entry of January 4, 1825, (Emmitsburg, Md.: Daughters of Charity, 1884), 140.
⁵¹ 7.289, Elizabeth Seton to Rev. Simon Bruté, P.S.S., n.d., in *CW*, 2:686. Cf. Mt 5:3.

her ever-present awareness of the sacred bond of Christian union forgotten—"He said, while the Soul was preparing: 'See the Blood I shed for you, is at this very hour invoked upon you by your Brother [Bruté presiding at the altar].'"[52] And again: "Watching night and cramp[ed] breast made heavy head for COMMUNION. As the tabernacle door opened—the pressing thought: This bread *should not be given to a dog*, Lord! Immediately, as the eyes closed, a white old shepherd dog, feeding from the shepherd['s] hand in the midst of the flock, as I have seen in the fields between Pisa and Florence, came before me. Yes, my Savior, You feed your poor dog, who, at the first sight, can hardly be distinguished from the sheep—but the Canine qualities You see!"[53]

In these two abject admissions of unworthiness, Elizabeth seems to express yet another insight into the poverty of the human family for whom Jesus came, that even His holiest disciples rightly count themselves as needy to attract His loving gaze and have His saving gospel preached to them. With her extraordinary talent for relating familiar objects to relevant divine truths, Elizabeth glorified the house chapel's common little tabernacle by simple reference to its spiritual significance and by urging Sisters and children alike to join actively in the sacred mysteries: "We who possess the actual presence of Our Lord in the Blessed Sacrament", she counseled, "should unite our homages to those which he offers day and night to his Father from our tabernacle in his quality of *Victim* and intercessor."[54] And she gave a delightful turn to the narrative of the Last Supper: " 'The disciple whom Jesus loved'—and 'who leaned on His breast at supper'—We—not on His breast,

[52] Ibid.

[53] 7.290, Elizabeth Seton to Rev. Simon Bruté, P.S.S, n.d., in *CW*, 2:687.

[54] 9.20, Exercise of the *Presence of God*, n.d., "In What Does the Exercise of the Presence of God Consist", in *CW*, 3a:404.

but He on ours, indeed".[55] Nor was she unaware that this disciple was the same John who represented all God's sons and daughters when Jesus entrusted them into the care of His Mother.

Elizabeth's intimacy with the divine Guest in the Sacrament grew so that it easily tolerated the weakness of human nature and even more of illness, and she admitted to Bruté without the slightest compunction, in the wake of her brush with death in 1818, that "I went to sleep before I had made any thanksgiving but *Te Deum* and *Magnificat* after Communion."[56] It was an intimacy shared by Saint Thérèse of Lisieux, who refused to worry when she, too, would fall asleep after Communion, because, she reasoned, God loved her as much when she was asleep as when she was awake.

No matter the "alarm and thoughts of fear" that sometimes preceded her Communions, Elizabeth experienced the solace of the Eucharist to the full—her *heavenly theme*.[57] For her the Real Presence was "as certainly true as that Bread naturally taken removes my hunger—so this Bread of Angels removes my pain, my cares, warms, cheers, soothes, contents, and renews my whole being."[58] Not alone a therapy of the soul but a therapy of the whole personality, healing physical sickness, banishing worry, bringing peace and contentment of mind. With what gladness, then, she clung to this solace through every twenty-four hours, without losing her awe of the Real Presence of Jesus in the Eucharist: "I sit or stand opposite his tabernacle

[55] 11.10, St. John, Valley, 1814, in *CW*, 3b:26.

[56] 7.170, Elizabeth Seton to Rev. Simon Bruté, P.S.S., July 2, 1818, in *CW*, 2:567.

[57] 7.289, Elizabeth Seton to Rev. Simon Bruté, P.S.S., n.d., in *CW*, 2:686.

[58] 4.55, Spiritual Journal to Cecilia Seton, August 10 to October 16, 1807, entry of October 16, in *CW*, 1:478.

all day"—her room adjoined the chapel—"and keep the heart to it as the needle to the pole, and at night still more, even to folly; since I have little right to be so *near* to him."[59] (The writer has never forgotten the same awe and humility in a senior religious who, recounting a trip in a car with a priest carrying Communion to the sick, said in wonder—she who had lived a busy and sophisticated life of service in high administrative positions—"Father, I rode in the same car with the *Blessed Sacrament!*")

For all her faith in the Eucharist, the elation of her Communions, Elizabeth never forgot the responsibility and ultimate accounting that went with so unbelievably intimate a gift. She did not hesitate to state both with uncompromising bluntness, even to her innocent audience: "I see you all around—at the foot of this tabernacle where the love of our Jesus has so long waited for many of you," she said fondly, "but also I see the awful and dreadful account in his judgment of the use of this grace. My dearest girls, if you should—even one of you—be so unhappy as to abuse it—but I rather hope every heart is in earnest—you know already when it was prepared for you, when it was merited for each Soul in particular."[60] It is not hard to detect the mother's anxiety yet also the mother's hope and trust.

Perhaps the crown of Elizabeth's countless fervent Communions in a fervent life was one of her last, just three months before her holy death. Confined to bed by her infirmities, she lay there day by day waiting for each new meeting with her Lord. On the night of October 5–6, 1820, she fought a raging thirst throughout a wakeful night, refusing steadfastly the glass of water that

---

[59] 7.285, Elizabeth Seton to Rev. Simon Bruté, P.S.S., n.d., in *CW*, 2:683–84.

[60] 4.75, Elizabeth Seton to Cecilia Seton, n.d., in *CW*, 1:511–12.

would bring her relief so that she might receive Communion in the morning (there were few concessions for persons who were sick in the fasting regulations of those days). When, at last, Father Bruté entered her room, he recounted:

> Her joy was so uncommon that when I approached, and as I placed the ciborium upon the little table, she burst into tears, and, sobbing aloud, covered her face with her two hands. I thought first it was some fear of sin and, approaching her, I asked, "Be still, Mother! Peace, peace be to you! Here is the Lord of Peace! Have you any pain? Do you wish to confess?"
>
> "No, no! Only give Him to me!" ... she said with an ardor, a kind of exclamation, and her whole face so inflamed that I was much affected.[61]

Here were the love and longing of a lifetime. They were surely fresh in Bruté's memory when he wrote, months later: "Will I ever forget that face, fired with love, melted in tears at His approach in Communion? To the last, exhausted death on that face—it was still inflamed, and blushed in ardent love, desire inexpressible of eternal union in Him."[62] The remembrance of such Communions was the cause of his reproaches on a spring evening after Elizabeth's death:

> "My Mother, O my Mother! What remembrance this evening of your fervent communions—why did I check your sobs, tears, almost cries, your whole countenance so inflamed—oh, why? I almost reproach it to my soul this evening—why not transports when *such* is our faith?—Our

[61] [Law], *Mother Seton: Notes*, 18.
[62] Ibid., 140–41.

Jesus present and received!" The next thought was logical for a priest as holy as Bruté: "O faith! And I the priest every day at the altar! Where is mine, my Lord? Do give me the faith of that woman to whom—me seems—coming to her, entering her heart you said well pleased, "O mulier, magna est fides tua!' "[63]

Our Lady

Elizabeth first came to know Mary, the Mother of God, while she was sheltered with the Filicchi in Livorno. She tells of it simply in a lengthy journal-like letter to Rebecca Seton:

A little prayer-book of Mrs. F[ilicchi]'s was on the table, and I opened [it to] a little prayer (the Memorare) of St. Bernard to the Blessed Virgin, begging her to be our *Mother*, and I said it to her with such a certainty that God would surely refuse nothing *to his Mother*, and that she could not help loving and pitying the poor Souls He died for, that I felt really I had a Mother—which you know my foolish heart so often lamented to have lost in early days. From the first remembrance of infancy, I have looked, in all the plays of childhood and wildness of youth to the clouds for my Mother, and at that moment it seemed as if I had found more than her, even in tenderness and pity of a Mother. So I cried myself to sleep in her heart.[64]

These are extraordinary words from a woman who, as a devout member of the Protestant Episcopal Church, just

---

[63] Ibid., 72–73. "O woman, your faith is great!"

[64] 2.11, Elizabeth Seton to Rebecca Seton, January 28, 1804, entry of February 24, in *CW*, 1:293, first brackets in published version.

days or weeks before had no concept of Mary as either universal Mother or Mediator of Grace. It is true that her grief for her husband, her loneliness, and her deep maternal instinct made her especially receptive to the maternal solicitude of Mary, but her instant responsiveness and accurate grasp of Mary's role in redemption suggest an exceptional grace of major importance. Certainly, Mary was to play a special role in her own conversion and perfection, as well as in the establishment and devotion of her apostolic community. There is, besides, an essential justice in the immediate and lasting rapport between the heavenly Mother and Patroness of the Church in America and the woman who was in so many ways its mother on earth.

It was this bond of motherhood that helped Elizabeth comprehend the Compassion of Mary, her role as Co-Redemptrix, even before it had been taught to her. As she stood before a masterwork in Florence:

> A picture of the Descent from the Cross [*Deposizione della Croce*], nearly as large as life, engaged *my whole soul*—Mary at the foot of it expressed well that the iron had entered into her, and the shades of death over her agonized countenance so strongly contrasted the heavenly Peace of the dear Redeemer's that it seems as if his pains had fallen on her. How hard it was to leave that picture, and how often, even in the few hours interval since I have seen it, I shut my eyes and recall it in imagination![65]

Unwittingly she had penetrated this sorrowful mystery as deeply as Saint Bernard of Clairvaux, whose Memorare had introduced her to the Blessed Virgin. "Truly, O

---

[65] 2.10, Florence Journal to Rebecca Seton, [January 1804], in *CW*, 1:287. The Church of Santa Maria Novella displays the painting, *Deposizione della Croce*, by Giovanni Battista Naldini (1535–1591).

blessed Mother, a sword has pierced your heart", the great
Father and Doctor had written.[66]

> For only by passing through your heart could the sword
> enter the flesh of your Son. Indeed, after your Jesus—who
> belongs to everyone, but is especially yours—gave up His
> life, the cruel spear, which was not withheld from His life-
> less body, tore open His side. Clearly it did not touch His
> soul and could not harm Him, but it did pierce your heart.
> For surely His soul was no longer there, but yours could not
> be torn away. Thus the violence of sorrow has cut through
> your heart, and we rightly call you more than martyr, since
> the effect of compassion in you has gone beyond the endur-
> ance of physical suffering.[67]

Bernard went on to question why anyone should be
"more surprised at the compassion of Mary than at the
passion of Mary's Son? For if He could die in body, could
she not die with Him in spirit? He died in body through
a love greater than anyone had known. She died in spirit
through a love unlike any other since His."[68]

These two first contrasting embraces of Mary by Elizabeth, in the relief of prayer and the starkness of crucifixion, are abundant proof that while Elizabeth's immediate
acceptance of the Mother of God was warm and even
impulsive in conformity with her nature, it was neither
sentimental nor sugary sweet but was forged in the steel
and sacrifice of that same nature.

The bond grew as Elizabeth returned to New York
and entered her own long passion of religious uncertainty.
"Anna coaxes me, when we are at our evening prayers, to

---

[66] Cf. St. Bernard of Clairvaux, "Sermo in dom. infra oct. Assumptionis",
14–15: Opera omnia, Edit. Cisterc. 5 (1968), 273–74.
[67] Ibid.
[68] Ibid.

say Hail Mary, and all say, 'Oh, do, Ma, teach it to us!' "[69]
she wrote Amabilia Filicchi.

> Even little Bec tries to lisp it, though she can scarcely speak;
> and I ask my Savior why should we not say it. If anyone
> is in heaven, His Mother must be there. Are the angels,
> then, who are so often represented as being so interested
> for us on earth, more compassionate or more exalted than
> she is? Oh, no, no. Mary, our Mother, that cannot be. So
> I beg her with the confidence and tenderness of her child
> to pity us and guide us to the true Faith, if we are not in
> it, and if we are, to obtain peace for my poor Soul, that I
> may be a good Mother to my poor darlings. For I know, if
> God should leave me to myself after all my sins, He would
> be justified; and since I read these books, my head is quite
> bewildered about the few who are saved. So I kiss her
> picture you gave me, and beg her to be a Mother to us.[70]

Yet even Elizabeth's reliance on Mary eventually felt
the suspicion of doubt as the clouds rolled thicker into
her soul. "I fell on my face before God (remember I tell
you all)", she confided to Antonio Filicchi in her agitation, "and appealed to Him as my righteous Judge, if hardness of heart, or unwillingness to be taught, or any human
reasons, stood between me and the truth; if I would not
rejoice to cast my Sorrows on the Bosom of the Blessed
Mary ... if once my soul could know it was pleasing to
Him."[71] With what feelings of guilt she must have asked
herself, "Could you believe that the Prayers and Litanies addressed to Our Blessed Lady"—she who had felt

[69] 3.31, Journal to Amabilia Filicchi, July 19, 1804, entry of August 28, in
CW, 1:369.
[70] Ibid.
[71] 3.8, Elizabeth Seton to Antonio Filicchi, September 19 [1804], in CW,
1:321.

their solace—"were acceptable to God though not com-
manded in Scripture?"[72] If only she had realized that "Our
Blessed Lady" was a telltale phrase, revealing how far she
had progressed in Catholic belief. But, if the mediation of
Mary had been held up to question, however reluctantly,
Elizabeth joyfully acknowledged its power in the crucial
Sunday of mid-January 1805, which turned her firmly
to the true Faith. "I became half crazy", she recalled for
Amabilia, "and for the first time could not bear the sweet
caresses of the darlings or bless their little dinner. O my
God, that day! But it finished calmly at last—abandoning
all to God—and a renewed confidence in the blessed Virgin, whose mild and peaceful love reproached my bold
excesses and reminded me to fix my heart above with better hopes."[73]

Years later, in the comfortable familiarity of settled faith,
Elizabeth turned with perfect naturalness to the Sorrowful
Mother as she nursed her dying daughter, Annina. On the
feast of Mary's Purification, she found herself "at the feet of
our sweet, happy Mother *Mary*, listening to dear old Simeon
doting on the darling babe—offering the precious sufferer in
my arms when He entered our chamber—and oh, to hold
them both up to the Eternal Father! The child offering the
mother, the mother the child. The sweet half-hour of love
and peace with Jesus between us, as she sits on her bed of
pain and I kneel beside her."[74] Surely she did not forget
that it was Simeon who had prophesied the sword that was
to tear the Virgin Mother's heart, or the awesome picture
of the Descent from the Cross that had "*engaged* [her] *whole*

[72] Ibid., 322.
[73] 3.31, Journal to Amabilia Filicchi, July 19, 1804, entry of January 1805,
in *CW*, 1:374.
[74] A-6.99a, Elizabeth Seton's Journal of Annina's Last Illness and Death,
[January–March 1812], entry of February 2, in *CW*, 2:750.

soul" in the Church of Santa Maria Novella at Florence.[75] The moving words of offering and sacrifice attest that she had entered into the Compassion of Mary. After Annina died, she continued to identify with that other Sorrowful Mother, "begging, crying to Mary to behold her Son and plead for us, and to Jesus to behold His Mother—to pity a Mother, a poor, poor Mother so uncertain of reunion".[76] The poignancy of the prayer and her trust are not lessened but given an agonized strength by the forlorn confession— made in humble honesty or agonizing grief—that darkness and uncertainty had engulfed her soul. "*My God, my God, why have you forsaken Me?*"[77]

The maternity that united the Virgin Mary with Mother Seton is especially strong in an exquisite meditation for the feast of the Assumption. "Jesus nine months in Mary, feeding on her blood—Oh, Mary! These nine months", Elizabeth wrote in remembrance of a similar joy she herself had known in carrying her children.[78] Now she was savoring it again in transcendent communion with the divine motherhood. "Jesus on the breast of Mary, feeding on her milk! How long she must have delayed the weaning of such a child!!!! The infancy of Jesus—in her lap—on her knees as on His throne, while the rolling Earth, within its sphere, adorned with mountains, trees, and flowers, is the throne of Mary and her blessed infant, caressing, playing in her arms. Oh, Mary, how weak these words!"[79] They were not weak in the remembrance of a mother's fondling and dandling

[75] 2.10 Florence Journal to Rebecca Seton, [January 1804], in *CW*, 1:287.

[76] 6.118, Elizabeth Seton to Rev. Simon Bruté, P.S.S., September 22, 1812, in *CW*, 2:228.

[77] Mt 27:46.

[78] 11.9, "Departed St. Teresa's Day," n.d., entry of Assumption 1813 Mt. St. Mary, in *CW*, 3b:19.

[79] Ibid.

her children—she had still the embraces and kisses of her growing brood—but they were weak in her groping to express the mystical endearments of that other Mother and her Divine Child that Elizabeth was privileged to experience in her soul. "The youth, the Obscure life, the public life of Jesus. Mary always, everywhere, in every moment, day and night, conscious she was His Mother!"[80] As she had once used her little Catherine's childish interplays with herself as models for her own relationship with God, she now called upon her love for and pride in her children to help her comprehend the divine Motherhood and Sonship, grace building on nature. "O glorious, happy Mother, even through the sufferings and ignominies of her Son".[81] How well experience had taught her that true happiness was impervious to suffering. Then, the awe, the delight in the maternal perfection that she could only strive to emulate as best she could: "Her full conformity to Him—What continual inexpressible improvement and increase of Grace in her—O virtues of Mary ... the constant delight of the Blessed Trinity—she alone giving them more glory than all heaven together. Mother of God! Mary! Oh, the purity of Mary! The humility, patience, love of Mary!—to imitate at humblest distance."[82]

Elizabeth's exquisite ending to her Assumption meditation was at the same time theological and illumined: "How happy the Earth to possess her so long—[a] secret blessing to the rising Church—the Blessed Trinity could not part so soon with the perfect praise arising from the Earth as long as she remained—how darkened in the sight of angels when she was removed from it."[83]

[80] Ibid.
[81] Ibid.
[82] Ibid.
[83] Ibid.

Elizabeth also pursued her maternal intuitions of Mary with her Sisters, as her notes from a sermon or meditation on the feast of the Assumption suggests: "The glory and happiness of the Catholic Church to sing the praises of Mary—the striking proof—She is the true Spouse of Christ ... whom Jesus Christ himself so much honors, loves, and cherishes."[84] "His 9 months [with]in her"—the thought inspired a fresh profusion of spiritual insights— "what passed between them—she alone knowing him"— there was indeed a time when Mary alone of all mankind knew that the Messiah had come—"His only tabernacle.... *Mary, full of Grace*, Mother of Jesus! Oh, we love and honor Our Jesus when we love and honor her."[85] How plain this truth was to her now that she was free of the constraints of her religious upbringing. "Virtues of Mary infinitely perfect, the constant delight of the Blessed Trinity, she alone giving them more glory than all heaven together—Mother of God! Mary!"[86] She finished with an abrupt transition, to bring the holy Mother into the very hearts of the Sisters: "Mary, the first Sister of Charity on Earth".[87] It was, indeed, and is, something for them to ponder.

Mother Seton delighted in contemplating the mutual love of Jesus and Mary as He lay hidden in her chaste womb for nine months. Elizabeth understood the precious bond between the Virgin Mary and her Infant, just like Saint Louise de Marillac (1591–1660), also a mother and widow, who wrote: "When we are filled with gratitude

[84] Ibid., 18.

[85] 10.1, St. Mary Magdalen de Pazzi Notebook, n.d., entry of Mary Our Mother, n.d., in *CW*, 3a:463.

[86] 11.9, "Departed St. Teresa's Day," n.d., entry of Assumption 1813 Mt. St. Mary, in *CW*, 3b:19.

[87] 10.1, St. Mary Magdalen de Pazzi Notebook, n.d., entry of Mary Our Mother, n.d., in *CW*, 3a:463.

for the graces that God has bestowed upon us through the Incarnation and the exemplary life of Jesus Christ, let us look upon the Blessed Virgin as the channel through which all these benefits have come to us and thank her by acts of love."[88]

Saint Louise de Marillac and Saint Vincent de Paul co-founded the Daughters of Charity in seventeenth-century Paris. Elizabeth embraced their legacy as the model for apostolic service for her Sisters of Charity of St. Joseph's, founded at Emmitsburg, Maryland, in 1809. Influenced and nurtured by her experience of motherhood, Elizabeth bore witness in a note to Bruté, perhaps at Christmastime: "Blessed, it will please your so kind heart to know that this week past or more, our soul's dear Baby has been much more present to me than the beloved Babes of former days, when I carried and suckled them. *He*, the Jesus Babe, so unspeakably near and close, hugged by his poor, Silently delighted wild one!"[89]

As Elizabeth's knowledge of sacred matters deepened daily, and her love for them took greater possession of her mind and heart, the place of Mary in the divine plan and consequently her place in every part of it became clearer to Elizabeth. Acknowledging Mary as Mediatrix, "returning our love to Jesus for us, our prayer [passing] through her heart with reflected love and excellence as from the heart of a friend, all delights us, Jesus delighting to receive our love embellished and purified through the heart of Mary"—she finishes by asking in happy abandonment, "How unhappy they who deprive themselves

[88] Document M.33 (Devotion to the Blessed Virgin), ed., trans., Louise Sullivan, D.C., *Spiritual Writings of Louise de Marillac* (New York: New City Press, 1991), 785.

[89] 7.198, Elizabeth Seton to Rev. Simon Bruté, P.S.S. [Christmas 1818], in *CW*, 2:597.

of such happiness—how can we honor the mysteries of our Jesus without honoring Mary in them all."[90] She now saw Mary everywhere in God, as she indeed is: "Jesus in Mary, Mary in Jesus, in our prayers—her name so often in the Divine Sacrifice."[91]

Elizabeth never gave herself to sleep, that prophetic sister of death, without "my crucifix under my pillow and the blessed Virgin's picture pressed on the heart".[92] She once described for her sister Mary Post how she clung to them during a frightful storm that seemed to her a warning of death and judgment:

Think of the contrast, to wake with the sharpest light-nings and loudest thunder succeeding each other so rap-idly that they seemed to stop but half a moment between, to give time for a sense of the danger. Every part of the house seemed struck in an instant, and the roarings of the winds and torrents through the mountain so impetuous, that it seemed they must destroy, if the lightnings should spare. Our God, what a moment! I had no power to rise, or to remember I was a sinner, or give a thought to the horrors of Death, or the safety of the children. God my Father in that moment so pressing—and the plunge in Eternity the next instant. Oh, my Mary! How tight I held my little picture as a mark of confidence in her prayers who must be tenderly interested for Souls so dearly pur-chased by her Son, and the crucifix held up as a silent prayer which offers all His merits and sufferings as our only hope—How you laugh at your poor, half-brained Betsy Seton, but never mind—

[90] 10.1, St. Mary Magdalen de Pazzi Notebook, n.d., entry of Mary Our Mother, n.d., in CW, 3a:463.

[91] Ibid.

[92] 7.271, Draft, Elizabeth Seton to Mary Bayley Post, [prior to 1816], in CW, 2:676.

Well, the decadence of the storm brought me down from the clouds, and I felt really, I suppose, as one who is drawn back from that door of Eternity, after having been half in, and I crept away to the choir window to see what had become of my little, peaceable Queen, who was wrapped in clouds alternately lightened as they passed over her with so much brightness that they appeared at first sight like balls of light hastening toward us, while she was taken [sic] her quiet course above them, to disappear behind the mountain. There again I found the soul which fastened on God. Storms or whirlwinds pass by or over it, but cannot stop it one moment. My Mary dear, how nice it would have been to have died then—if it had been the right time. But since it was not, here I am, very happy to meet all the countenances of terror and wonder this morning, and the repeated appeal of: "O Mother, what a night!"[93]

When, years later, "the right time" had come, Elizabeth knew only the happy contentment all those nights with the "crucifix under my pillow and the Blessed Virgin's picture pressed on the heart" had earned.[94] "If this be the way of death, nothing can be more peaceful and happy," she said one day, chatting with a Sister attending her, possibly Cecilia O'Conway, "and if I am to recover, still how sweet to rest in the arms of Our Lord!"[95] Peace and happiness and the absence of all fear were not the only rewards prepared for her who had loved her Lord and His Blessed Mother so dearly and faithfully. "It seems as if Our Lord stood continuously by me in a corporeal form to comfort, cheer and encourage me in the different weary

[93] Ibid., 676–77.
[94] Ibid., 676.
[95] [Law], *Mother Seton: Notes*, 41.

and tedious hours of pain", she went on, and her words are not to be taken lightly.[96] "Sometimes sweet Mary, also, gently coaxing me—but you will laugh at my imagination."[97] Sister Cecilia O'Conway did not laugh. Nor did anyone else. Elizabeth's assistant, Sister Mary Xavier Clark, testified of her blessed death: "I do not know if you will give the name of superstition to what I experienced at this sorrowful moment. I felt our Lord was there, close by waiting to receive that beautiful soul. Never have I felt so impressed with His presence."[98]

[96] Ibid., 41–42.
[97] Ibid., 42.
[98] Ibid., 35.

6

If You Would Be My Disciple

One of the mysteries of today's contrary world is the silent disappearance of the words *penance* and *mortification* from the Christian and even the religious vocabulary. There is much talk of self-fulfillment, little of self-discipline; much talk of attaining human justice, little of satisfying divine justice. Yet penance and mortification have been urged as instruments of self-purification, perfection, and salvation by ascetical masters from the earliest Christian times, indeed, since Jesus Christ Himself insisted, "If any man would come after me, let him deny himself and take up his cross daily and follow me."[1]

Elizabeth Seton understood from the beginning the necessity of taking up her cross and did so willingly. She learned early that the cross was the mark and abiding providence of Christians. Thus, she recorded a remarkable reflection the week of her beloved father's last illness and untimely death: "The cup that Our Father has given us, shall we not drink it? Blessed Savior, by the bitterness of thy pains we may estimate the force of thy love. We are *sure* of Thy kindness and compassion. Thou wouldst not willingly call on us to suffer. Thou hast declared unto us that all things shall work together for our good, if we

[1] Lk 9:23.

are faithful to Thee. Therefore, if Thou so ordainest it: welcome, disappointment and Poverty; welcome, sickness and pain; welcome, even shame and contempt and calumny!"[2] She left out nothing. Nor was she speaking from an ivory tower of lofty sentiments, safe from the harsh realities she welcomed. She had already suffered them all with her husband in his financial disaster and bankruptcy. Nor was it superhuman stoicism, however admirable, but earnest, humble recognition of the Christian way. "If this be a rough and thorny path, it is one which Thou hast gone before us. Where we see Thy footsteps, we cannot repine."[3] And her confidence was sure and unafraid. "Meanwhile, Thou wilt support us with the consolations of Thy Grace, and even here Thou canst more than compensate us for any temporal sufferings by the Possession of that Peace which the world can neither give nor take away."[4]

Elizabeth understood, too, that "temporal sufferings" were most often caused by fellow creatures, by-products of the daily give-and-take of imperfect beings with wounded natures, and she sought to offset their harm by striving, she wrote, "not in any instance or by any provocation to retaliate anger or passion—to speak harshly or severely, *even if the truth*, of any fellow creature, and in all difficulties and situations contrary to the bent of my inclination, to *remember my cross* and for what purpose I wear it—in the name of my Savior and in firm reliance and trust in His assistance."[5] The cross she referred to was a gift from her father, and she loved it, describing it as "the mark of my captain and Master whom I was to follow so valiantly".[6] Most significant

[2] 8.7, "O tarry thou thy Lord's leisure ..." July 26, 1801, in *CW*, 3a:21.
[3] Ibid.
[4] Ibid.
[5] 8.5, "Not in any instance ...", April 18, 1800, in *CW*, 3a:19.
[6] 10.4, *Dear Remembrances*, n.d., in *CW*, 3a:514.

was her use of it as a reminder that she was to imitate her Lord in meeting trials, but especially in self-discipline by abandoning all out of love, as He did.

Elizabeth understood well the reason. She was as imperfect, her nature as wounded, as her nearest neighbor's, and from the realization came that honest sense of sin that is essential to common goodness, to say nothing of the holiness Elizabeth was to attain. On an August afternoon in 1802, she put it in words: "Solemnly in the presence of my Judge—I resolve *through His grace*—to remember my *Infirmity* and my *Sin*—to keep the door of my lips—to consider the causes of Sorrow for Sin in *myself* and *them* whose souls are as dear to me as my own."[7]

Elizabeth never lost the sense of sin. Indeed, the more she pondered it in her mature spiritual years, the sharper it became and the more she was able to probe its depths. Thus she came to the terrible truth that "when we sin, we not only sin in the Presence of God, *but in God Himself*; for since He is the source of motion and life, it follows that the sinner uses the concurrence of God Himself to offend and sin against Him, turning the means of life, health, time, etc., *powers of nature and grace*, to this horrid perversion and abuse against their Almighty Giver"—and she finished thoughtfully, "which explains to us in some degree the eternity of Hell torments".[8]

The practice of living habitually in God's Presence helped refine the sense of sin, Elizabeth discovered, for "all things shall work together for our good."[9] "A Soul

---

[7] 8.11, "Solemnly in the Presence of my Judge ...", August 1, 1802, in *CW*, 3a:25. It is obvious from the date that it was all part of the practical working out of the covenant made with her Lord the preceding May, and the reference to loved ones indicates, even in something so intimate as blame, that apostleship was always part of anything Elizabeth did.

[8] 9.20, Exercise of the *Presence of God*, n.d., in *CW*, 3a:395.

[9] 8.7, "O tarry thou thy Lord's leisure", July 26, 1801, in *CW*, 3a:21.

faithful to this holy exercise becomes so timorous and tender toward God", she told her Sisters, "that the least fault it commits is a pain to it, the smallest wound of conscience a torment, till it has humbled itself before Him and had recourse to His infinite mercies."[10] A *real* turning to God in sorrow, she cautioned, "not like those who are restless till they go to Confession, and afterward are neither better nor more humble"—she was a shrewd judge of souls—no, that kind of restlessness had nothing to do with the honest emotions of regret that were perfectly natural in the circumstances.[11] "Far from suffering our faults and imperfections to turn us from the Presence of God through the uneasiness and chagrin they cause us," she continued reassuringly, "we should return to it as quickly as a little child to its Mother after it has had a fall by letting go her hand, and hold to that dear hand with new care and fidelity."[12] The soul practiced in seeking God after some momentary lapse of attention, or even of strayed loyalty, will become so wonderfully used to being with God that nothing can take His place, like Mary Magdalen, who "at the Sepulchre was not dazzled or stopped by the beauty of the angels there, but went on seeking her God and could find no rest but in Him"; in the same way, "a heart which loves God truly will stop at nothing created, because nothing can supply for its God, which it seeks everywhere and in all things."[13]

When young Cecilia Seton had been drawn by Elizabeth's example of Christian devotion and practice and committed to emulate her, the older sister-in-law—now more than her friend but de facto her *second* mother, since William

---

[10] 9.20, Exercise of the *Presence of God*, n.d., "In What Does the Exercise of the Presence of God Consist", in *CW*, 3a:403.

[11] Ibid.

[12] Ibid.

[13] Ibid., 400.

Magee Seton had at his father's death assumed care of all his young half brothers and half sisters and moved his own family into his father's large home—cautioned her: "If you find that [t]here are any obstacles in your way—and doubtless you will find many, as every Christian does in the fulfillment of his duty—Still Persevere with yet more earnestness, and rejoice to bear your share in the *Cross*, which is Our Passport and Seal to the Kingdom of our Redeemer."[14]

Elizabeth gave only advice she herself followed. In the agony of the lazaretto, she wrote: "Not only willing to take my cross, but kissed it too."[15]

The difficulty of Elizabeth's submission is revealed in a flare of passion when the long confinement was almost over. Talking in thought to the absent captain of the quarantine, she scolded:

> The dampness about us would be thought dangerous for a person in health—and my W[illiam']s sufferings—Oh well, I know that God is above. Capitano, you need not always point your silent look and finger there; if I thought our condition the Providence of man, instead of the "weeping Magdalen"—as you so graciously call me—you would find me a lioness, willing to burn your Lazaretto about your ears, if it were possible that I might carry off my poor prisoner to breathe the air of Heaven in some more seasonable place.[16]

The pain of submission is equally evident in a poignant passage written for her eyes alone, days before the death of

[14] 1.177, Elizabeth Seton to Cecilia Seton, October 1, 1803, in *CW*, 1:224.

[15] 2.7, Journal to Rebecca Seton, November 19, 1803, entry of [November 23], in *CW*, 1:257.

[16] 2.7, Journal to Rebecca Seton, November 19, 1803, entry of December 14, in *CW*, 1:270.

Rebecca Seton, Elizabeth's sister-in-law whom she called her *soul's sister*:

> The dear, faithful, tender friend of my Soul through every varied scene of many years of trial, gone—only the shadow remaining, and that in a few days must pass away!
>
> The Home of plenty and comfort, the Society of Sisters united by prayer and divine affections, the Evening hymns, the daily lectures [readings], the sunset contemplations, the Service of holy days, the Kiss of Peace, the widows' visits—all, all gone forever! And is Poverty and Sorrow the only exchange? My husband, my Sisters, my Home, my comforts—Poverty and sorrow. Well, with God's blessing, you, too, shall be changed into dearest friends.[17]

Unlettered as yet in asceticism, Elizabeth was nevertheless affirming in word and deed that life lived in conformity to God's Will is a mortification. Certainly, hers had been. That she did not realize that her constant, willing acceptance of it had already had its effect on her soul was a grace. She never gloried in the hardships of her life but only in the Cross of Our Lord Jesus Christ.

Nor did Elizabeth complain. Her love for God had made her the complete realist in matters spiritual and temporal. When she told Julia Scott, "God has given me a great deal to do", she was stating a simple fact.[18] When she told her, " 'I rise up early and late take rest,' you may be sure—never before after 12, and oftener one. Such is the allotment", she was stating a simple fact.[19] That she added, "And as everybody has their *Pride* of some sort, I cannot deny that this is mine", she was not boasting, only acknowledging her artless satisfaction in fulfilling her responsibilities by doing what

[17] 3.1, Journal to Rebecca Seton continued, June 4, 1804, in *CW*, 1:308.
[18] 3.5, Elizabeth Seton to Julia Scott, July 15, 1804, in *CW*, 1:313.
[19] 1.149, Elizabeth Seton to Julia Scott, January 7, 1802, in *CW*, 1:197.

was expected of her.[20] The truest assessment of her daily life and attitude was in the vignette of one of her days: "I have cut out my two *suits* today and partly made one. Heard all the lessons, too, and had a two hours' visit from my Poor Widow Veley—no work, no wood, child sick, etc.—and should I complain, with a bright fire within, bright, bright *Moon* over my Shoulder, and the darlings all well, hallooing and dancing?—I have played for them this half hour."[21] A classic example of "count your blessings", but elevated— the piety of her life bears witness to it—to the plane of true mortification and prayer.

With this love of the Cross long Elizabeth's only way of life, she pounced with delight on a new revelation of its power in her Catholic friends of Livorno. "Why, Rebecca," she wrote in wonderment,

> they believe all we do and suffer—if we offer it for our sins—serves to expiate them. You may remember when I asked Mr. [John Henry] H[obart] what was meant by fasting in our prayer book—as I found myself on Ash Wednesday Morning saying so foolishly to God, "I turn to you in fasting, weeping, and mourning," and I had come to church with a hearty breakfast of buckwheat cakes and coffee, and full of life and spirits, with little thought of my sins—you may remember what he said about its being *old customs*, etc. Well the dear Mrs. F[ilicchi], who I am with, never eats, this Season of Lent, till after the clock strikes three. Then the family assembles. And she says she offers her weakness and pain of fasting for her sins, united with Our Savior's sufferings. I like that very much.[22]

---

[20] Ibid.

[21] 1.150, Elizabeth Seton to Rebecca Seton, n.d., in *CW*, 1:198.

[22] 2.14, Journal to Rebecca Seton continued, April 18 [1804], in *CW*, 1:296, brackets in published version.

I like that very much—a startling sentiment, humanwise, in one who had just suffered the draining trial of the lazaretto and who might be expected to flee from even the thought of pain, for the human frame naturally shrinks from it, but sure proof that Elizabeth was not accustomed to wasting her pain, indeed, that she had penetrated the mysterious relationship of sin and suffering, and sure proof, further, that the soil of her soul lay fertile for the great tree of faith the Lord had ready for it. *A humble and contrite heart, O Lord, you will not spurn.*

Sin and its punishment were very much in Elizabeth's thoughts at the time. On the voyage to Italy she had set Anna crying by telling her that "we offended God every day", and had herself, in a kind of Calvinist terror, penned a desperate resolution.[23] "Considering the Infirmity and corrupt Nature which would overpower the Spirit of Grace", she had reasoned,

> and the enormity of the offense to which the least indulgence of them would lead me—in the anguish of my soul, shuddering to offend my Adored Lord, I have this day solemnly engaged that, through the strength of His Holy Spirit, I will not again expose that corrupt and Infirm nature to the Smallest temptation I can avoid; and, therefore, if my Heavenly Father will once more reunite us all, that I will make a daily sacrifice of every wish, even the most innocent, lest they should betray me to a deviation from the Solemn and sacred vow I have now made.[24]

The extravagance of the bargain betrays Elizabeth's depression and desperation, but there is no mistaking the clear

---

[23] 2.5, Journal to Rebecca Seton, November 8, 1803, entry of November 11, in *CW*, 1:247.

[24] Ibid.

vision and determination. On the voyage home, with the opening of her spiritual horizon in Italy, the vision was even clearer, and she cried out in a fright inspired by the sight of Nelson's warships off Cape Trafalgar, "Oh, my God, if I should die in the midst of so much sin and so little penitence! How terrible it will be to fall into thy hands!"[25]

The sense of sin, thus, still brought Elizabeth terror, but her own seasoned love of God and the new revelation of it learned from her devout Catholic friends in Livorno would soon begin to change things. In the fresh crucible of troubles, she might tell Antonio, "Our God is pleased to hammer me like a truly poor sinner"[26]—but she was about to put aside any religion of fear. Symbolic of the happy change was her description of her first Confession: "So delighted now to prepare for this GOOD CONFES- SION which, bad as I am, I would be ready to make on the house top to insure the GOOD ABSOLUTION I hope for after it."[27] Her eagerness for what to many con- verts is an object of fear was rooted in a deep longing for an authentic forgiveness of her sins. Two months before, she had described her dejection in her last attendance at an Episcopalian service: At "the bowing of my heart before the Bishop to receive his Absolution—which is given pub- licly and universally to all in the church—I had not the least faith in his Prayer, and looked for an Apostolic loos- ing from my sins, which by the books Mr. H[obart] had given me to read, I find they do not claim or admit."[28] As Elizabeth prepared now for that apostolic fiat, she looked

[25] 2.14, Journal to Rebecca Seton continued, April 13, [1804], entry of April 24, in CW, 1:302.

[26] 7.81 Elizabeth Seton to Antonio Filicchi, April 1, 1817, in CW, 2:471.

[27] 3.31, Journal to Amabilia Filicchi, July 19, 1804, entry of [March 14, 1805], in CW, 1:376.

[28] Ibid., entry of January 1805, 373, brackets in published version.

forward to setting "out [on] a new life, a new existence
itself. No great difficulty for me to be ready for it, for truly
my life has been well [culled] over in bitterness of Soul,
these months of sorrow past."[29] Then: "IT IS DONE!
Easy enough .... Oh, Amabilia, how awful those words of
unloosing after a 30 years' bondage! I felt as if my chains
fell, as those of Saint Peter at the touch of the divine messenger. My God, what new scenes for my Soul!"[30]

Elizabeth did not, however, in her newfound innocence
forget the lesson of satisfaction for sin she had learned in
Livorno, as she confided to Amabilia: "Much he [Anto-
nio] says of my bringing all the children to you[r] Gubbio
to find peace and abundance, but I have a long life of
Sins to expiate."[31] She was still conscious of the debt years
later, in remonstrating with her son William for his silence:
"February your last date, and here 25th July. Eyes fill and
heart aches, but Our God is God, and the hardest penance
I can pay in this life is separation from you, and I must bear
it. Oh, if but at last to be FOREVER UNITED!"[32]

Nor did Elizabeth fail to teach the lesson to her daughter Annina, who, though her sins were scarcely "as scar-
let", yet freely offered a most painful expiation for them.
Gasping for breath on her mother's knees the night before
she died in March 1812, the young girl scribbled this moving prayer of consecration at the foot of the Cross.

Amiable and adorable Savior, at the foot of Your Cross I
come to consecrate myself to You forever.... O dear Jesus,
I offer You all my sufferings, little as they are now, and

[29] Ibid., entry of [March 14, 1805], 376.
[30] Ibid.
[31] Ibid., entry of [April 14, 1805], 378, second brackets in published version.
[32] 7.100, Elizabeth Seton to William Seton, [July 24 or 25, 1817], in *CW*,
2:490.

will accept with resignation—oh, by Your grace, let me
say with love—whatever You will please to send in future.
I offer in union with Your blessed merits all the sufferings I
ever suffered, those which I endured at a time I did not
know how to unite them to Yours; those I have experienced during this last sickness I offer more particularly to
Your glory and in expiation of the offenses and grievous
sins committed during my life. O my Jesus, pardon the
impatience, ill humor, and numberless other faults.[33]

The love of the Cross, which Elizabeth found at every
turn, remained a constant in her soul. She was sometimes
awkward in accepting it, perhaps because it presented
itself in the most surprising places. For example, when her
employment as a house mother to pupils boarding at Saint
Mark's School ended abruptly, she was obliged to take refuge with her sister Mary Bayley Post, and pride and the natural tension between siblings obscured the Cross. Catholics
were obliged to abstain from meat on Fridays at that time.
"My sister procures fish with so great expense and difficulty (really as if for the greatest stranger!)", she complained
to Antonio, "that my Bread and Water Spirit is ashamed to
partake of it."[34] And again: "Some proposals have been
made me of keeping a Tea store or China Shop, or small
school for little children (too young, I suppose, to be taught
the 'Hail Mary'). In short, Tonino, they do not know what
to do with me, but God does; and when His blessed time is
come, we shall know."[35] Despite her all-too-human indignation, the apprehension of God and His ways was not lost,
and she begged Antonio not to give her "the scolding I

[33] Annina Seton, The Last Words of A. M. Seton Consecration at the Foot
of the Cross, March 12, 1812, 1-3-3-9:40b, APSL.

[34] 4.7, Elizabeth Seton to Antonio Filicchi, [October 11, 1805], in CW, 1:391.

[35] 4.10, Elizabeth Seton to Antonio Filicchi, October 25, 1805, in CW, 1:394.

know I deserve".[36] Her friend Eliza Craig Sadler, however, did not spare her and asked, "Does your sister and her husband really desire your remaining with them?"[37]

> Of this I think there can be little doubt, however some inequalities of temper may seem to contradict it.... Perhaps not even *I* have it in my power to conceive how hard (in your situation) such inequalities are to submit to. But let us only repeat ... that the harder they are to bear, the greater will be your reward if you bear them as a cross at the foot of which feelings of worldly considerations must be sacrificed when we resolve to do all for the glory of God. Now this can only be done from a conviction that your duty is to remain where you are, or rather that you are placed there by the divine will.[38]

Elizabeth confessed the understandable truth to Julia Scott: "It seemed as if there was no escape from the Inconveniences and trouble I was necessitated to give the family of my brother[-in-law] [Wright] P[ost]. The more kind they were to me, the more painful was my sense of it."[39] As might be expected of a soul normally composed, Elizabeth soon recovered her equanimity. "The rubs, etc., are all past", she assured Julia. "No one appears to know it except by showing redoubled kindness—only a few knotty hearts that must talk of something, and the worse they say is: 'So much trouble has turned her brain.' Well, I kiss my Crucifix, which I have loved for so many years, and say they are only mistaken."[40]

[36] 4.5, Elizabeth Seton to Antonio Filicchi, October 2, 1805, in *CW*, 1:386.
[37] Eliza Sadler to Elizabeth Seton, [Aug./Sept. 1805], Saint Elizabeth Ann Seton, 1-3-3-11(B1), APSL.
[38] Ibid.
[39] 4.11, Elizabeth Seton to Julia Scott, November 20, 1805, in *CW*, 1:396, second and third brackets in published version.
[40] 4.13, Elizabeth Seton to Julia Scott, January 20, 1806, in *CW*, 1:401.

Elizabeth had rightly professed in the same letter, "I am gently, quietly, and silently a good Catholic."[41] She had become so in large measure through the sensible, steady direction of Father Jean Tisserant, an itinerant, émigré priest from France, who had discerned the basic docility of her soul and relied upon it. For example:

You tell me you were deprived of the satisfaction of going to church on Ash Wednesday.... Your Lent began by a sacrifice and a mortification of the will (which submitted itself to the motivations you indicate), and by good resolutions. I ask God to accept, bless and strengthen these resolutions. Sustain them by the practices that the Church prescribes in this holy time.... Allow me to tell you, be careful about exaggerating what is of duty and giving in to suggestions of zeal on what is only advised. Remember always that you owe yourself entirely to the duties of motherhood and the job with which you are charged.[42]

The surprise of the Cross came again, even in the first days of Elizabeth's joy of having attained her desire for consecrated life in community, with the petulant leave-taking of Father William Dubourg and the arrogance of his successor, Father John David. Her own inclination was to avoid conflict, but her conscience told her what she had to do, to advocate for the Sisters in her community. "Circumstances have all so combined as to create in my mind a confusion and want of confidence in my Superiors which is indescribable", she wrote desperately to Archbishop Carroll.[43] "If my own happiness was only in question, I should say: 'How good is the cross for me; this is my opportunity

[41] Ibid.

[42] Rev. Jean Tisserant to Elizabeth Seton, March 9, 1806, Saint Elizabeth Ann Seton, 1-3-3-1(22), APSL.

[43] 6.23, Elizabeth Seton to Archbishop John Carroll, January 25, 1810, in CW, 2:106.

to ground myself in patience and perseverance': and *my reluctance to speak* on a subject which I know will give you uneasiness is so great that I would certainly be silent. But as the good our Almighty God may intend to do by means of this community may be very much impeded ... it is absolutely necessary [that] You as the head of it ... should be made acquainted with it before the evil is irreparable."[44] The distinction between personal concerns and the common good and the consequent responsibilities were clear in her mind, as well as the personal suffering demanded.

Carroll, as the representative of Christ and His Church, responded by making this very point while at the same time sanctifying Elizabeth's suffering by identifying it positively as her way of the cross. "The proposal, if renewed, will not create any uneasiness on your account", he said confidently—the crisis had now reached the point where David actually considered removing the foundress from office—

> You have gone through many trials in overcoming the obstructions, interior and exterior, which were interposed to your change of religion. To these, other difficulties equally or more painful succeeded; but it has still pleased God to reserve another which must naturally disappoint your expectations more than any preceding one. That is, you are destined to be tried by disapprobation and humiliation, where you expected to meet confidence and tranquility. This was wanting, perhaps, to perfect your other sacrifices, and to operate in your heart an entire disengagement from human things and expectations—even the consolations of religious retirement.[45]

[44] Ibid.

[45] Archbishop John Carroll to Elizabeth Seton, July 18, 1810, Saint Elizabeth Ann Seton, 1-3-3-1(44), APSL.

Elizabeth took the proffered cross to her heart and with it not only the exterior assaults on her and her Sisters of Charity, which would pass in time, but also the day-to-day demands on her as its Mother, which would not. "I am at peace", she told Eliza Craig Sadler, just days after receipt of the archbishop's letter.[46]

A lazy, sleepy soul, give me but quiet, and all is given; yet that quiet is in the midst of 50 children all day, except the early part of morning and the last of the afternoon. But *quiet it is*. Order and regularity cannot be skipped over here, and I am in the full exercise of that principle which in the world passed either for hypocrisy or a species of it. You know, that manner of looking upon twenty people in the room with a look of affection and interest, showing an interest for all and a concern in all their concerns.[47]

With her usual vividness, Elizabeth went on to draw the picture of some challenges of her days: "You know I am as a Mother encompassed by many children of different dispositions, not all equally amiable or congenial; but bound to love, instruct, and provide for the happiness of all, to give the example of cheerfulness, Peace, resignation, and consider individuals more as proceeding from the same Origin and tending to the same end than in the different shades of merit and demerit."[48]

The common life requires humility, self-discipline, and mutual support to nurture peace and promote union of hearts among the members. The most committed community is made up, after all, of persons with human personalities and imperfections—all obliged by their acceptance

[46] 6.54, Elizabeth Seton to Eliza Sadler, [August 3, 1810], in *CW*, 2:153.
[47] Ibid., 153–54.
[48] Ibid., 154.

of the Rule to live together cordially and minister collaboratively. In such a way of life, the smallest eccentricity of the one becomes the most insufferable irritant to the other. The Little Flower, Saint Thérèse of Lisieux, confessed that a companion in the laundry splashed her with water to the point of utter distraction. But the common life is especially difficult for the superior who, because of the evenhandedness and example demanded by the office, is constrained more than others in word and deed.

Elizabeth's courage in taking up the cross unceasingly for the good of the community was a model for her Sisters, and she must have had a just pride in their imitation of it, for example, when they willingly accepted the hardships of their first mission beyond Saint Joseph's Valley during the turmoil of the War of 1812. The community minutes record their valor:

> A letter was read from the Archbishop which seemed for a moment to raise obstacles to the Sisters taking charge of the orphan establishment—yet leaving it in our power to decide. These obstacles only presenting personal inconveniences, the Sisters generously determined to meet them and begin the good work. Another letter to the same purport was read from the Vicar General and one from Reverend Mr. Hurley [both of Philadelphia], the present menacing aspect of public affairs rendering it dangerous and disagreeable to the Sisters—unanimously agreed that no personal inconvenience should prevent Sisters of Charity doing what duty and charity required.[49]

The measure of the heroicity of these young Sisters of Charity was in their use of the word *inconveniences* to describe the dangers and trials they were to face in living the spirit of

---

[49] Sisters of Charity of St. Joseph's Council Minutes, August 20, 1814, Saint Elizabeth Ann Seton, 3-3-5-1, APSL.

Saint Vincent de Paul and Saint Louise de Marillac "to serve the sick poor as ... mothers, procuring for them for soul and body all the good you can because often they have no one [else] ... to care for them".[50]

The mission's first local superior, a Sister servant in the Vincentian tradition, Sister Rose Landry White, wrote with the simplicity of the deprivations of the first year: "The Asylum was in debt $5,000. The subscriptions for its support were few; the embargo made goods double price, and it was often told us to reflect that the sum allowed for support was only $600 a year. They had no occasion to remind us, for our fears were so great that we would not be able to make out that for three months we never ate bread at dinner, but used potatoes; no sugar in our coffee, which was made of corn."[51] Even the orphans suffered. "The poor children had not been accustomed to get any sugar in their morning beverage; breakfast was weak coffee and dry bread, sugar being very high. However, Rev. Mr. Hurley, hearing of our not using sugar, commanded us to use it, and some was sent."[52] There can be little doubt that the appalling mortifications forced on these pioneer Sisters in their utter poverty and hard lives earned the success and spread of the Sisters of Charity of St. Joseph's. The sufferings of the little innocents did their part too!

Elizabeth did not hesitate to urge the cross on those she loved. "Look up!" she rallied her friend and benefactor George Weis.[53] "The highest *there* were the lowest *here*. . . . Now, my friend, we are in the true and sure way of

[50] Document 70, Explanation of the Common Rules, September 29, 1655, *Vincent de Paul: Correspondence, Conferences, Documents*, ed., trans., Marie Poole, D.C. et al., 14 vols. (New York: New City Press, 1983–2014), 10:94.

[51] A-6.3a, Sister Rose White's Journal, "[Philadelphia]," n.d., in *CW*, 2:734.

[52] Ibid.

[53] 6.57, Elizabeth Seton to George Weis, August 9, 1809 or 1810, in *CW*, 2:156.

salvation for that long, long eternity before us; if only we keep courage, we will go to heaven on horseback instead of idling and creeping along.... George, George, be a man! but a supernatural man crucified in Christ."[54]

Lest Weis miss the depth of her meaning, Elizabeth drew graphic pictures of the bloody union the words "crucified in Christ" signified: "If you sink so soon in the days of trial, My friend, how will we be able to keep in the bloody footsteps of our Leader—oh, look upon Him, see His look of love and sorrow while He looks behind after you and calls, 'Come, follow Me'—Calvary is the rendezvous—there, my dear George, both you and I *must* meet Him—meet Him—we must be crucified—it is in vain to start, or think of escaping."[55] And again: "As often as I look at the crucifix, I think of you as if I could see your name was written there on our crucified Lord, as indeed it is, my poor xxx [sic]."[56]

Elizabeth included herself in the exhortation, not only to encourage her suffering friend by her company but also because she was truly and completely united to him and his suffering. First of all by prayer: "Oh, that the Adored would give you a spark of the fire He has put in my heart since I bid you the last *A Dieu*," she wished aloud with childlike simplicity, "but I will use that fire to beg you may be supported or carried through this deluge of sorrow which has beset you."[57] Then, by full intention: "Happy w[oul]d I be to take the sorrow and trouble of you all, if you might have the merit"[58]—here, indeed, was unselfish

[54] Ibid.

[55] 6.38, Elizabeth Seton to George Weis, May 13, 1810, in *CW*, 2:125.

[56] 6.153, Elizabeth Seton to George Weis, March 19, 1814, in *CW*, 2:264.

[57] 6.38, Elizabeth Seton to George Weis, May 13, 1810, in *CW*, 2:125.

[58] 7.277, Elizabeth Seton to George Weis, n.d., in *CW*, 2:679, brackets in published version.

affection, spiritual affection even more telling than the giving of life—"Our Lord knows, my good friend, I would gladly give my life to do you any real good," she assured him, "but you know well what I think of the troubles of this life. I wish them even to be the portion of inheritance of my children, so how can I desire my poor friend to be without them?"[59]

The wish for her children and all her loved ones to be burdened with the cross did not dispel Elizabeth's compassion for them. In fact, their suffering weighted down her own but at the same time increased the bond of their love, as she assured George Weis: "I know you suffer more for your dear wife than for your[self], which is the double trouble, poor friend, and you will have the double blessing, too, if only you will persevere."[60] Most of all, however, to bear the sufferings of loved ones increased union with Jesus. "If Our Lord suffered us to bear our misery alone without affecting the dearest part of ourselves," she explained to Weis, "we would not suffer like Himself whose whole suffering was for us, and the injuries endured by His Eternal father."[61]

Elizabeth was not so insensitive to weak human nature, either in herself or in others, as to forget the promised rewards of suffering. "Our cross will soon be taken off", she assured Weis, "look only forward to our long, long Eternity—Annina cries to all from her grave how quickly everything passes—my poor, poor George, take courage—sow in tears to reap in joy, look to the Master Carpenter you follow after—I would be very sorry [if] He would

[59] 6.137, Elizabeth Seton to George Weis, August 20, 1813, in *CW*, 2:249.
[60] 6.130, Elizabeth Seton to George Weis, March 1813, in *CW*, 2:243, brackets in published version.
[61] 6.57, Elizabeth Seton to George Weis, August 9, 1809 or 1810, in *CW*, 2:156.

divide our lot from His and treat us better than He did him-self."[62] And again she exclaimed: "That bright and glorious Cross which we now drag through the mud and dirt, how beautiful and lovely it will appear when we find it opens the door of our eternal happiness to us. ... Remember, there is but one place of true *rendezvous* for true souls."[63]

Indeed, Elizabeth insisted, the rewards were often bestowed here and now, as if God could not wait to indulge those in whom He was well pleased. "Your trou-bles I find, like my own, are multiplied," she admitted to George, "and so will our comforts be when this dark night of life is over. Won't we sing Alleluia in the morning!— You may depend."[64] Even now, although "I do not grow *very fat* nor strong in the body—yet the soul is so well at liberty that everything except Eternity seems but a dream, a teasing tiresome dream—sometimes—at others it thirsts for Jesus and knows no pleasure but in suffering."[65]

Nonetheless, wherever the reward, Elizabeth loved her friend too dearly and rightly to wish his sufferings away. On the contrary: "I hope your cross may increase till it purifies you like pure gold," was all her comfort, "and woe to you if you, knowing as well as you do how rich a treasure you have, do not let [it] work its effect in you."[66]

Elizabeth could not forbear to season her uncompro-mising counsel with wit and teasing. She suggested that Weis tell a mutual friend "that we have adopted his motto: 'Well enough to work, and bad enough to suffer'".[67] And

[62] 6.114, Elizabeth Seton to George Weis, July 30, 1812, in *CW*, 2:225. George Weis was a carpenter by trade.
[63] 6.58, Elizabeth Seton to George Weis, August 28, 1810, in *CW*, 2:157.
[64] 7.278, Elizabeth Seton to George Weis, n.d., in *CW*, 2:680.
[65] Ibid.
[66] Ibid.
[67] Ibid.

she wondered whether "our little mischievous Cecil [Seton] has procured you all these blessings for having so tenderly received and waited on her in her last days of exile—indeed she is capable of all that spiritual malice could do, for you may depend, [she] would not be ungrateful."[68]

A truly remarkable memorial to Elizabeth's love of the Cross of her Lord Jesus Christ is a unique meditation entitled "Of the Communion of the *Cross*", in which she contrasts and unites both infinite mysteries. "It is strictly true that although there is no possible advantage to be compared with the happiness of receiving Our Lord and Savior in the Holy Eucharist, who is our very life in all our sufferings," she begins, "yet we also receive Him by the Communion of His Cross, that is to say, we may *unite with Him, we draw His spirit in us*, and it is very certain that we receive no grace in the communion of the Holy Eucharist but in proportion, as we receive it in the communion of *the Cross*. We can know the value of neither, it is true, without Faith"—she continues, building her analogy of the sacred on the divine and indispensable common denominator of all religious belief and practice—"and as when we are called to participate at Our Lord's table we go joyfully, not stopping on what *we see*, but on what *we believe*, so when He invites us to come and receive Him in afflictions and sufferings, we should receive His chalice with the same ardor and *drink His blood by Faith*, without looking at the veils under which it is hidden."[69] In Elizabeth's day, of course, the Holy Sacrament was received under only one species, the species of bread, which made

---

[68] 6.129, Elizabeth Seton to George Weis, March 26, 1813, in *CW*, 2:243, brackets in published version. Cecilia Seton had died in the home of George Weis three years prior.

[69] 9.20, Exercise of the *Presence of God*, n.d., "Of the Communion of the *Cross*", in *CW*, 3a:419–20.

easier the comparisons between receiving the Lord's Body in joy and His Blood (the Communion of the Cross) in suffering; nevertheless—"Without this firm *Faith*, we see nothing but a cross of *wood* in the *Cross* of Our Lord, as we see nothing but *Bread* in the Sacrament of His Body."[70]

Certain aspects of the Communion of the Cross are favorable to our weakened nature because they preclude mistaken self-interest and self-indulgence: "The great advantage of the Communion of the Cross is that we receive it when *Our Lord* Himself pleases and at the time He sees best ... we may go to the table of Our Lord when He did not call us there, when He only bears with our presence, but we never receive Him in the Communion of the Cross without being called by Himself; it is a mandate from heaven itself we Obey. ... We need not go to church to make this Communion of Suffering", she urges. "Our Savior comes to find us wherever we may be."[71] Furthermore, "angels can praise and love Him with us, but angels cannot suffer for Him with us; this glory of suffering with and for our head is for us alone as His happy members."[72]

This was the center of all penitential argument and action, the Suffering Servant prophesied by Isaiah, the crucified Lord: "When Our Savior offers us His Cross in any way, it is Himself, it is His own blood He offers. Approach, then, to participate [in] it", she pleads, "and do not overturn the chalice on its altar, or lose one drop of the Precious Blood it contains in order to spare our own."[73]

To spare our own! Elizabeth spoke now with the unerring eye of a spiritually wise woman and the sadness it brought:

[70] Ibid., 420.
[71] Ibid.
[72] Ibid.
[73] Ibid., 421, brackets in published version.

Unhappily, we are apt to think the very least suffering is too much, because we are lovers with our lips rather than our heart, while a true lover of Christ can never have enough of His Cross.... We open the door when He comes to us as the spouse in the canticles, crowned with lilies, but when He wears his garment of ignominy or His blood-stained robe of which the prophet speaks, we are struck with dread, and would be tempted to shut out our blessed *Spouse of Blood*, although He is covered with it but to save us.... This is because we love ourselves much more than we love Him.[74]

Despite the sad truth, Elizabeth was too knowledgeable and compassionate of human nature to leave it at that. "All He asks of us is our good will", she coaxes.[75]

We are never strong enough to bear our cross—it is the cross which carries us—nor so weak as to be unable to bear it, since the weakest become strong by its Virtue.

Our God is a great Physician ... who pays His patient, and gives a great recompense for the smallest pains, though we owe those pains to His Justice....

It is God alone we must look at in all that befalls us, small or great, and be persuaded that men and devils combined can do nothing ever so small but what He permits, and He permits no pain or trial whatever to befall us, but for the exercise of our Virtue and His Glory.[76]

In one sentence she encompasses this wondrous communion of the Cross, with the regret and the ardor it generates: "Our Lord, it is true, is content with our docility and resignation," she admits reluctantly, "but to this high

[74] Ibid., 421–22.
[75] Ibid., 422.
[76] Ibid.

mystery of our eternal union with Him, we should bring the burning fire of love and gratitude."[77]

Elizabeth's lessons in mortification were turned back on her on one occasion when she admonished Annina—now doubly her child, since the young woman had committed herself to the Sisterhood—"for the little care of her health: rising at the first bell and being on the watch to ring it the moment the clock struck, washing at the pump in the severest weather, often eating what sickened her stomach—'Ah, dear Mother,' was the dying girl's reply, 'if Our Lord called me up to meditate, was I wrong to go? If I washed at the pump, did not others more delicate do it? If I ate what I did not like, was it not proper, since it was but a common Christian act to control my taste?'"[78] That the Mother recorded it in her journal is proof of her personal satisfaction.

When the last weeks of her own dying were upon her, the Mother, forgetting her remonstrances to her dying daughter, pursued with the wonderful perverse logic of an oracle the same mortified path she had protested. The authority for this is no less than her spiritual director, Father Bruté. "She continued to follow as closely as possible the exercises and rules of the house, being assisted in doing so by a Sister who read and prayed with her", he told Antonio Filicchi.[79]

> This she did until her death, with great fidelity and perseverance—manifesting her uneasiness when some point of rule could not be fulfilled and supplying it as

[77] Ibid., 421.

[78] A-6.99a, Elizabeth Seton's Journal of Annina's Last Illness and Death, [January–March 1812], in *CW*, 2:748–49.

[79] Rev. Simon Bruté, P.S.S., to Antonio Filicchi, May 5, 1821, Saint Elizabeth Ann Seton, 1-3-3-12(108), APSL.

soon as there was an opportunity. Being obliged to make use of mitigations and necessary exemptions, she avoided them as much as she could without affectation. Sometimes she made excuses to her Sisters for what she termed her weakness, and she reproached herself for paying attention to it; and she endeavored as much as possible to repair what she considered a fault by mortifying herself the more. On one occasion she sent for me and lamented so earnestly, with tears that elicited mine, the relief that she experienced and the comparative comfort she enjoyed in the use of a mattress that had been provided for Rebecca when she suffered too much to bear the hardness of the ordinary bed—and this mattress they had given to her.[80]

Elizabeth herself corroborated Bruté's testimony in the very last letter she wrote, which took her "near a day to write ... blowing and puffing all the time", to Sister Elizabeth Boyle, "dearest old partner of my cares and bearer of my burdens": "When I used to hear of their sending children's bills to Superior or paying out money, in the lowest moments when I could not turn on the pillow without hartshorn," she confessed, "I would stop them; for as Jane and I only had known, they were all in the dark. It soon pleased God I could answer and see to those things without letting them go out of their own old track."[81]

The inward mortification of the mind and will was supreme in Elizabeth Seton's practice and teaching. "You must be in right earnest, or you will do little or nothing", she told her Sisters with her usual energy.[82]

[80] Ibid.

[81] 7.266, Elizabeth Seton to Sister Elizabeth Boyle, October 25, 1820, in *CW*, 2:673, 671. Jane is probably Sister Joanna Smith, who entered the Sisters of Charity in 1812.

[82] 9.9, Mother Seton's last writings, [1820], in *CW*, 3a:254.

What sort of interior life would you lead, if every time the door opens, or if any one passes you, you must look up; if you must hear what is said, though it does not concern you? Or, if you remain silent and in your modest attention to your duty, what would be your *interior life*, if you let your thoughts wander from God?

I once heard a silent person say that she was listening to everything round her, and making her *Judas* reflections on everything that was said and done.

And another, that she delighted in silence because she could be thinking of her dear people.[83]

And she ended wisely, "But you know better than that."[84]

In another conference, Elizabeth kindly but relentlessly exposed the pretensions of self that sapped all good at its source. "You wish so much to be good and to please our dear Lord", she acknowledged with compassion, "that you will not be tired if I tell you what the *Spiritual Guide* says of the obstacles to our interior life."[85] Note that she herself makes no pretensions to originality. Her teaching was accepted ascetism of the spiritual masters, which she had absorbed in spiritual direction and reading; but how vividly she salted it with her eye and ear for the homely and simple, the colorful, telling word or phrase! "The first", she continued, "is the little knowledge we have of ourselves and of our faults; for, as by an interior life we wish to be united to Our Lord, a *pure* heart must be prepared, in which He may reign as in His own kingdom. Self-love does not like to hear it, but our heart is very corrupt, and we must do continual violence to [our] bad nature to keep it in order."[86]

Elizabeth would not leave her Sisters the false peace engendered by their agreement with so general a statement

[83] Ibid.
[84] Ibid.
[85] Ibid., 259.
[86] Ibid.

but uncovered one by one specific flaws they were forced to recognize in themselves: "Our love of God is always opposed by our self-love", she stated flatly,

> our love of one another by the miserable pride and pretension which creates jealousy, rash judgments, and the pitiful dislikes and impatience which so often trouble us and *wound Charity*.
>
> Curiosity, too, which keeps us engaged in what is doing and saying, brings home many a foolish companion for our thoughts, to break the silence and peace Our Lord desires to find in us. Who that reflects on their own nature can doubt of its corruption and misery? You know ... how unwilling [we are] to deny ourselves, how unwilling to be reproved or contradicted, how trifling a thing will make us sad, how we delight to be commended, while, with a sort of natural cruelty, we see blame and fault in others which we are scarcely willing to excuse.[87]

Elizabeth then asked the totally honest question and drew the uncompromised conclusion:

> How should we live an interior life until some of our natural rubbish is removed? How walk valiantly with our dear Savior, dragging our foolish attachments after us, and ready to faint if the least weight of His Cross presses on us?
>
> The less sensible we are of our misery, the greater our evil is; for an unmortified soul cannot bear *to hear the truth* nor to be reproved even for its evident faults; so it remains buried in its darkness, and the enemy tries to double its blindness, while, sick and weak, it scarcely struggles against its imperfections, much less thinks of entering the sanctuary of *interior life*.[88]

[87] Ibid.
[88] Ibid., 259–60.

Having exposed the maladies they would recognize, Elizabeth proceeded to the remedy: "You will never receive any lively impressions of grace until you overcome this dissipation of mind.... If you are ever so fervent at your prayers, or desire ever so much to be good, it will be all like putting hartshorn in a bottle and leaving the cork out. What will it be worth?"[89] The echo of the parables of her Lord was here. "So all the prayers, readings, and good talk you love so much will be to little purpose, unless you place a sentinel at the door of your heart and mind. You often lose in ten minutes by your dissipation of mind more than you had gained a whole day by mortification."[90]

Elizabeth showed also how this lack of self-control at the source could ravage the entire spiritual structure built so laboriously. "How is it that many of us keep the rule as to the letter of it", she asked with a muted exasperation, restrained,

and also look pious enough—there is no want of good will, nor idleness indulged—and in a house where it would seem so easy to become Saints, you would say, what is the matter? Why are we not Saints? Why is there so little progress in perfection, or rather, why are so many tepid, heavy, discouraged, and going along more like slaves in a workhouse than *children in their own* home and the house of their Father? Why? Because we do not watch over our *Interior*, do not watch the impulse of *nature* and *grace* in our actions, nor avoid the occasions of the habitual faults we live in, when it is in our power, or keep a good guard on ourselves when it is not. Frequent indulgence of *useless* thoughts, inconsiderate words, expressions of natural feelings, and changes of temper all stand at variance with

[89] Ibid., 256.
[90] Ibid.

our sweet interior life, and stop the operations of grace, too often indeed even to grieving the divine Spirit and sending it away.[91]

Elizabeth was particularly concerned that the novices and young Sisters should get started early on the right road: "Young people ..., especially, should fight cheerfully, since Our Lord has so kindly called you in the morning of your days, and not exposed you to the anguish and remorse we feel after so many years of sin", she pleaded.[92] "It moves my very soul to see you young ones taken and sheltered by Our dear Lord, and yet you often look so ungrateful. Can you expect to get [into] *heaven* for *Nothing*? Did not our dear Savior track the whole way to it with His tears and blood?—and yet you start at every little pain."[93]

Elizabeth well knew the sincerity of her listeners, however, and the weakness of human nature and did not fail to remind them of a traditional help and safeguard always at hand: "The rule given us for securing the heavenly practice of pure intention is to be careful of our morning offering, which seals the whole day; since Fénelon says, that after it is made fully and sincerely, if we should forget to renew it from hour to hour (as all good souls commonly do) and not retract it by any act of our will (if no mortal sin comes in the way), our first good offering secures all we do for the day. What a comfort that is!"[94]

The most agonizing form of mortification endured by Elizabeth Seton was one she shared with all the saints,

[91] Ibid., 260.
[92] Ibid., 261.
[93] Ibid.
[94] Ibid., 258–59. Elizabeth Seton refers to François Fénelon, P.S.S., an eighteenth-century archbishop, theologian, poet, and writer.

indeed with all good souls earnestly persevering in the struggle for perfection—aridity. It is sometimes a lassitude of soul, sometimes the searching for a hidden God, sometimes a blankness of spirit, sometimes a positive distaste for devotion, sometimes an aching depression, sometimes the shadow of quiet desolation, but always an anguish of mind and soul. Elizabeth suffered it in its various disguises, often nurtured by physical weakness and the relentless illness that ate at her lungs or by the pangs and disappointments of natural and spiritual motherhood.

This scourge attacked Elizabeth's unremitting efforts to practice the highest virtue. "I am atom! You are God! Misery all my plea!"[95] she cried piteously to her Lord.

> So few saved! If we are lost, are You less justified? The patience so long waiting, less adorable? And the soul, burying itself in the chaos of mystery, always rested in stupidity within; but without, played with children, amused with the Sisters, yielding to all minutiae, attentive to all necessities.... Not one spark of grace can the soul discern in it all, but rather a continuation of the original fault, of desire to do, to be loved, to please! And so far from the simplicity of grace which would turn every instant to gold, it felt ashamed when [it] returned to the tabernacle, as if it had played the fool, or acted like those women who try to please company and show all their ill humors at home.[96]

Yet, with the sure instinct of the wholly dedicated soul, helped perhaps by the example of the great heroines of her spiritual reading—such as Saint Teresa of Avila, who endured more than twenty years of complete aridity yet never neglected a prayer, a devotion, or a duty though

---

[95] 7.318, Elizabeth Seton to a Clergyman, n.d., in *CW*, 2:704.
[96] Ibid.

"not one spark of grace can the soul discern in it all"—
Elizabeth clung faithfully to prayer and to work.[97]

"Poor, poor poverina, obliged to preach", she lamented
at a time when illness weighed her down.[98]

> If you knew only one-half my reluctance to give an instruc-
> tion or a catechism (formerly the heart's delight), it seems to
> me even yourself would be tempted to turn away with dis-
> gust from the ungrateful culprit: but the Dearest says, "You
> shall, you must, only because I will it; trust your weak breast
> and turning head to Me; I will do all." And *Sam* is so cruel,
> whenever there is an evident success, he pushes and says,
> "See how they are affected, how silent and attentive; what
> respect, what look of love!"—and tries to make distractions
> in every way. The poor, poor soul doesn't even look toward
> him, but keeps direct forward with Our Dearest, but with
> such a heavy, heavy heart at this vile mixture. So, in the
> refectory sometimes, the tears start and the weakness of a
> baby comes over me, but Our Dearest again says, "Look
> up, if you had your little morsel alone, of another quality,
> no pains of body or reluctance to eat, what part would I
> have in your meal? But here is your place: to keep order,
> direct the reader, give example, and eat cheerfully the little
> you can take—in the spirit of love, as if before My taber-
> nacle. I will do the rest. Abandon all." Abandon all! All is
> abandoned! But pray, pray for your poor one continually.[99]

Elizabeth, with her native good sense and spiritual sight,
recognized her torments as temptations and dealt with
them accordingly, but with what heroism and humility!
"Yet it might be a grace," she admitted,

---

[97] Ibid.
[98] 7.326, Elizabeth Seton to a Clergyman, [after 1810], in *CW*, 2:708.
[99] Ibid., 708–9.

for as often He saw, it was no more in my choice to hinder
these evaporations than to stop the giddiness of my head
in a fever. And they [the Sisters] are so loving, so fixed on
Mother's every look, clouds or sunshine, so depending,
sometimes I would shudder at the danger of such a situation if it was not clear as light that it is a part of the mate-
rials He takes for His work; and so little did He prepare
the composition that He knows, if nature was listened to,
I would take a blister, a scourging, any bodily pain, with
a real delight, rather than speak to a human being—that
heavy sloth which, hating exertion, would be willing to
be an animal and die like a brute in unconsciousness! O,
my Father, all in my power is to abandon and adore. How
good He is to let me do that![100]

Elizabeth once expressed it in another way, extraordinary for its ecstasy amid the dejection and pain of divided
human nature: "It is not the soul that is guilty of all this:
The evil spirit is most active, it is true; but the good one
sits in anguish at the foot of the Cross, looking over all this
desolation, adoring, subjecting, abandoning all to Him,
seeing only Him, annihilating itself and all creatures before
Him, saying *amen* to the resounding *alleluias*, and willing
any moment to go into hell itself, rather than add one more
offense to the mountain it has laid already upon Him."[101]

Nowhere does Elizabeth ask that the persistent sadness
of soul that she hid from the world be lifted from her.
Early in her final years of illumination and union, she deliberately made her choice. "Understand, Blessed," she
asked Father Bruté,

and let not your too kind, too patient heart *in its turn* "be
sad". The sadness of mine I cherish as a grace, and do

[100] 7.318, Elizabeth Seton to a Clergyman, n.d., in *CW*, 2:704–5.
[101] 7.320, Elizabeth Seton to an Unknown Person, n.d., in *CW*, 2:705.

hope to have it to my *last hour*, because it makes me so watchful that I cannot open my lips since St. Raphael's Day without fear. A blessed fear! Would that I had had it these forty years—how short *my account* would be! And be assured that sorrowful mixture which works in every prayer, *sleeping* or waking, and asks Our God continually, "Am I indeed in full charity with *ALL*?" Pure, delicate, sincere charity is no work of temptation; because, after the looking, the whole and repeated act of contrition (such as poor I can offer), I give up all to Our dear God of mercy and compassion.[102]

She strove to share her choice with her Sisters to alert them to the "grace", to instill in them the "blessed fear". She continued, "Besides, it is a Community grace, for I have said to our Betsy [Boyle] and Margaret [George] since: 'Do you know what you do? Mind—I have agonies of soul for less than that.' They both are quite too easy, as well as myself, on this edge of mortal sin. O my God—if He was not my God, I should go crazy in heart as well as the poor Body!"[103]

The sense of sin, as has been noted, pervaded Elizabeth's life of grace. It was not a scrupulousness or an exaggeration. It was the realism of the genuine self-awareness. Certainly, Elizabeth's consciousness of imperfection kept her in constant sorrow and penitence. "You see I say not a word to you of my poor interior world", she once broke off a recital of local and community news to Bruté.

The poor little Atom in darkness, clouds, and continual miseries—going like a machine in the beautiful round of graces—a sad month, the past—but yet another begun in the same stupidity and weariness of soul and body.

---

[102] 7.189, Elizabeth Seton to Rev. Simon Bruté, P.S.S. [November 1818], in *CW*, 2:588.

[103] Ibid., brackets in published version.

Communion itself but a moment of more indulgence for this state of torpor and abandonment, *wanting all* and asking nothing—for after so much asking and so much granted, to remain still the same unfaithful thing so long! Poor, poor soul, where will it end? *There* the point of *dreadful* uncertainty. I look over to the little Sacred woods, then up to the clear Vault—all is silent. Poor, poor soul![104]

The truly terrible cross and mortification of soul called aptly by spiritual writers the "dark night" is described by Elizabeth in a paragraph that is chilling in its simple directness: "Writing on a table opposite the door of the chapel, looking at the tabernacle"—this fixing of the sacred place of abandonment has its own cold terror—

the soul appeals to Him if this is not a daily martyrdom. I love and live, and love and live, in a state of separation indescribable. My being and existence, it is true, are real, because I meditate, pray, commune, conduct the community, etc., and all this with regularity, resignation, and singleness of heart; but yet, this is not I; it is a sort of machinery, no doubt acceptable to the compassionate Father, but it is a different being from that in which the soul acts. In meditation, prayer, Communion, I find no soul; in the beings around me, dearly as I love them, I find no soul; in that tabernacle I know He is, but I see not, feel not; a thousand deaths might hang over me to compel me to deny His Presence there, and I would embrace them all rather than deny it an instant; yet it seems that He is not there for me—and yesterday, while for a few minutes I felt His Presence, it was only to make me know that hell was gaping under me and how awful His judgment would be.[105]

[104] 6.195, Elizabeth Seton to Rev. Simon Bruté, P.S.S., Journal 1815, entry of [May 25], in *CW*, 2:328.

[105] 7.317, Elizabeth Seton to a Clergyman, [after 1810], in *CW*, 2:703–4.

There is nothing to be said in the face of such utter penitential and mortified suffering; but, how joyful to remember that Elizabeth's last words were the prayer of submission to God's plan by Pope Pius VII, who, exiled and imprisoned by Napoleon, had suffered greatly. Elizabeth savored this prayer and probed its depths of meaning in her dying months: "May the most high and ... [the most amiable will of God be accomplished forever.]"[106]

[106] A-7.268, Account by Rev. Simon Bruté, P.S.S., of Elizabeth Seton's Last Days, January 2, 1821, entry of January 4, in *CW*, 2:769, brackets in published version.

7

"A Kind of John the Baptist"

It has been reported that a brother-in-law once described Elizabeth to her grandchildren as "a kind of John the Baptist".[1] That description was apt, for she was indeed a voice crying in the wilderness of a new land, "Prepare the way of the Lord, make his paths straight."[2] That she felt this mission and its starkness was evident in her joy at the arrival of the first Vincentian priests and brothers in America: she received Holy Communion, she told Bruté, and "directed those of the Sisters to [give] thanks for the blessed Missioners sent to enlighten our savage land".[3] She was herself a born minister and missioner, initially for the lay apostolate; her life was wholly apostolic in its efforts and its fruits, particularly through service to persons in need, religious formation, and female education. It was her predestination.

It has been noted that saints are canonized not for what they *do* but for what they are—*who* they become in the

---

[1] Rev. Joseph I. Dirvin, C.M., cites ASJPH (now APSL) for this assertion in the original published edition (1990) of this work, but after much research, I have been unable to document a source. Whether this was truly said or not, therefore, remains unknown.

[2] Mt 3:3; Cf. Is 40:3.

[3] 7.47, Elizabeth Seton to Rev. Simon Bruté, P.S.S. [September 2], in *CW*, 2:420. Elizabeth's comment referred to the newly arrived priests and brothers of the Congregation of the Mission, whom William Dubourg, bishop of Louisiana (1815–1826), had invited to the United States.

eyes of God. Yet what they do and what they are profoundly interrelate: *holiness of soul* spilling over in good
works, as creation is the superabundance of God's goodness, and the good works continuously influencing and
building up holiness of soul. Both holiness and good works
express themselves in apostolic work, ministries, that are at
first the paths and then the fruits of vocations or callings.

Elizabeth had two essential vocations, first to the married state and then to consecrated life in community—
numerous apostolic ministries flowed from each. When
she was a married woman, her main obligations were
familial—private, personal, and intimate—not only to be
a good wife and mother in the temporal sphere but also to
be a bearer of salvation to her husband and children.

Elizabeth Ann Bayley and William Magee Seton married for love. Their love was mutual and deep. Away on
business, he could only wish "that tomorrow was come,
that might bring me nearer to that little heart";[4] and she
could assure him that his children "cannot understand that
Papa is not to come [this afternoon], nor tomorrow—
nor next day, nor the day after—that is for their Mother
to feel".[5] On her last visit to his grave in Livorno, she
"wept plentifully over it", she told his sister Rebecca,
"with the unrestrained affection which the last sufferings
of his life, added to the remembrance of former Years,
had made almost more than precious. When you read my
daily memorandums since I left home, you will feel what
my love has been, and acknowledge that God alone could
support [it, by His assistance,] through such proofs as has
been required of it."[6]

[4] Copy of William Magee Seton to Elizabeth Seton, June 10, 1801, 28–29
Mother Seton Guild Collection, Convent Station Correspondence, 12, APSL.
Original in Archives Sisters of Charity of Convent Station.

[5] 1.189, Elizabeth Seton to William Magee Seton, n.d., in *CW*, 1:231.

[6] 2.12, Elizabeth Seton to Rebecca Seton, March 5, 1804, in *CW*, 1:294.

For all the love between Elizabeth and her husband, it was unrequited in their lack of sharing fully and mutually in the love of God. A good and upright man, William Magee was a nominal Christian. He was tolerant enough of his wife's devotion, but it was her constant complaint to Rebecca that "Willy did not understand".[7] His lack of understanding provoked her, on at least one occasion, to impatience and sarcasm. *"Our H[enry] H[obart] was at St. Mark's* instead of St. Paul's," she informed Rebecca, "and Willy says those who heard him said he was a great contrast to the gentleman *we had*, who had given them, in the morning, a *Schism* sermon. Surely *H. H.* knew nothing of *Schism* yesterday! Willy regretted very much he did not hear him. *Regrets are idle things.*"[8]

There was a change in Will's attitude, to which his rapidly declining health may have contributed, two months before the Setons sailed on their hope-filled voyage to Italy; that it was important is evident from Elizabeth's excitement. "Willy says he *will dine at home* tomorrow, with a significant smile", she wrote Rebecca. "I shall be too happy if he means to keep his promise *freely* and without any persuasion from me."[9] Hard on the heels of this came another note, detailing further developments that seem to be concerned not so much with Will's going to church—there are indications that he did not neglect such an amenity—but with his approaching the Sacrament: "Since a *quarter* before three I have been, oh, how happy! Come, come, 'Soul's Sister,' *let us Bless the day together—one Body, one Spirit, one hope, one God*—the Father of *All*! I think our Willy will go—he has not left

[7] 1.102, Elizabeth Seton to Rebecca Seton, n.d., in *CW*, 1:144.

[8] 1.162, Elizabeth Seton to Rebecca Seton, August 16, 1802, in *CW*, 1:208, brackets in published version. "H.H." refers to the Episcopal priest Rev. Henry Hobart.

[9] 1.160, Elizabeth Seton to Rebecca Seton, August 7, [1803], in *CW*, 1:207.

me five minutes since yesterday's dinner, and has had *Nelson* in his hand very often.[10] If he does, what a dinner will *today's* be to me!"[11] And then, when Rev. Hobart had come to visit and share her joy: "I told him the last twenty-four hours were the happiest I had ever seen or could ever expect, as the most earnest wish of my heart was fulfilled. Dear Rebecca, if you had known how sweet last evening was—Willy's heart seemed to be nearer to me for being nearer to his God. From absolute weariness of body I fell asleep at *11*, and left him with *Nelson* in his hand."[12]

It was not, however, the ultimate, for some twelve days into their shared anguish in the lazaretto, Elizabeth wrote of her dying husband in her journal:

> My William's Soul is so humble, it will hardly embrace that Faith, which is its only resource. At any time, whom have we but Our Redeemer? But when the spirit is on the brink of departure, it must cling to Him with increased force, or where is it?
>
> Dear W[illiam], it is not from the impulse of terror you seek your God. You tried and wished to serve Him long before this trial came. Why, then, will you not consider Him as the Father who knows all the different means and dispositions of His children, and will graciously receive those who come to Him by that way which He has appointed? You say your only hope is in Christ; what other hope do we need?
>
> He says that the first effect he ever felt from the calls of the Gospel, he experienced from our dear H[obart]'s pressing the question in one of his sermons: "What avails gaining the whole world and losing your own Soul?" The

---

[10] 1.191, Elizabeth Seton to Rebecca Seton, n.d., in *CW*, 1:232. Robert Nelson was an Anglican spiritual writer in the eighteenth century.

[11] Ibid.

[12] 1.202, Elizabeth Seton to Rebecca Seton, n.d., in *CW*, 1:239.

reflections he made when he returned Home were, "I toil and toil, and what is it? What I gain destroys me daily, Soul and Body. I live without God in the world, and shall die miserably." Mr. F.D., with whom he had not been in habits of business, offered to join him in an Adventure; it succeeded far b[e]yond their expectation. Mr. F.D. said, when they wound it up: "One thing, you know, I have been long in business—began with very little—have built a house and have enough to build another. I have generally succeeded in [my] undertakings and attribute all to this: That, whether they are great or small, I always ask a blessing of God, and look to that blessing for success." William says, "I was struck with shame and Sorrow that I had been as a Heathen before God." These he called his two warnings, which awakened his Soul, and speaks of them always with tears.

Oh, the promises he makes, if it pleases God to spare him![13]

Elizabeth need not have worried over this "humble" soul, whom suffering and the inevitability of death had brought face-to-face with truth and who was only passing through the last phase of clinging without conviction to deceptive hopes and fruitless promises. Another two weeks, and the journey to peace was completed. On December 12, the doctor arrived, and William, "as soon as he saw him," said that "he was not wanted, but I must send for Him who would minister to his Soul", Elizabeth recorded sadly. William "looked in silent agony at me, and I at him," she continued, "each fearing to weaken the other's Strength. At the moment, he drew himself toward me and said, 'I breathe out my Soul to you.' "[14]

---

[13] 2.7, Journal to Rebecca Seton, November 19, 1803, entry of November 30, in *CW*, 1:261–62, second and third brackets in published version.

[14] Ibid., entry of December 12, 267.

From that moment on, Will's only concern was to prepare himself well to meet God: "No sufferings, nor weakness, nor distress (and from these he is never free in any degree) can prevent his *following* me daily in Prayer, portions of the Psalms and generally large portions of the Scriptures", Elizabeth wrote, herself in newfound peace. "If he is a little better, he enlarges his attention. If worse, he is the more eager not to lose a moment.... [He] often talks of his darlings, but most, of meeting, *ONE family, in heaven.*"[15]

Despite Elizabeth's heartsore human grief, how filled with joy was her soul to watch Will run now so swiftly in search of God. "Was so impatient to be gone that I could scarcely persuade him to wet his lips, but continued calling his Redeemer to Pardon and release him", she wrote of his truly blessed deathbed.[16]

> Every promise in the Scriptures I could remember and suitable Prayer I continually repeated to him, which seemed to be his only relief. When I stopped to give [him] anything: "*Why do you do it? What do I want? I want to be in heaven. Pray, pray for my Soul....*"
>
> At four, the hard struggle ceased. Nature sunk into a settled sob: "*My dear Wife—and little ones—and—My Christ Jesus, have mercy and receive me,*" was all I could distinguish; and again, repeated, "*My Christ Jesus,*" until a quarter past seven, when the dear Soul took its flight to the blessed exchange it so much longed for.[17]

While William Magee Seton may be said to have had little to do with his children's spiritual upbringing in life,

[15] Ibid., entry of December 13, 269–70.
[16] Ibid., entry of December 26, 274.
[17] Ibid.

his truly holy death surely did much to make up for it, especially as a sacrifice and unceasing prayer before God both for their salvation and in support of their mother, who now had the awesome responsibility of both their upbringing and their salvation entirely and alone. It struck her most forcibly as she rode out of the cemetery in Livorno: "Poor, high heart ... in the clouds, roving after my William's soul and repeating: 'My God, You are my God'; and so I am now alone in the world with You and my little ones"—yet to be alone with Him was everything, for "You are my Father, and doubly theirs".[18]

Some months later, as Elizabeth was struggling with religious conversion and leaned toward the truth of the Catholic faith, she asked the Blessed Virgin "to obtain peace for my poor Soul that I may be a good Mother to my poor darlings".[19] To be a good mother had always been as paramount with her as to be a good wife; now that her children were fatherless, it overrode all. They held priority in everything, temporal and spiritual. She made this very clear when the option of living a consecrated life in community was opening before her and a spiritual motherhood could be added to her, and she especially pondered it when the moment of truth arrived in the adoption of a Rule to guide their mission and way of life. "The thought of living out of our Valley would seem impossible if I belonged to myself," she told Julia Scott, "but the dear ones have their first claim, which must ever remain inviolate. Consequently, if at any time the duties I am engaged in should interfere with those I owe to them, I have solemnly engaged with our good

---

[18] 2.11, Elizabeth Seton to Rebecca Seton, January 28, 1804, in *CW*, 1:289.

[19] 3.31, Journal to Amabilia Filicchi, July 19, 1804, entry of August 28, in *CW*, 1:369.

Bishop Carroll, as well as my own conscience, to give the
darlings their right, and to prefer their advantage in everything."[20] There was no ambiguity as to what their "right"
and "advantage" entailed. "By the law of the Church I
so much love," she assured Catherine Mann Dupleix,
"I could never take an obligation which interfered with
my duties to them, except [if] I had an independent pro-
vision and guardian for them, which the whole world
could not supply to my judgment of a mother's duty."[21]
And she asked Archbishop Carroll, in reference to the
Daughters of Charity, who were expected from France
to mentor the infant community in the spirit of Saint
Vincent de Paul and Saint Louise de Marillac, "How can
they allow me the uncontrolled privileges of a Mother to
my five darlings?"[22]

Elizabeth had especially cultivated knowledge and love
of God in her children from their births. The Setons had
each child baptized in infancy at Trinity Church. The
parents promoted daily family prayers, even for the tod-
dlers, and regular attendance at Episcopal worship services
as each grew old enough. Along with their schooling at
home, Elizabeth taught them the stories of David, Dan-
iel, Judith, and other biblical heroes and heroines. She led
them in singing hymns. After Elizabeth joined the Catholic
Church, she gradually introduced the children to Catholicism and raised them in the faith. When she put them to
bed, she possibly laid her hand in blessing on them, made
the Sign of the Cross on each little brow, and whispered

[20] 6.50, Elizabeth Seton to Julia Scott, July 20, 1810, in *CW*, 2:146.

[21] 6.70, Elizabeth Seton to Catherine Dupleix, [February 4, 1811], in *CW*, 2:172.

[22] 6.76, Elizabeth Seton to Archbishop John Carroll, May 13, 1811, in *CW*, 2:185.

a silent prayer "with a humble hope" that God would not forsake the family.[23]

When Anna was to make her first Communion, Elizabeth sent her daughter to stay with friends who were part of the Catholic community in the parish for a week of instruction and preparation led by Father Michael Hurley, an Augustinian priest at Saint Peter's parish. Elizabeth wrote her an endearing note on the occasion of this memorable experience: "My darling daughter, you must not be uneasy at not seeing me either yesterday or today. Tomorrow I hope to hold you to my heart, which prays for you incessantly that God may give you grace to use well the precious hours of this week.... Remember that Mr. Hurley is now in the place of God to you. Receive his instructions as from heaven, as no doubt your dear Savior has appointed them as the means of bringing you there."[24] That Anna kept to these and to her mother's instructions brought her through an adolescent infatuation in absolute innocence, as Elizabeth learned and confided raptly to Julia Scott: "Music of heaven—that my darling should have had the virtue and purity of an angel in the first dawn of youthful and ardent affection (for she certainly is not without passion) is a joy to her Mother, which a Mother only can know."[25]

Named after her maternal grandmother, Catherine Charlton, Elizabeth's second-born daughter, began to use the moniker Josephine, instead of Catherine or Kit, her nickname, as early as March 1810, perhaps to identify with her new home in Saint Joseph's Valley, or maybe she

[23] 3.9, Elizabeth Seton to Antonio Filicchi, September 27, [1804], in *CW*, 1:324.
[24] 4.23, Elizabeth Seton to Anna Maria Seton, July 23, 1806, in *CW*, 1:413–14.
[25] 6.50, Elizabeth Seton to Julia Scott, July 20, 1810, in *CW*, 2:147.

hoped to take it for her Confirmation name. Elizabeth penned an appealing note for her thirteenth birthday:

> Birthday of my Josephine, and Mother's heart rejoices. It will look a little to the uncertainty of her crown, yet the good angel looks so smiling and points to the tabernacle. How can I help hoping my dear one will be safe? But, my darling, you must renew every good resolution, and keep close by your Good Shepherd. You know, the little lamb only stepped aside to crop the spear of grass, and then a little farther, and a little farther, 'till it could no longer hear the voice of the Shepherd; and then, when entangled in briars and thorns—you know the rest. My dear, dear one, think well of the little lamb. And take care of our dear little lamb, our little limping dear one [Rebecca]. Oh, yes, take care and be a good angel to her! Bless, bless you forever![26]

To Rebecca, the "little limping dear one", Elizabeth wrote in the same affectionate vein before a Communion day: "With the little pen I answer my dear, every day dearer darling. How much I desire she should go and unite still closer to our only beloved.... Make your careful preparation of the purest heart you can bring Him, that it may appear to Him like a bright little star at the bottom of a fountain. Oh, my Rebecca! Child of Eternity, let Peace and love stay with you in your pains, and they will brighten and sweeten them all."[27]

Elizabeth surely had no intention of imposing a religious life on any of her children, as she once protested humorously to Mrs. Scott about the girls: "Dearest Julia,

[26] 6.132, Elizabeth Seton to Catherine Seton, [June 28,] 1813, in *CW*, 2:244–45, brackets in published version.

[27] 6.109, Elizabeth Seton to Rebecca Seton, July n.d., in *CW*, 2:221.

you talk of making nuns like making bread. How can I make my dear ones love the life I love ...?"[28] It was solid faith and virtue she wished to pass on to them; what they were to do with it was up to God and themselves. It is true that Anna died as the first vowed member in her mother's community, and Catherine became a Sister of Mercy about forty years after her mother's death, but these were their personal choices, not their mother's.

Indeed, Elizabeth confided to Julia: "I never look beyond year to year for either myself or them, as you know how much my constitution was long ago impaired, and my children have the most marked symptoms of our family complaint [tuberculosis], and look forward themselves with cheerfulness and pleasure to an early reunion where there is no separation—especially the girls."[29] It was a hardheaded appraisal and revealed an exceptional frankness between mother and children.

When Rebecca's illness was in an advanced stage, Elizabeth sent her, in a last desperate measure, to Philadelphia to see Dr. Philip Syng Physick, an eminent practitioner in new methods of treating hip-joint diseases. Knowing how frightened the child would be at the separation, the mother tried to keep close to her by daily accounts of everything that went on at home. However, she did not hesitate to close one such letter with these exalted words: "My Rebecca, *we* will at last, at last unite in His eternal praise, lost in Him, you and I, closer still than in the nine months so dear when, as I told you, I carried you in my bosom as He in our Virgin Mother's—*then*, no more separation."[30] The young adolescent raised in the countryside

[28] 6.121, Elizabeth Seton to Julia Scott, [October 29,] 1812, in *CW*, 2:232.
[29] Ibid., 233.
[30] 6.206, Elizabeth Seton to Rebecca Seton, September 25, [1815], in *CW*, 2:343.

was, of course, enchanted by the great city, where she visited "the museum, the Bank of Pennsylvania, [the] Bank of the United States, the water works and I do not know where else"; but—her mother's true daughter—"What was better than all, Sister Rose [White] took me to the Poor house. You must know what a coward I am, as you have experienced all. I do not dare to think of my own sufferings after having seen theirs, though Sister Rose tells me I have seen but the best part of it."[31]

Elizabeth watched over Rebecca's soul as carefully as her wasted body to the last. "Poor beloved!" the mother wrote Father Bruté five months before the girl's death. "We examine much together if she is in the good disposition of *the will*. She is so sure—only she says, 'Perhaps I indulge my feelings too much, not stay[ing] in bed at night, but I do suffer so in it.' Strange indulgence! Yet do pray for the poor lamb: it has so many little old and even fancy ways of pride, pretensions (Seton maladies), etc."[32]

Dearly as Elizabeth's sons, William and Richard, loved her, they were too restless of nature to want to remain in the rural valley she loved. They were eager to try the world, and their mother was too sensible to prevent them. But advise and guide and pray she did. "Be not, my dear one, so unhappy as to break willfully any command of Our God", she begged William on his first venture abroad, "or to omit your prayers on any account. Unite them always to the only merits of our Jesus and the Maternal prayers of our Mother and His. With them you will always find your own poor, poor mother. You cannot even guess the

[31] Rebecca Seton to Elizabeth Seton, [October 1815], Saint Elizabeth Ann Seton, 1-3-3-9(46), APSL.

[32] 7.34, Elizabeth Seton to Rev. Simon Bruté, P.S.S., June 28, 1816, in *CW*, 2:406, brackets in published version.

incessant cry of my Soul to them for you."[33] She grew more insistent as she wrote:

> Don't say Mother has the rest to comfort her. No, no, my William. From the first moment I received you in my arms and to my breast, you have been consecrated to God by me, and I have never ceased to beg Him to take you from this World, rather than you should offend Him or dishonor your dear Soul; and, as you know, my stroke of Death would be to know that you have quitted that path of Virtue which alone can reunite us forever. Separations, everything else, I can bear—but that, never. Your Mother's heart must break, if that blow falls on it.[34]

Richard was less mature and more careless and therefore more of a worry to his mother. "Richard ... does not give poor Kit and me as much comfort in a year as *one of your letters*", she told William. "His heart is not turned like yours, my Son, and I dread, yet hope, everything.... You may guess if I have any other hopes but to look up to God, *Your Father and Mine*."[35] Four years later she was still hoping, still "looking up". "You can have no idea [of] our anxiety to hear from you", Elizabeth scolded in a letter to Richard, who was then with the Filicchi in Livorno. "Six, seven, eight months pass without one line.... What a heartfelt consolation, my Soul's Richard, it would be to me if you could write me in full sincerity before the Searcher of hearts (and not merely to comfort mine): 'Mother, I preserve my faith entire amidst all the dangers and scandals I meet—*Your* Faith, Mother, the one so dear to *you*.'"[36]

---

[33] 6.182, Elizabeth Seton to William Seton, [January 1815], in *CW*, 2:298.
[34] Ibid.
[35] 7.69, Elizabeth Seton to William Seton, [early 1817], in *CW*, 2:459.
[36] 7.246, Elizabeth Seton to Richard Seton, May 8, 1820, in *CW*, 2:650.

Some weeks later, when Richard had finally written, it was only to cast down his mother's soul. He was "full of schemes about settling on the Black River", she confided to a friend, "black indeed will it be to him if he carries it through. He says, 'Commerce is [a] dead loss of time at present.' Poor fellow, I fear his Faith is dead by the whole tenor of his letters; yet he puts change aside 'till another year—so, we will see—nothing from William. You hear my sighs, and they go to your dear Heart, I know; but never mind, my Ellen, Our God will pity."[37] And she besought Father John Hickey, a priest at Mount Saint Mary's, "You pray, I hope, for my poor, very poor, dear boys. My tears for them smart more and more day and night."[38] She was dying now, which made her heartbreak even more poignant.

Elizabeth did her best to give the three children who would survive her a start in life. She sent Catherine to visit with friends and relatives in Philadelphia and New York that she might get to know the wide world outside Saint Joseph School in Emmitsburg. Prior to her death, Elizabeth entrusted Catherine to the care of good friends, Major General Robert Goodloe Harper and his wife, Catherine Carroll Harper. Elizabeth prevailed on the faithful Filicchi brothers to guide and prepare both her sons for business, though neither pursued commercial interests, preferring the high seas. She importuned her many influential friends in behalf of William's commission in the United States Navy, much as she dreaded the possible effect on his soul.

There was Elizabeth's constant, chief concern—her children's souls. She felt, of course, the natural maternal pull on

---

[37] 7.250, Elizabeth Seton to Ellen Wiseman, [June 29, 1820], in *CW*, 2:657, brackets in published version.
[38] 7.252, Elizabeth Seton to Rev. John Hickey, P.S.S., [July 2, 1820], in *CW*, 2:659.

her heart, a pull aggravated by the loss of their father as provider and role model and their far-from-normal upbringing amid schoolchildren and Sisters of Charity. But the importance of their salvation was supreme, and she never left off urging it at every possible opportunity. She put it all in proper perspective in a few lines to Antonio Filicchi concerning William: "I cannot hide from Our God, though from everyone else I must conceal, the perpetual tears and affections of boundless gratitude which overflow my heart when I think of him secure in his *Faith* and your protection. Why I love him so much I cannot account, but own to you, my Antonio, all my weakness. Pity and pray for a mother attached to her children through such peculiar motives as I am to mine. I purify it as much as I can, and Our God knows it is their Souls alone I look at."[39]

The mother's prayers and tears were neither requited nor rewarded while she lived, but they were not wasted. Richard died aboard the *Oswego* off the coast of Liberia, just two years after his mother; it was a noble death of a fever contracted by nursing to health Jehudi Ashmun, the United States consul there. William lived into his seventies and died at his home in New York with his children around him.

There are curious hints of Elizabeth Seton's ultimate religious vocation even in her early life. She writes retrospectively of "passionate wishes that there were such places in America as I read of in novels, where people could be shut up from the world and pray, and be good always. Many thoughts of running away to such a place over the seas, in disguise, working for a living."[40] Young romanti-

---

[39] 6.214, Elizabeth Seton to Antonio Filicchi, November 20, 1815, in *CW*, 2:356.

[40] 10.4, *Dear Remembrances*, n.d., in *CW*, 3a:512.

cism beyond a doubt, yet suggestive of an inchoate yearning that took form and intensity bit by bit in later years and the proper environment.

More significant, however, was Elizabeth's special bond with her sister-in-law Rebecca Seton, an exceptionally spiritual soul. The two quickly became "soul sisters" united by mutual devotions and good works that earned for them the nickname "Protestant Sisters of Charity", primarily because of their benevolence as volunteers with the Society for the Relief of Poor Widows with Small Children. When the two came together under the direction of Rev. John Henry Hobart, the earnest curate of Trinity Church, they leaped forward in a "sacred circle" to which they later invited Catherine Mann Dupleix. As the older, Elizabeth was the one who did not hesitate to admonish when the occasion called for it. When Rebecca had broken their pact to remain at home in prayerful reflection on Sacrament Sunday by reluctantly fulfilling a social obligation, Elizabeth scolded her gently but firmly in words that, for all their apparent rigor, made a certain religious sense: "The misfortune of the afternoon will, I hope, be a *lesson for life* to my Darling Sister", she wrote soothingly,

that you never should violate a strict rule, not to leave Home on any persuasion on *Sacrament Sunday*, and to say openly to whoever may request it that it is *your rule*. It can never be a breach of civility or seem unkind ... if you say it with the firmness of one who has been at *His table* who refreshes and strengthens the Soul in well-doing. I have often asked myself the question: Why should anyone be more earnest in prevailing with me for a trifle or a thing of no consequence in itself, than *I*, in maintaining the thing I know to be right and that touches the interests of my Soul's Peace.[41]

[41] 1.135, Elizabeth Seton to Rebecca Seton, July 24, 1801, in *CW*, 1:178.

It was to Rebecca that Elizabeth poured out her heart from the abyss of her sufferings in the lazaretto of Livorno, to Rebecca that she confided her wonder and delight in the dawning faith she found among her newfound Catholic friends in the months that followed, to the dying Rebecca that she went in dismay directly on landing home in New York. Elizabeth's special messages had fallen on willing eyes and ears, and although the dying young woman could not do anything to formalize them—Elizabeth herself was not ready for such a step—she showed her heart by gasping faithfully the words of Ruth to Naomi, "Your people are my people, your God, my God."[42]

A further indication of Elizabeth's early influence as a spiritual model and mentor was the immediate impact her conversion to Catholicism had on her youngest sisters-in-law, Cecilia (fourteen) and Harriet Seton (sixteen), and their cousin Eliza ("Zide") Farquhar (nineteen).[43] The rest of the family reacted with anger and intense hostility; Zide soon lost all will to resist them, and even Harriet faltered. Cecilia was not to be intimidated, young as she was. Elizabeth became her spiritual guide, bringing down on herself the Setons' fury and, indeed, the disapproval of everyone who knew the Setons. Despite really harrowing persecution, Cecilia, with Elizabeth's encouragement and firm backing and the counsel of Father Jean Cheverus, persevered, and on June 17, 1806, voluntarily left her family. "My dear Charlotte," she announced quietly to her sister in a note,

> in consequence of a firm resolution to adhere to the Catholic faith, I left your house this morning; and can only repeat that, if in the exercise of *that* faith my family will again receive me, my wish is to return and give them

---

[42] 10.4, *Dear Remembrances*, n.d., in *CW*, 3a:518. Cf. Ruth 1:16.

[43] See Annabelle M. Melville, *Elizabeth Bayley Seton 1774–1821*, ed., Betty Ann McNeil, D.C. (Hanover, Pa.: The Sheridan Press, 2009), 161.

every proof of my affection by redoubled care to please them and submission to their wishes in every point consistent with my duty to *Him* who claims my *first* Obedience. Under these circumstances, whatever is the Providence of Almighty God for me, I must receive it with entire resignation and confidence in his protection—but in every case must be your affectionate sister, Cecilia.[44]

Three days later, Cecilia was received into the Catholic Church. Harriet accompanied Cecilia to Baltimore when the latter went to visit Elizabeth there and join the nascent Sisterhood. Harriet intended to return to New York to marry Elizabeth's half brother Andrew Barclay Bayley, who was in Jamaica in the West Indies, but he proved to be faithless.

The unhappy Harriet lingered in Emmitsburg, where, under the guidance of Father Pierre Babade, she made her profession of faith as a Catholic in September 1809. Harriet had made her decision during a late-night visit to Saint Mary's Church on the Mountain of the same name two months previously. Elizabeth has left a description of her "stealing up to the Church by the light of a full moon, in deepest silence, her arms crossed upon her breast, and the moon's reflection full on her pale but celestial countenance". Elizabeth recalled, "I saw the falling tears of love and adoration, while we said, first *Miserere* and then *Te Deum*, which from her childhood had been our family prayers. Descending the mountain, she burst forth the full heart: 'It is done, my sister: I am a Catholic! The cross of our dearest is the desire of my soul. I will never rest till He is mine.'"[45] Although

---

[44] Cecilia Seton to Charlotte Seton Ogden, n.d., 1806, Saint Elizabeth Ann Seton, 1-3-3-4:168, APSL.

[45] 10.2, Red Leather Notebook, n.d., in *CW*, 3a:480.

seemingly in the bloom of health, the young woman was unexpectedly stricken with a violent type of brain fever, lingered four weeks, and died on December 23, 1809. Cecilia died in Baltimore on April 28, 1810, at the age of nineteen, the first of Mother Seton's spiritual daughters in the Sisters of Charity to be given back to God.

Elizabeth's role in these conversions was most appropriate, for her own long and hard conversion was the first giant step toward her call to consecrated life and public ministry. The second was the series of trials it precipitated, trials that were in fact cleansing agents sweeping the past out of the way of her progress into the future: the ostracism of family and friends and ultimately the hostility of all in her orbit, which defeated her efforts to support her children financially and finally convinced her that she must leave New York for their welfare and for love of her children's very souls.

That God's intent was much more pervasive than one little family, however good and precious, is evidenced in the prophetic note that now appeared in the advice of Elizabeth's spiritual guides. "Your perseverance and the help of grace will finish in you the work which God has commenced", Father Matignon assured her, "and will render you, I trust, the means of effecting the conversion of many others."[46] And, since Elizabeth, influenced by Antonio Filicchi, had evinced serious thought of relocating to Montreal, he sought to dissuade her: "You are destined, I think, for some great good in the United States," he stated flatly, "and here you should remain in preference to any other location."[47]

[46] Rev. Francis Matignon to Elizabeth Seton, September 22, 1806, Saint Elizabeth Ann Seton, 1-3-3-1(34b), APSL.

[47] Rev. Francis Matignon to Elizabeth Seton, November 25, 1806, Saint Elizabeth Ann Seton, 1-3-3-1:37, APSL.

These solemn words must have sounded fatefully in Elizabeth's ears, but she did not yet give them, or rather herself, undue importance, for she continued to press Antonio Filicchi with her thoughts of a future much more private. She seems to have alerted him to the possibility nearly a year before, when she wrote that she had "a little secret to communicate ... when we meet (a sweet dream of imagination)".[48] Now she grew more specific in an allusion, possibly only understood by the Filicchi: "If you were now here, my dear brother, I think you would exert your friendship for us and obtain the so-long-desired refuge of a place in the Order of St. Francis for your converts."[49]

From this time on, Elizabeth's future outside of New York was roundly discussed and reasoned. The real call came from God in April 1808. As she told Julia Scott, Father William Dubourg of Baltimore "offered to give me a formal grant of a lot of ground [land] ... and procure me immediately the charge of a half-dozen girls, and as many more as I can manage".[50] Elizabeth answered the call at once. The needed advice had been sought and opinions given long before, and only the opportunity had been awaited. She arrived at Saint Mary's Seminary, Baltimore, to begin the next phase of her life's work on the feast of Corpus Christi, June 16, 1808.

There was the momentary, and again curious, distraction of her meeting Samuel Sutherland Cooper, a convert and retired sea captain, who had come to Baltimore to study for the priesthood, and their mutual attraction. However, Elizabeth had answered her call, and there was no turning aside. "You may be sure though I have always

---

[48] 4.7, Elizabeth Seton to Antonio Filicchi, [October 11, 1805], in *CW*, 1:391.
[49] 4.24, Elizabeth Seton to Antonio Filicchi, August 10, 1806, in *CW*, 1:415.
[50] 4.73, Elizabeth Seton to Julia Scott, April 25, 1808, in *CW*, 1:506.

considered him as a consecrated being—as he did me", she told Julia Scott, "and the only result of this partiality has been the encouragement of each other to persevere in the path which each had chosen."[51]

Elizabeth paid attention now to insights and their importance for others. "It is expected I shall be the mother of many daughters", she wrote quite simply to Cecilia Seton.[52]

> A letter received from Philadelphia where my Blessed Father, Our Patriarch [Father Pierre Babade], now is on a visit, tells me he has found two of the Sweetest young women, who were going to Spain to seek a refuge from the World—though they are both Americans, *Cecilia* and *May*—and now wait until my house is opened for them: Next spring, we hope. He applies to me the Psalms in our Vespers: "The Barren Woman shall be the joyful Mother of children", and tells me to repeat it continually, which you must do with me, my darling.[53]

Prophetically, the highly esteemed and future bishop of Boston, Father John Cheverus, wrote Elizabeth: "I see already numerous choirs of virgins following you to the Altar", he told her solemnly. "I see your holy order diffusing itself in the different parts of the United States, spreading everywhere the good odor of Jesus Christ and teaching by their angelical lives and pious instructions how to serve God in purity and holiness. I have no doubt, my beloved and venerable Sister," he finished, echoing his friend Father Francis Matignon, "that He who has begun this good work, will bring it to perfection."[54]

[51] 5.21, Elizabeth Seton to Julia Scott, March 23, 1809, in *CW*, 2:61.
[52] 5.10, Elizabeth Seton to Cecilia Seton, October 6, 1808, in *CW*, 2:34.
[53] Ibid., 2:34–35.
[54] Rev. John Cheverus to Elizabeth Seton, April 13, 1809, Saint Elizabeth Ann Seton, 1-3-3-1(10), APSL.

Elizabeth herself was wonderfully happy in all that had come to pass, culminating in making private annual vows for the first time in the presence of Archbishop Carroll on the feast of the Annunciation and causing her to cry out to Julia Scott: "To speak the joy of my soul at the prospect of being able to assist the Poor, visit the sick, comfort the sorrowful, clothe little innocents, and teach them to love God!"[55] These few words sum up the vocational call of Elizabeth Ann Seton and reveal her as a spiritual daughter of Saint Vincent de Paul and Saint Louise de Marillac. Elizabeth would be the first to enculturate the Vincentian charism in North America. The mission of the American Sisters of Charity had two main thrusts: service to those in need and education, particularly for girls and young women.

From childhood Elizabeth had a heart for her neighbors in need—the poor, the sick, the helpless, and the unfortunate—a heart of total service, an apostle's heart. By her own testimony, at eight she took "delight in being with old people", at twelve she loved to "nurse the children and sing little hymns over the cradle", at eighteen, she recalled with amusement, she had "fine plans of a little country home, to gather all the little children round and teach them their prayers, and keep them clean, and teach them to be good".[56]

Grown up, married, and a mother at twenty-three, Elizabeth helped found the Society for the Relief of Poor Widows with Small Children in Lower Manhattan, an association of Christian matrons who, in unwitting emulation of Saint Vincent de Paul's Ladies of Charity, not only gave their own money and coaxed others to give

---

[55] 5.21, Elizabeth Seton to Julia Scott, March 23, 1809, in *CW*, 2:62.
[56] 10.4, *Dear Remembrances*, n.d., in *CW*, 3a:511–12.

but also visited widows in their homes, taking them food and clothing and assisting them to earn some income through piecework.

Family and friends called Elizabeth first to the bedside of the grief-stricken, sick, and dying.[57] She responded promptly and, in addition to her attentive presence, often brought the consolations of religion along with the medicines and little treats. When the end came and she could do no more, she stayed behind to console the bereft. She gave Eliza Craig Sadler a graphic description of her ministrations to Julia Scott at the death of Julia's husband: "I have not left her night or day during the excess of her Sorrows, and such scenes of terror I have gone through as you nor no one can conceive. 'Tis past. Little Julia goes to Philadelphia next week where she is to fix her residence, as her Family connections are all there. And I am once more *Home*, ten thousand times more delighted with it than before, from witnessing the Horrors of a Separation and derangement in that of my friend."[58] Mrs. Sadler was herself to be the beneficiary of Elizabeth's solace three years later, when her own husband died. Now it was Julia's turn to hear about Elizabeth's compassionate accompaniment of Eliza in her time of loss: "I have borne *my part* in the melancholy scene ... and I was (as seems my lot to be) her only Earthly Support."[59]

Charity did begin at home for Elizabeth, as the adage has it; she was often shouldering responsibilities thrust upon her that few others are called to assume. After William Francis Seton, Elizabeth's father-in-law, passed away in 1798, his six minor children were left orphaned. Elizabeth's husband,

[57] 1.14, Elizabeth Seton to Eliza Sadler, March 27, 1798, in *CW*, 1:20. See also 1.97, Elizabeth Seton to John Wilkes, October 9, 1800, in *CW*, 1:138n2, and 4.3, Elizabeth Seton to Julia Scott, August 28, 1805, in *CW*, 1:384.

[58] 1.14, Elizabeth Seton to Eliza Sadler, March 27, 1798, in *CW*, 1:20–21.

[59] 1.147, Elizabeth Seton to Julia Scott, October 27, 1801, in *CW*, 1:193.

being the oldest of the blended family, had to take responsibility for them. As a result, the young couple was forced
to leave their first little townhouse on Wall Street and
move to the more spacious Seton family home on Stone
Street in order to care for the children. Even the magnanimous Elizabeth, who was eight months pregnant at the
time, admitted candidly that "for me, who so dearly loves
quiet and a small Family, to become at once the Mother
of six children [besides her own two and a third on the
way] ... is a very great change".[60] When the yellow fever
struck New York that autumn, they all had to take refuge
in the Seton country cottage, along with Will's sister Eliza
Seton Maitland and her brood, causing the young wife
to remark ruefully to Julia Scott, "You may imagine that
eighteen in [the] Family, in a House containing only five
small rooms, is rather more than *enough*."[61] She was not
complaining, just stating facts, as she always did. Indeed,
the Maitlands were often the objects of the Setons' charity; even when the Setons were themselves on the edge of
poverty, they fed the struggling family, "*six in number ...
from our own storeroom and every day marketing, as no
other part of the family will keep them from starving, or
even in firewood*".[62]

    In serving persons in need, Elizabeth learned, first of all, a
profound gratitude. "Had a two hours' visit from my Poor
Widow Veley", she wrote Rebecca Seton, "no work, no
wood, child sick, etc.—and should I complain, with a bright
fire within, bright, bright *Moon* over my shoulder, and the
Darlings all well?"[63] It was a holy gratitude, for she remembered in later years that her Widows' Society made her

[60] 1.22, Elizabeth Seton to Julia Scott, July 5, 1798, in *CW*, 1:36.
[61] 1.28, Elizabeth Seton to Julia Scott, [October 13, 1798], in *CW*, 1:46.
[62] 1.155, Elizabeth Seton to Julia Scott, February 1, 1802, in *CW*, 1:202.
[63] 1.150, Elizabeth Seton to Rebecca Seton, n.d., in *CW*, 1:198.

"delight in the continual contrast of all my blessings with the miseries I saw, yet always resigning them".[64]

Elizabeth learned, as well, how to be poor in spirit and detached from her possessions. Amid bankruptcy of the Seton family firm and preparations for the voyage to Italy for her husband's health, she described taking "delight in packing up all our Valuables to be sold, enjoying the *adieu* to each article to be mine no more".[65]

Elizabeth learned that love for those who are poor had to come from a heart in love with God. As she was to tell her Sisters, "*We sanctify ourselves for others.*"[66] And she probed the sacred truth more deeply during the memorable retreat in preparation for the community's vows for the first time: "The Daughter[s] of Charity," she noted, "led by their beloved into solitude, look at Him and their own souls with their most religious and loving thoughts, and express also to Him their tender concerns for other souls.... Thy Kingdom come ... let Thy Kingdom be founded forever in our hearts—ah! we pledge them all to spread it also the most we can in others."[67] And the means right at hand, she assured the Sisters of Charity, was their own good example: "We must be a shining and brightening light of edification to all, that they may say, 'See how pure, holy, and glorious is religion in the souls truly sanctified by its best spirit.' O my God, this is our vocation."[68]

This led naturally to the further lesson that love of those suffering from poverty and desiring their material relief

---

[64] 10.4, *Dear Remembrances*, n.d., in *CW*, 3a:513.

[65] Ibid., 514.

[66] 9.1, Instructions on Religious Life, "Sisters of Charity meditate the means of making well their retreat", n.d., in *CW*, 3a:235.

[67] 9.15, [Retreat Meditations], n.d., in *CW*, 3a:317, 316, brackets in published version. At this time, the terms Daughters of Charity and Sisters of Charity were interchangeable colloquially by francophone and anglophone Americans.

[68] Ibid., 319.

must be entirely motivated by the desire for their eternal salvation. "And the Souls of others, will we forget them in our retreat?" Elizabeth asked.[69] "O my God! We are the Daughters of Charity. From our happy solitude, we look with desolation to the misery of the souls at large; we know how many do not know Thee, do not serve Thee."[70] Elizabeth had clear-sighted vision of both the physical and spiritual poverty of so many men and women (a spiritual poverty overwhelming in what is so often and so justly called the post-Christian age), and she was just as clear-sighted in recognizing her own and her Sisters' responsibility toward them: "Our name", she insisted, "devotes us to their service in any manner that we could truly serve them." But "we must bring them to the knowledge of and the practice of Thy holy religion, to the habits of a good life".[71]

This, Elizabeth told her Sisters, was their goal, to be achieved through the relief of temporal ills: "We must display for them the tender compassion of Thy goodness, be the ministers of Thy providence for the relief of their miseries, a relief which disposes so well every heart to Thy better service."[72] After Elizabeth's death, her director, Father Bruté, marked this goal as central to the very existence of the community. "Around her assembled other hearts, zealous as her own", he wrote. "With her they lived the life which shows to the world that light of holiness which Jesus Christ tells us we should offer to our brethren."[73] The most uncompromising lesson Mother

[69] Ibid.
[70] Ibid.
[71] Ibid.
[72] Ibid.
[73] [Sister Loyola Law, D.C., ed.], *Mother Seton: Notes by Rev. Simon Gabriel Bruté*, entry of May 19, 1821, (Emmitsburg, Md.: Daughters of Charity, 1884), 68.

Seton learned was that no matter how her heart went out to those in need, no matter their priority in that same loving heart, no matter how eager she was to serve them, it was up to God whether she did so or not. The supreme example, a classic case of God's bending personal desires to the accomplishment of His Will, was the establishment of Elizabeth's life work itself.

There can be no doubt of what Elizabeth desired. Father Dubourg, whom God had sent to guide her to the consecrated life and her ultimate apostolate, has testified that he "had thought for a long time of establishing the Daughters of Charity in America; and as the duties of this institute would be compatible with the cares of her family, [Mrs. Seton] expressed a most ardent desire of seeing it commenced and of being herself admitted into it."[74] When the *Common Rules of the Daughters of Charity* had arrived from Paris, and Elizabeth had read it carefully, she "never had a thought discordant" with the document.[75] The initial ministries of the Sisters of Charity were indeed Vincentian—visiting the poor and the sick in their homes and teaching "little innocents ... to love God".[76] Saint Louise de Marillac and Saint Vincent de Paul instructed their Daughters of Charity in Paris about their mission: "You have a vocation obliging you to help equally all sorts of persons: men, women, children, and in general, every poor person who needs your assistance."[77]

[74] Rev. William Dubourg to Abbé Henri Elévès, July 15, 1828, Saint Elizabeth Ann Seton, 1-3-3-2 (102), APSL.

[75] 6.83, Elizabeth Seton to Archbishop John Carroll, September 5, 1811, in *CW*, 2:195.

[76] 5.21, Elizabeth Seton to Julia Scott, March 23, 1809, in *CW*, 2:62.

[77] Document 92, Saint Vincent de Paul, January 6, 1658, *Vincent de Paul: Correspondence, Conferences, Documents*, ed., trans., Marie Poole, D.C. et al., 14 vols. (New York: New City Press, 1983–2014), 10:363.

In February 1810, Elizabeth established free education for poor girls from the surrounding countryside. Those day pupils formed the nucleus of Saint Joseph School, which, by May, expanded to include boarding students, whose parents paid tuition. The Sisters of Charity had "the entire charge of the religious instruction of all the country round"[78] and were able to visit the sick, although Elizabeth admitted wistfully, "The Villages round us are not very extensive."[79]

These ministrations, over time, became ancillary because circumstances initially made education the principal apostolate of Elizabeth and her Sisters of Charity. She told her friend and benefactor the stark truth at year's end in 1811: "The promising and amiable perspective of Establishing a House of plain and useful Education, retired from the extravagance of the world," she wrote, "connected also with the view of providing Nurses for the sick and poor, an abode of Innocence and refuge of Affliction, is, I fear, now disappearing under the pressure of debts contracted at its very foundation."[80]

God rewarded Elizabeth's patient and persevering docility, even in her lifetime. She was able to send Sisters of Charity to manage an orphanage in Philadelphia in 1814, establish another in New York in 1817, and establish a free school for German Catholics in Philadelphia in 1818—all this despite Archbishop Carroll's conservative outlook: "A century at least will pass before the exigencies and habits of this country will require, and hardly admit of the charitable exercises toward the sick, sufficient to employ any number of the sisters out of our largest cities; and therefore,

---

[78] 6.39, Elizabeth Seton to Antonio Filicchi, May 20, 1810, in *CW*, 2:127.

[79] 6.18, Elizabeth Seton to Eliza Sadler, January 9, 1810, in *CW*, 2:99.

[80] 6.93, Elizabeth Seton to Robert Goodloe Harper, December 28, 1811, in *CW*, 2:206.

they must consider the business of education as a laborious, charitable, and permanent object of their religious duty."[81]

Elizabeth herself admitted, "Our orphan asylums ... promise more than we could have hoped."[82] Within a few years of Elizabeth's death, the Sisters of Charity of St. Joseph's opened their first hospital; then in quick succession came one new social work after another—to the point that, just as the Church has named Saint Vincent "Patron of All Organizations of Charity" and Saint Louise de Marillac "Patroness of All Christian Social Workers", Elizabeth herself can well and truthfully be called a Mother of Christian Social Work in America.

Elizabeth continued to instruct pupils and Sisters about the gospel mandate and the Vincentian mission of service to the neighbor. On one occasion she reminded a former pupil that Advent was "so sweet a season for comforting the poor and in everyone, Our *coming Lord*".[83] On another occasion, she was happy to send the news to Bruté: "So many of your Mountain children and poor, good Blacks came today for first Communion instructions. They were told from *the pulpit*, all to repair to the Sisterhood—so they came as for a novelty, but we will try our best ... poor, dear souls so unconscious—!!!"[84] Sister Cecilia O'Conway recalled some Sisters brightening Elizabeth's last days with tales of their visits to "several poor [families] around the mountains". Elizabeth was so absorbed that, "finding one had yet something more to tell, she eagerly said, 'O!

---

[81] A-6.83a, Archbishop John Carroll to Elizabeth Seton, September 11, 1811, in *CW*, 2:747.

[82] 7.175, Elizabeth Seton to Antonio Filicchi, August 8, 1818, in *CW*, 2:573.

[83] 6.217, Elizabeth Seton to Ellen Wiseman, [November 27, 1815], in *CW*, 2:361.

[84] 6.195, Elizabeth Seton to Rev. Simon Bruté, P.S.S., Journal 1815, entry of [June 10], in *CW*, 2:329.

do tell me, it delights me so much to hear such things!' "[85]
And Sister Cecilia finished fondly: "Yes, blessed soul, truly
dear were the poor and unfortunate to your heart."[86] It is
fitting that the Church recognized at Elizabeth's canonization her zeal to serve those who are suffering. Through
her efforts, God planted this love for the sick, the poor,
and the dejected in the hearts of her Sisters. "We pray",
said Paul VI, "that the Church in the United States will
indeed be faithful to her [Elizabeth's] mission on behalf
of those who endure suffering in various forms—spiritual
and material poverty, sickness, loneliness, lack of understanding, deprivation of rights—on behalf of those on the
margin of society, those without hope."[87]

The second, and in the beginning the dominant, thrust
of Mother Seton's calling as a Catholic educator also had
prophetic roots in her earlier life as a Manhattan matron.
By her own recollection, at age six, she taught Emma, her
half sister, about God.[88] In the fall of 1798, she began to
homeschool the youngest Seton girls, Harriet and Cecilia,
and her daughter, Anna Maria, because sending them out
"through snow and wet will give me more trouble than
keeping them at Home".[89] As her sons grew, they joined
the class.

In that little parlor on Stone Street in Lower Manhattan was primary education, not playacting. The teachers
were Elizabeth and Rebecca Seton (eighteen), her oldest,
unmarried sister-in-law. School began at ten o'clock each

---

[85] [Law], *Mother Seton: Notes*, 39.

[86] Ibid., 40.

[87] Paul VI, Address to the Cardinals and Bishops from the United States
of America, September 15, 1975, https://www.vatican.va/content/paul-vi/en
/speeches/1975/documents/hf_p-vi_spe_19750915_cardinali-vescovi-usa.html
(hereafter cited as Paul VI, Address).

[88] 10.4, *Dear Remembrances*, n.d., in *CW*, 3a:510.

[89] 1.33, Elizabeth Seton to Julia Scott, November 25, 1798, in *CW*, 1:54.

morning, and the subjects studied were "grammar, reading, writing, spelling of large and small words, marking, sewing, and figures".[90] Even the prekindergarten tots recited "their lessons: little Pieces, names of the United States, Divisions of the Globe, *some* of the commandments".[91] Elizabeth also included age-appropriate, basic religious instruction. Inclined to imitate Elizabeth's piety, Cecilia received a little packet of religious maxims and words of wisdom, addressed: "To Cecilia B. Seton from her own sister, E.A.S., 19th November 1802. Let your chief study be to acquaint yourself with God, because there is nothing greater than God, and because it is the only knowledge which can fill the Heart with a Peace and joy, which nothing can disturb."[92]

A few months after becoming Catholic, Elizabeth accepted a position to teach in a school being established by Mr. and Mrs. Patrick White that had the "prospect of Eminent success".[93] She was pleased with the financial arrangements and delighted that her sons could also attend. However, the school failed financially before it began, and the anti-Catholic bigotry of the townsfolk toward her helped defeat the enterprise. Within months, the young widow became a housemother for boarding students at Saint Mark's School. The opportunity, which included washing and mending, seemed ideal. Eventually, the boarders bullied the Seton boys because they were Catholic. Then the parents became dissatisfied and complained to the schoolmaster. Again, Elizabeth experienced another "sad trial".[94]

[90] 1.108, Elizabeth Seton to Julia Scott, March 10, 1801, in *CW*, 1:150.
[91] Ibid.
[92] 1.166, Elizabeth Seton to Cecilia Seton, November 19, 1802, in *CW*, 1:214.
[93] 3.27, Elizabeth Seton to Julia Scott, May 6, 1805, in *CW*, 1:361.
[94] 4.58, Elizabeth Seton to Eliza Sadler, November 13, 1807, in *CW*, 1:484.

Elizabeth was surely ready when the invitation to Catholic Baltimore came "at this very moment of solicitude for our destination when the present means fails", and she rightly attributed it to "the Providence that overrules us".[95] What gave her the most joy was that the house provided for her was "almost joining the chapel ... Mass from daylight to eight ... Vespers and Benediction every evening", and that her school was to be a Catholic boarding school for girls.[96] She heartily concurred with her Sulpician patron, Father William Dubourg, that "there are in this country enough, and perhaps too many ... schools, in which ornamental accomplishments are the only objects of education; we have none that I know where the acquisition [of useful knowledge] is connected with, and made subservient to, *pious* instruction—and such a one you certainly wish yours to be."[97]

Elizabeth herself put it even more directly when she reminded Antonio Filicchi that "the subject of my letter to you ... so nearly concerns all my hopes and expectations for this world, which is to do something if ever so little toward promoting our dear and holy Faith."[98] In a letter to his brother Filippo, she explained the proposed "plan of establishing an institution for the advancement of Catholic female children in habits of religion, and giving them an education suited to that purpose".[99]

From the beginning, Elizabeth and her Sisters were happy in the ministries God provided for them. One of

[95] 4.73, Elizabeth Seton to Julia Scott, April 25, 1808, in *CW*, 1:506.

[96] 5.1, Elizabeth Seton to Cecilia Seton, June 9, 1808, entry of [June 17], in *CW*, 2:7.

[97] Rev. William Dubourg to Elizabeth Seton, May 27, 1808, Saint Elizabeth Ann Seton, 1-3-3-2:S3, APSL.

[98] 5.14, Elizabeth Seton to Antonio Filicchi, January 16, 1809, in *CW*, 2:45.

[99] 5.18, Elizabeth Seton to Filippo Filicchi, February 8, 1809, in *CW*, 2:54.

the Sisters has left a memorable record of that happiness in describing the first high Mass in the yet unfinished Saint Joseph House, later called the "White House", on March 19, 1810: "So poor was the little altar, that its chief ornaments were a framed portrait of Our dear Redeemer which Mother had brought with her from New York, her own little silver candlesticks, some wild laurel, paper flowers, etc.—yet what a happy, happy company, far from the busy, bustling scenes of a miserable, faithless world!"[100]

Hindsight makes plain God's purpose in directing Elizabeth to Maryland for the apostolate of Catholic education. It was essential for inculcating the faith in a vast country that would continuously expand its borders and welcome immigrants seeking a brighter future. It was essential for protecting the faith of so many of these same immigrants and their children, cast ashore amid a populace opposed to or ignorant of Catholicism. In time the Catholic school became the bulwark for the Church in North America, developing into a unique and successful system of thorough secular and religious education. Mother Seton was a pioneer not only in female education but also in free and affordable Catholic education. The Sisters of Charity of Saint Joseph's, not the parish, sponsored and staffed Saint Joseph School; hence it was a Catholic school but not a parochial school. The first pupils, all from the Emmitsburg area, were admitted *gratis* as day students February 22, 1810; boarding pupils were accepted by mid-May. The Sisters of Charity comprised the faculty for Saint Joseph School, which offered two programs: one *gratis* for day scholars and another for boarding students, whose families paid tuition. It was something she

---

[100] Charles I. White, *Life of Mrs. Eliza A. Seton: Foundress and First Superior of the Sisters or Daughters of Charity in the United States of America* (Baltimore, Md.: John Murphy & Co., 1859), 262.

did quite consciously, for Father Dubourg had assured her earlier that "far from objecting to your plan of opening a day school at St. Joseph's, Mr. [John] David [a Sulpician] and myself beg it should be done without loss of time".[101]

Elizabeth, being perceptive and insightful, was swift to perceive the workings of Divine Providence in the unfolding events. She believed that the "hand of the chief Shepherd" was behind the focus on the apostolate of female education and acknowledged that the resulting success and blessings were a direct result of God's work alone.[102] Indeed, she foretold with great content its eternal worth in the "precious souls which we cherish and prepare in silence and under a rather common look of no pretension to go over our cities like a good leaven".[103] Pope Paul VI spoke the definitive and official word in telling the American bishops present in Rome for Elizabeth Seton's canonization how his thoughts "turn spontaneously to parochial and other Catholic schools in your nation. We bless the providence of God that raised up Mother Seton to inaugurate this important work. We render homage to those who have expended their lives to communicate Christ through the apostolate of the school, and to give to generations of young Americans true education imbued with Christian principles."[104]

On this same occasion, the Holy Father had first paid tribute to the holy mother's all-embracing charism, her call to consecrated life. It was as foundress of the first native Sisterhood in the United States that she provided

---

[101] Rev. William Dubourg to Elizabeth Seton, December 28, 1809, Saint Elizabeth Ann Seton, 1-3-3-2:S6, APSL.

[102] 6.54, Elizabeth Seton to Eliza Sadler, August 3, [1809], in *CW*, 2:153. Cf. 7.87, Elizabeth Seton to Antonio Filicchi, June 1, 1817, in *CW*, 2:479.

[103] 7.175, Elizabeth Seton to Antonio Filicchi, August 8, 1818, in *CW*, 2:573.

[104] Paul VI, Address.

the means of serving both the nation's poor and its school-children. "The very meaning ... of the Canonization of St. Elizabeth Seton", the pope said with notable emphasis,

> impels us to express our good wishes, filled with loving hope, for Religious Life in the United States. Through you, the Bishops, we say to all the Religious: "Let us keep our eyes fixed on Jesus, who inspires and perfects our faith" (*Hebr.* 12:2). Jesus, and Jesus alone, is our wisdom, our justice, our sanctification, our redemption (Cfr. *1 Cor.* 1:30).
>
> Through the powerful example of joyful love and of selfless service rendered by Religious, may the young people of America again find attraction in Christ's invitation to follow him and to be witnesses of the transcendence of his love. Our earnest prayer therefore for all Religious is that they may base all their activity on the power of God and not on the deceptive wisdom of the world, and that they may recognize for their lives the absolute necessity of prayer and of the transforming power of the Eucharist: source of all the Church's power (Cfr. *Sacrosanctum Concilium*, 10). After the shining example of Elizabeth Seton may they have renewed conviction that Christ offers them complete fulfillment in their vocation of consecrated love and ecclesial service.[105]

It would have been very difficult for Elizabeth Ann Seton, in her lifetime, to have imagined the Holy Father in faraway Rome even knowing her name, let alone extolling her as a model for consecrated life.

Elizabeth took her academic duties as principal or headmistress very seriously, visiting each classroom and making a detailed study of each regularly, with particular attention to the quality of the teaching and the aptitude

[105] Ibid.

of the pupils.[106] As for her spiritual duty to instruct young souls, her wholehearted devotion to it was one of the chief contributions to her sainthood, for she was a constant, shining light to all, her sanctity not only illuminating what she taught but also showing concretely how to love God. The love that united Mother and alumnae is evident in their correspondence such as this: "Mother begs Our Lord to bless her dear Eliza that she may be an ever-blooming Rose in His Paradise. Come under the Shawl this morning, and love and bless Our Jesus—your poor, affectionate Mother."[107]

Elizabeth had an unwavering dedication to her work. She took great care in teaching the older girls twice a week, making sure they fully understood the purpose of their journey right from the start. Not only her wisdom, but also her empathy and compassion shone through in every lesson, making her an exceptional teacher and mentor.

"Your little Mother, my darlings, does not come to teach you how to be good nuns or Sisters of Charity, but rather I would wish to fit you for that world in which you are destined to live; to teach you how to be good ... mothers of families."[108] Like Jesus, she used parables, metaphors, and similes to impress minds so young. Warning of the allurements of the world they were preparing for, she recounted how "the fable says that a butterfly asked an owl what she should do to keep from burning her wings, since she could never come to the candle without singeing them. The owl counselled her to abstain from looking even at the smoke of it.... You will first burn your wings, poor little moth[s]", she drew the lesson, "before you will

---

[106] Cf. 12.8, Regulations of the School of St. Joseph, n.d., in *CW*, 3b:124–27.
[107] 7.24, Elizabeth Seton to Eliza Wyse, May 18, 1816, in *CW*, 2:396.
[108] White, *Mrs. Eliza A. Seton*, 344.

withdraw from the flame. In all these cases, there is more safety in our fear than in our strength; it is ever easier to abstain from such pleasures than to use them well."[109] The heart duly prepared for the reception of Holy Communion she depicted as "a crystal vial filled with clear water, in which the least mote of uncleanness may be seen".[110] Her spiritual nurture of young souls was summed up in an unforgettable word of advice: "Love God, my dear children, and you may forget there is a hell."[111]

The bond of love forged was a lasting one, as evidenced by the extensive correspondence engendered by pupils long graduated seeking their Mother's advice in each new upsetting experience. To Sarah Cauffman of Philadelphia, troubled by a letter left by an admirer at her door, the Mother replied by asking,

> Is it not more simple and consistent to hear and answer its contents with the respect and gratitude due to an amiable being who gives us an unmerited preference, than to play the part of a proud woman receiving an homage she thinks her due? If you must *reject*, my precious child, do it with reason, and a candid statement of your reasons. Then, if they are approved or condemned, you will have acted like a Christian and your mind will be at peace, however painful the exertion ... and reject you will, unless there is a fund of uncommon Virtue in the person in question. Your poor little Mother can only pray for you, my beloved.[112]

Ellen Wiseman was especially beloved, and the two were faithful correspondents. "Try and keep all your *intentions*

[109] Ibid., 346.
[110] Ibid., 346–47.
[111] Ibid., 348.
[112] 7.140, Elizabeth Seton to Sarah Cauffman, February 19, 1818, in *CW*, 2:528.

with Our Lord", Elizabeth advised this dear daughter. "When you go to your dearest companions, go in His name and send up the little sigh to beg Him to stay with you, even *most* in your liveliest moments. Dearest Ellen, it will soon become so easy *and so sweet,* and when death come[s]—Oh, then the blessed practice will be your great consolation."[113] Once Elizabeth wrote Ellen in alarm, occasioned by a note that had warned her, "Pray for your Philadelphia children, Mother; they want it. *Kitty* Wiseman and R. Mallon alone resist the torrent—" She responded: "Much as to say my Ellen goes with it. Oh, my God! What a hard world to steer through with innocence! My Ellen, Ellen, chosen, beloved child of my heart, I must leave you to Our God. You are as far out of my reach as my soul's William is. What is all I can say? How can I even guess your trials, circumstances, affairs of the heart, temptations of all kinds? But Our God will protect and save my beloved ones (I trust)."[114] This trust, invoked over and over for those she loved, was well placed precisely because she placed it without faltering.

Two years later, Elizabeth was rallying Ellen about receiving the Sacrament of Reconciliation (Confession): "Think how I would beg you, supplicate you, this day"—it was the feast of Saint Peter, the holder of the keys—

> to keep near to Him by the *only means,* and not let the wall of partition be raised again in your dearest heart as it was before our last happy meeting. Wake up your *Faith.* You know Our Lord never meant us to mind who we go to, if they do but take us to Him. And the longer you stay back, you will know, the harder it is for you to go forward.

[113] 6.211, Elizabeth Seton to Ellen Wiseman, [October 14, 1815], in *CW,* 2:352, brackets in published version.

[114] 7.216, Elizabeth Seton to Ellen Wiseman, [June 1819], in *CW,* 2:616.

And, at last, what does it end in, dearest, to go through double thrible [sic], pain, and examins [sic], which will not be pains of grace and merit, but of your own weakness and want of courage in *delaying*? Oh, do, dearest, write me [how] you have been.[115]

The trust of her "old girls" gave Elizabeth great joy and encouraged her to urge them to even greater goodness because, as she said, "It is *you young ones* He delights in who have so many sacrifices to offer Him."[116] In return, she could reassure them with complete honesty that "Our Lord who sees the deep heart knows with what pleasure I would give my life to prove my true love to any of you."[117]

Mother Seton extended her care to the students at Mount Saint Mary's in a friendly and caring way. She didn't just send the Sisters of Charity to the Mount in 1815 to establish a mission and be responsible for the laundry, clothes room, chapel, and infirmary to nurse them when they were sick, but Mother Seton also personally visited them. Her kindness and affection toward them individually are inspiring, a reminder of the importance of being friendly and compassionate toward everyone. She was partial to poor families and individuals whether in goods or in heart. She scraped together fifty dollars a year from her own meager funds to help pay the tuition of Charles Grim, son of a poor New York widow who had been her friend in former years. She tried to lighten the loneliness of little Jerome Bonaparte, left behind when his parents went to Paris at the command of his uncle Napoleon. "My dear Mother," the boy once wrote her earnestly, "I

---

[115] 7.250, Elizabeth Seton to Ellen Wiseman, [June 29, 1820], in *CW*, 2:656.
[116] 6.135, Elizabeth Seton to Ellen Wiseman, August 12, 1813, in *CW*, 2:248.
[117] 7.83, Elizabeth Seton to Ellen Wiseman, [April 6, 1817], in *CW*, 2:474.

am very anxious to get an Agnus Dei before I go home, in order to preserve me in the vacations from the dangers that will surround me.... I will keep it as a memorial of kindness and love for your little child, who always thinks of you with respect and love", he continued with a child's instinctive trust in and attraction to goodness, "and who will think of you with gratitude also", he finished with a child's instinctive slyness, "especially if I shall have an Agnus Dei from you as a present."[118] Elizabeth responded graciously: "Dear Jerome: It is a great pleasure to me to send you the *Agnus Dei*. I wish I had one handsomely covered, but you will mind only the Virtue of the prayers our Holy Father has said over it. I earnestly beg Our Lord to preserve in you the graces He has so tenderly bestowed on you." She continued, seizing on the boy's reason for the request to remind him, "Take care yourself not to lose them. Pray for me, and I will for you. Your true friend, E.A.S."[119]

Elizabeth personally prepared many of the Mount boys for their first Holy Communion. Her *Notebook* for February 2, 1813, records a meditation for the first Communion day of Michael du Burgo Egan, perhaps a summary of topics she had taught him and his classmates as they made ready for this day: "Piety must be habitual, not by *fits*. It must be persevering, because temptations continue all our lives—and *perseverance* alone obtains the crown. Its means are—the Presence of God—good reading, prayer,

---

[118] Jerome N. Bonaparte to Elizabeth Seton, June 21, [1816], Saint Elizabeth Ann Seton, 1-3-3-4(100), APSL. The *Agnus Dei* is an ancient sacramental, a sacred object, or an action that the believer uses for intercession to obtain spiritual favors. An *Agnus Dei* (literally "Lamb of God") refers to a small piece of pure wax bearing the impress of a lamb supporting the standard of the cross, which is encased in precious metal. It is worn devoutly around the neck or hung in a glass frame.

[119] 7.30, Elizabeth Seton to Jerome Bonaparte, [June 1816], in *CW*, 2:401.

the Sacraments, good resolutions often renewed—the remembrance of our last ends—and its advantages—habits which secure our predestination, making our life equal, peaceable, and consoling—leading to the heavenly crown where our perseverance will be eternal!!!"[120] The urging to perseverance and the means of assuring it are standard spiritual advice, but the stamp of deep perception growing out of holiness is on the sure theological insight that these habits *secure* predestination, and the recognition of its signs, an "equal, peaceable, and consoling" life—imparted with the enthusiasm of holiness, the saint's habitual underlining (shown here with italics), and exclamation points.

Elizabeth's holiness was not lost on Egan and his companions. "I remember Dearest Mother's repeated expression of Faith and *Love*", he wrote Catherine Seton, long afterward:[121]

> How well she possessed them. Faith enlightened her, Love inflamed her, and the more I reflect on it the more I perceive how justly she insisted on those two great virtues.... I cannot help thinking it is harder for a priest to get to heaven than anyone else—though indeed surrounded and loaded with graces—yet beset with dangers and overwhelmed with difficulties also.... Would to Our Lord I had some small share of that holy love which inflamed the heart of our Dear Mother—Love would sweeten everything—Love would triumph over everything.[122]

Egan's easy assumption that Elizabeth was *his* mother as well as Catherine's is in itself a lesson in the power of love. Michael had known Elizabeth since he entered Mount

---

[120] 11.9, "Departed St. Teresa's Day", n.d., entry of The First Communion at Mount Saint Mary's, February 2, 1813, in *CW*, 3b:12.

[121] Rev. Michael du Burgo Egan to Catherine Seton, January 6, 1826, University of Notre Dame Archives.

[122] Ibid.

Saint Mary's College at age seven. His older sister Mary had frail health but a few years later enrolled in Saint Joseph School as a boarder. She soon entered the Sisters of Charity but died at seventeen during her novitiate. Michael and Mary Egan and many others thrived because of Elizabeth's maternal solicitude. Her own experience enabled her to nurture the best in others.

Elizabeth's special affection was reserved for seminarians like Egan, and it grew out of her "religious respect for the ministries of the Lord", cited by Bruté in a tribute after her death.[123] She herself laid the ground for this "religious respect" in a letter to a young man who had left the Mount in a flurry of doubts as to his vocation. "My dear Smith, my heart has gone home with you", she assured him, "as a Parent follows the child she loves when she sees it treading in uncertain steps, doubtful whether it will find the right way."[124] She had no doubts herself:

To be engaged in the service of Our Adored Creator, to be set apart to that service, and thereby separated from all the contentions, the doubts, and temptations that surround the man whose lot is cast in the busy scene of the World, is in itself a sufficient plea on the side which I wish you to engage, but to be placed as a representative of God Himself, to plead for Him, to be allowed the exalted privilege of serving Him continually, to be His instrument in calling home the wandering Soul and sustaining, comforting, and blessing your fellow creatures, are considerations which bear no comparison with any other; and should lead you to consider the very possibility of your realizing the Hope they present as the most precious and valued gift this life can afford.[125]

[123] Bruté, *Memoir*, Saint Elizabeth Ann Seton, 1-3-3-12(87), APSL.
[124] 7.304, Draft, Elizabeth Seton to Mr. Smith, n.d., in *CW*, 2:695–96.
[125] Ibid., 696.

Much as Elizabeth wanted this young man to continue his studies for the priesthood, she did not fail to point out that "the grace of even wishing to belong to God must come from Himself."[126] At the same time, she warned, "Be cautious, my dear, dear friend, how you damp or check that good gift, which should be cherished as the richest mercy."[127] Nevertheless, she insisted that for one on whom God has bestowed the grace of vocation, the priesthood has a spiritual security beyond all others: "A man may be a very good man in the pursuit of any other Profession; but certainly that of a clergyman is the easiest, surest road to God"—she was taking a different tack than Egan, who actually felt the burdens of the priesthood—"and the first, the highest and most blessed that can adorn a Human Being— the Peace of God is the full, the sure and certain compensation for any discouragement or obstacles the World may throw in the way—and His guidance and favor 'till Death, in Death, and after Death, the reward and crown of him who faithfully served Him."[128]

Even as an Episcopalian, Elizabeth had hoped that at least one of her sons might be a devout servant of the Lord as was her highly respected Rev. John Henry Hobart. When William was only five, Elizabeth told Rebecca Seton how "Bill called out, as he opened his Eyes this Morning, 'Dear Henry Hubbard [Hobart], I wish you would preach for me.' Just those words. They woke me from my sleep and occasioned a long, heavy sigh ... the anxious presage and hope, that he might teach the wisher to be a preacher—oh, what a thought!"[129] At Emmitsburg she rejoiced to see both William and Richard as acolytes serving Mass. "To have seen

---

[126] Ibid.
[127] Ibid.
[128] Ibid., 696–97.
[129] 1.146, Elizabeth Seton to Rebecca Seton, [1801], in *CW*, 1:191–92.

my own two Boys in his sanctuary this day", she once exclaimed to Bruté, "at the moment of the elevation, each holding the chasuble—then Communion—the fears and hopes and desires of a Mother—what is the heart made of, to hold so much?"[130] The sanctuary was not, however, to be their home, and that was one of her private griefs. "He sees the torrents [of tears] at the thought that I bore and suckled them for anything but His service", she confided to Bruté. "Oh, do, do pray."[131]

This grief surfaced anew when a chance meeting with a former seminarian set off a passionate lament for the thin ranks of seminarians and the priesthood. "May you be spared the agony of heart", Elizabeth cried out to Bruté,

> to see the poor, good *Lipp*, who once adorned Your Sanctuary in Baltimore where I had last seen him, now with wife and child. I burst in tears at the sad Reverse ... to Our Jesus redoubled. Oh, his Kingdom! Laborers for his vineyard! My poor, poor, poor Richard, William—My God, Oh if the bleeding of a Mother's heart can obtain! Poor, poor, poor blind ones! Such a Lord! Such a master! Such a divine and glorious service!—but blind, blind, and lost to love and duty, groping along through the bright, heavenly light which shines so lovely to the happy ones who *comprehend*. Blessed, blessed G., most blessed, you are *His* and in that, at least, [the] grateful Soul of your own Mother rejoices. And, oh, remember those who are not.[132]

---

[130] 6.160, Elizabeth Seton to Rev. Simon Bruté, P.S.S., [after Easter 1814], in *CW*, 2:270.

[131] 6.195, Elizabeth Seton to Rev. Simon Bruté, P.S.S., Journal 1815, entry of [May 21], in *CW*, 2:326.

[132] 7.103, Elizabeth Seton to Rev. Simon Bruté, P.S.S., August 1, 1817, in *CW*, 2:494, brackets in published version. Elizabeth frequently refers to Father Bruté as familiarly as "G". His middle name was Gabriel.

Those who persevered to priestly ordination never forgot the part Elizabeth played in their perseverance. Thus, William Gillespie asked John Hickey, "Give my respects to Mother Seton when you see her again; tell her to pray for her son as she kindly used to call me."[133] And Egan confided to William Seton, "I often imagine I see ... our Dearest Mother looking down on us here below and afflicted when we do wrong—rejoicing when we do well and praying hard for us to obtain a seat [in heaven]."[134]

Saint Elizabeth's awe for the office of the priesthood goaded her to its defense when she saw priests of her acquaintance take it lightly, as in her sharp rebuke to John Hickey when he had preached badly because of his laziness and poor preparation.[135] Indeed, her anguish at their shortcomings compelled her, as Bruté once suggested: "Oh that priests felt for themselves as Mother Seton felt they ought to be! How much did she not suffer in witnessing their imperfections! How sorrowfully, yet how charitably, did she consider their faults!"[136] She took a special interest in Hickey, whom she had known from the time he was a student at the Mount, and counted him as a friend and correspondent. For these reasons her advice to him was as frank as it was wise, and surely it made him a better priest. When he had been harshly judgmental in rebuking his sister, who was a pupil at Saint Joseph's, Elizabeth told him bluntly,

[133] William L. Gillespie to Rev. John Hickey, July 21, 1817, Rev. John F. Hickey, P.S.S., Papers, Box 1, Folder 9, Archives of the Associated Sulpicians of the United States, Associated Archives at St. Mary's Seminary & University.

[134] Rev. Michael du Burgo Egan to Catherine Seton, June 19, 1822, University of Notre Dame Archives.

[135] Cf. 6.195, Elizabeth Seton to Rev. Simon Bruté, P.S.S., Journal 1815, entry of [May 8], in CW, 2:323.

[136] White, Mrs. Eliza A. Seton, 418.

I do not like ... some things you wrote Ellen lately. You and I speak all for Eternity; but take an advice from your old mother—I am a hundred to your thirty *in experience*, that cruel friend of our earthly journey.

When you ask too much at first, you often gain nothing at last. *And if the heart is lost, all is lost.* If you use such language to your family, they cannot love you, since they have not *our* Microscope to see things *as they are.* Your austere, hard language was not understood by Ellen who, dear Soul, considers your letters as mere curiosities. She loves and venerates you, but do not push her away.... Gently, gently, my Father in God and son in heart.[137]

Then the swift larger, telling question: "Do you drive so in the tribunal? I hope not."[138]

"The faults of young people, especially such faults as Elinor's," Elizabeth explained patiently, "must be moved by prayers and tears, because they are *constitutional* and cannot be frightened out. I have said much harder things to her than you do, but turning the tune in her own heart, and not"—here she could not forego derision—"on her poor, dear family quite as respectable even—as to the point you press on so valiantly—as half our Legislature, Senate, etc. How can you, in such a country as ours, dwell on such a motive of humility?"[139]

Another time, Elizabeth spiritedly defended Hickey's brother William, a student at the Mount, again contrasting the privileged graces the priest had received from God's hand: "William is surely one of the most estimable young men in the world. What a precious diamond, to be so covered with the cares of this world! But how can he help it?

[137] 7.147, Elizabeth Seton to Rev. John Hickey, P.S.S., [before March 19, 1818], in *CW*, 2:536.
[138] Ibid.
[139] Ibid.

Be you gentle and considerate to him," she warned, "you blessed man of God, feeding on sweetmeats every morning and rejoicing your heart with the choicest wine. Had his dispositions to Virtue and religion been cultivated as yours have been," she finished mischievously, "he would be already your equal, I believe—but not sure."[140]

The one with whom Elizabeth shared most deeply her passionate love for Christ's priesthood was, naturally, her closest priest friend, Father Simon Bruté. In a very true sense, they directed each other's souls in an intimate sharing of their intense love for God. Frequently, in fact, she assumed the natural role of maternal mentor, for he was young and new to North America. It was she who largely taught him the difficult language of his adopted land—she had spoken his native French from childhood—with the Bible and *The Imitation of Christ* for his textbooks, taking him through them laboriously and patiently, line by line, sentence by sentence. It was she, also, who unlocked for others his beautiful concepts of God's love by giving them full-blown expansion in the sentences and paragraphs he could not yet write; but he, for his part, did not shirk the ordeal of preaching them, "bad preaching as it may be", ignoring humbly the half-stifled smiles at mispronunciations and awkward choice of words, for it was his solemn calling as well as the only practical way, he admitted, "to force this dreadful English into my backward head".[141]

When Bruté was summoned to the Sulpician motherhouse in Paris, Mother Seton made sure the recognition would not go to his head. "Mr. Tessier writes in such triumph that his darling was called for even by the Superior

---

[140] 7.214, Elizabeth Seton to Rev. John Hickey, P.S.S., [June 14, 1819], in *CW*, 2:612–13.

[141] James Roosevelt Bayley, *Memoirs of the Rt. Rev. Simon Wm. Gabriel Bruté, D.D.* (New York: D. & J. Sadler, 1861), 40.

overseas *on particular business*", she teased, "and how happy that this precious pearl was esteemed and confided in equally by *both*. The clearer eye of the Mountain [Father Dubois] and old microscope of the Valley [herself] must laugh at these doting Grandpapas, though so Venerable. The darling himself must smile at these poor, blind optics [that] Our Lord permits; let it pass. *Tu es sacerdos in aeternum secundum ordinem Melchisedech*. There the soul's grand triumph—all else but smoke."[142]

Whatever Bruté's business abroad, the recognition by his superiors in Baltimore and Paris was deserved. The aged and ailing Father Charles Duhamel, C.S.Sp. (1753–1818), pastor at Saint Joseph's Parish, Emmitsburg, until 1818, attested to it in his grumbling way as Elizabeth, highly amused, reported to Bruté: "Poor Hickey got a great compliment this morning", the elderly pastor had told her.

> An Irishman told him the three priests at the Mountain all put together are not worth one Bruté. Poor creatures, . . . they tell me to my face—now Bruté's gone, all is gone! Some say they will not go to Confession till he comes again. Poor, dear, good Bruté! Did you see his letter, Ma'am, *to everybody* to *save souls*? Poor, crazy Bruté! He says he will be on the high seas—he would be much better *here*, attending his congregation. He could tend six congregations at least. He can do what would kill ten men, if you only give him bread, and two or three horses to ride to death, one after t'other. Poor gentleman, if he was but steady![143]

There is no mistaking Elizabeth's affection and trust shining through her amusement. In fact, she put it plainly in

---

[142] 6.195, Elizabeth Seton to Rev. Simon Bruté, P.S.S., Journal 1815, entry of [May 25], in *CW*, 2:327. Translation: You are a priest forever after the order of Melchizedek. Ps 110:4.

[143] Ibid., entry of [April 25], in *CW*, 2:320–21.

recounting for the traveler in France, with the same mischievous delight, Father Dubois' retreat for her pupils: "Almost I laughed out at his opening, telling [them] ... to be as many little stumps—no, '*chunks*'—of fire put together. *One*, he said, if left *alone*, would soon go out. My eye fell on an old black stump in the corner [herself]—and a big, inward sigh to the live coal far away which used to give it the blaze in a moment."[144]

Elizabeth's underlying sorrow at this long separation from her soul's director and friend was renewed when, shortly after his return, he was off again to Baltimore to take over new duties as president of Saint Mary's College. There was no teasing this time. "In this *little* life of your Mother, not a moment since I saw you to write a word but the meditation," she lamented,

> ᴏɪ ᴀ Volume would have not been enough to say half the heart that fastens to yours mᴏʀᴇ and mᴏʀᴇ, if possible—but with such freedom of the local circumstances, or posɪtɪᴏɪɪ of the moment, that I shall see you go again to fulfill your big *Presidentship* (oh, bad omen, G., I did not know that tear was there)—Well, I will see you go to do *His Will of the present moment* with no other sighs or desires but for its most full and complete *accomplishment*.
>
> Your little silly woman in the fields (most happy name and place for her, my G.), your little woman, silly of our dear silliness of prayers and tears, will now hold closer and closer to *Him* who will do *all in you*, as He does in my poor little daily part, and try always to bring you the (*tut!* there again my candle is so dim I cannot see)—try always every moment to bring to you the *support* [of] Mother's prayers, her cry to Him for *your* full fidelity as for our poor William's "deliverance from *Evil*".[145]

---

[144] Ibid., entry of [February 10], 315–16.
[145] 7.31, Elizabeth Seton to Rev. Simon Bruté, P.S.S., [June 1816], in *CW*, 2:401–2, brackets in published version.

The teasing spirit that disguised so much love and wisdom returned in a dialogue between "Sam"—the name Elizabeth typically applied to the devil—and Bruté's "Good Angel":

> *Sam*—now we'll catch *Monsieur le President*! First, we will fill his head with plans of reformation—every successor improves on his predecessor, to be sure! Of course, with the *Succession* comes multiplied distractions of thought, complaisances, etc.—that alone a fine trap, if there was no other, but (Oh, joy to the grinner!) we will catch him, too, by endless conversations and opinions (to be sure, a president must be *full* of opinions!). This seraphim's wings shall be clipped; and the modest, retiring, devout spirit shall swell and fill and push, [we] insist.
>
> (Oh, be joyful, what a change we will see!), and this Simple heart, loving now to serve but his God in, and the Salvation of Souls, shall be plunged in the labyrinths of science and grow fat as a doctor (oh, we will have fun this next year, *1816*!)—short thanksgivings, quick preparations, forced offerings....
>
> "2nd *good Angel*"—Well, at least he will have abundant Sacrifice of dearest, choicest consolations. He will act in full opposition to his own choice. His daily bread will be dry and hard. He will be a bond of union and peace to his Confreres, a *spirit* of purest, ardent piety to worldlings, and an example of cheerful and tender forbearance to his pupils—poor, dear G., after a little while of subjection and patience to his wild heart, it *shall* be set free from the yoke, improved and experienced, to return with new ardor to its more Simple and heavenly delights.[146]

Unquestionably, Elizabeth viewed Bruté's new appointment as curious and questionable, for he is certainly the

---

[146] 7.3, Elizabeth Seton to Rev. Simon Bruté, P.S.S., n.d., in *CW*, 2:367–68, brackets in published version.

second person contrasted in the following comment on the vagaries too often encountered in the religious life: "While I say our *Te Deum* in union with your thanksgiving, my heart fills at 'O Lord, save *Thy* people,' thinking how things are shared in this world", she confided to him. "I see a quiet, moderate, *experienced* man put in the center of a Congregation who is not 'SAVED' for want of an active, zealous, driving man, because they must have 'fire' cried in their ears; and I see a zealous, driving man without *experience* put in a Seminary where he will '*SAVE*' none, because he cannot wait to gain a heart or unfold a temper, and his zeal, instead of bedewing the plant in the thirsty ground, crushes it underfoot. Alas, well if he does not root it out forever!"[147] That her comments were comments and nothing more, neither resentment nor criticism and certainly not a quarrel with God, is evident in the close: "O Lord, then '*SAVE*!' Save the Redeemed of thy precious blood, and send 'wisdom from above'. 'Blessed,' I am truly *downhearted* this day, poor Leper! Yet, 'Glory to the Father, Son, and Holy Ghost [*sic*, Spirit]!' has been my incessant prayer with one hundred meanings. Too sick to do anything but pray."[148]

Much as Elizabeth admired the "active, zealous, driving man" in Bruté, she knew from experience of her own nature that the holiest zeal had at times to be tamed.[149] It was indeed the exuberance of both their souls that made them such a unique pair in God. She had once confided to him that it would be

like changing an Ethiopian to pretend to preserve the spirit of detail which the charity and natural disposition of our Superior [Father Dubois] has made the Spirit of

[147] 7.121, Elizabeth Seton to Rev. Simon Bruté, P.S.S., [October 1817], in *CW*, 2:512.
[148] Ibid.
[149] Ibid.

our Community. Long may Our Lord spare him to it, for who could ever be found to unwind the ball as he does, and stop to pick out every knot? Too happy I to break the knot and piece it again! And it does seem to blind eyes like mine, so far from the spirit of Simplicity to be obliged to spell every word and feel the pulse with your Sisters, but I will try more and more.[150]

Elizabeth did not hesitate, then, to bring her beloved priest-director-son up short when nature overstepped its bounds, resulting in runaway enthusiasm or foolish sensitivity. "My *Blessed*, all is a true mystery to me in your disposition, much greater mystery than any of *FAITH*", she once lectured him bluntly.[151]

A man of your particular principle *on paper*, who has evidently the most dear and special graces—not given drop by drop as to other souls, but poured over your head in a daily torrent—yet I seldom see you but in such wild enthusiasms of your own particular impression of the moment that you can see nothing, hear nothing, but that one object; or else quite *reserved, hurt*, and *anxious* because you have not been consulted in things *which spoke for themselves*, or others which we would not dare take your advice about without knowing the Superior's will, or others again which, like the poor German Smiths, go over in our blind ignorance and I never even guess I have not done well 'till someone points it out.

How troubled, too, because Mr. [John] Dubois doesn't come, and what responsibility have you? Is it your zeal and desire of the good you imagine he will do?[152]

---

[150] 6.169, Elizabeth Seton to Rev. Simon Bruté, P.S.S., [August 6, 1814], in *CW*, 2:281.

[151] 7.191, Elizabeth Seton to Rev. Simon Bruté, P.S.S., [November 1818], in *CW*, 2:591.

[152] Ibid., brackets in published version.

Elizabeth asked pointedly, and then got down to the points of practical administration with which, she strongly hinted, Bruté was familiar:

> You ought to know our Reverend Superior [Dubois] by this time and see that he is not to be *pushed* anywhere; and your urging him cannot but keep him away. When anything *essential* happens, I always inform him of it; and if the thing is not essential, his absence often hinders a fuss about nothing, and suffers pets and little passions to drop in silence.
>
> You speak as if your Mother's confidence is deficient, but it is surely not at this time. I am to open your eyes on my situation in this community.[153]

While the good man must have been properly chastened after such a relentless scolding, he must at the same time have been humbler and wiser, which was Mother Seton's whole purpose.

In the final months of Saint Elizabeth Ann's life, the fires of that deeply spiritual friendship that had warmed the hearts of Bruté and herself in its lighthearted familiarity and humor on her part—she knew no other way with her friends—and the sacred lights and flashes of mysticism it ignited in both were deliberately banked by mutual consent as a final sacrifice of purification. "We have broken our old bonds", she told John Hickey. "I seldom speak to him but in the tribunal. What a lofty Grace for this low earth, but it is to be nearer in heaven, I hope."[154]

Elizabeth spelled out their motivation by indirection in another letter to Hickey, who wanted to return to Mount Saint Mary's from Baltimore:

[153] Ibid.

[154] 7.252, Elizabeth Seton to Rev. John Hickey, P.S.S., [July 2, 1820], in *CW*, 2:659.

My heart and soul this week past has been under *the press* of the Beatitude: "Blessed are the pure of heart—they *SHALL SEE GOD.*" ... Happy, happy are you to love *All for Him.* Every bent of your heart's affections, every power of your Soul, turned Wholly to Him without even the mixture of the innocent sojourning awhile with your old Father [Dubois] and dear Brother [Bruté]. How much *Purer* is your service where you are above the mist of earthly attraction. One thing I hope you are convinced of (I as a wretched sinner know it well), that wherever we meet a little prop of *human* comfort, there is always some subtraction of Divine Comfort. And for my part, I am so afraid to cause any such Subtraction, that I feel a reserve and fear in every human consolation that makes them more my pains than my pleasures.[155]

She was not, however, pressing such difficult sublimity on others: "Yet the liberty of the Children of God I hope in all. I only mean to say we should be too happy when the Providence of Our God keep[s] us wholly to *Himself.*"[156]

The saint once gave definitive tongue to the ardent apostolic spirit that fueled her life and works in an ecstatic response to Bruté's thoughts of going with Father Samuel Cooper to preach the gospel to indigenous peoples in Canada, members of the First Nations. "Blessed you, Your little *Bête*-Mother [foolish Mother] is lost these days past in your *Canada* letters", she began.

Oh my! To see Man a *wild Savage*, a *polished* savage, *Man* in any state, *what a Savage!*—unless he be in Christ. Oh, Blessed, I gasp with the desires to Him whom you are now carrying in and on your breast for *your full, whole* accomplishment of His blessed will. I glance a fearful look

[155] 7.237, Elizabeth Seton to Rev. John Hickey, P.S.S., [February 28, 1820], in *CW*, 2:640–41.
[156] Ibid., 641, brackets in published version.

at you and Mr. [Samuel] Cooper and say secretly: if I was
one or the other! Then *adore* and think, I know nothing
about it; only it seems to me that those who have light and
grace already might be trusted to keep it: and I would not
stop night or day till I reached the dry and dark wilderness
where neither can be found, where such horrid crimes go
on for want of them, and where there is such a glorious
Death to be gained by carrying them. Oh, G., if I was light
and life as you are, I would shout like a madman alone to
my God, and roar and groan and sigh and be silent alto-
gether till I had baptized a thousand and snatched these
poor Victims from Hell.[157]

There can be no doubting the sincerity and depths of
Elizabeth's desire, for she turned immediately and honestly
to her everyday calling:

And pray, *Madame Bête*, say you, why does not your zeal
make its flame through your own little Hemisphere?
True—but rules, prudence, subjections, opinions, etc.—
dreadful walls to a burning SOUL wild as mine and *some-
body's*.... I am like a fiery Horse I had when a girl, whom
they tried to break by making him drag a heavy cart; and
the poor beast was so humbled that he could never more
be inspired by whips or caresses, and wasted to a skeleton
till he died. But you and Mr. Cooper might waste to Skel-
etons to some purpose, and after wasting be sent still living
to the glories of the kingdom.

In the meantime, that Kingdom come. Every day I ask
my *bête*-soul what I do for it in my little part assigned, and
I can see nothing but to smile, caress, be patient, write,
pray, and *WAIT* before Him.

Oh, G., G., G., my blessed God, that Kingdom come![158]

[157] 7.193, Elizabeth Seton to Rev. Simon Bruté, P.S.S., [November 1818],
in *CW*, 2:593–94, second brackets in published version.
[158] Ibid., 594.

8

My Blessed Faith

The mystery of the Church was the central fact and factor of Saint Elizabeth Ann Seton's life and holiness. Without it she never would have lived the fullness of her apostolic life, reached the pinnacle of sanctity, or been hailed by that same Church in the loving gesture of canonization.

Elizabeth was not born into the totality of the mystery that, the Fathers of Vatican II confirmed, "subsists in the Catholic Church".[1] Rather, she was the heir of "many elements of sanctification and of truth ... found outside of its visible structure" in her native Episcopal Church.[2] However, she was thankfully to become a memorable witness that "these elements, as gifts belonging to the Church of Christ, are forces impelling toward catholic unity".[3] Pope Paul VI paid tribute to their unifying power in thanking the Episcopal Church, based in the United States, for the gift of Elizabeth Bayley Seton. "To this Church goes the merit of having awakened and fostered the religious sense and Christian sentiment which in the young Elizabeth were naturally predisposed to the most spontaneous and lively manifestations", he

[1] *LG* 8.
[2] Ibid.
[3] Ibid.

acknowledged.[4] "We willingly recognize this merit, and, knowing well how much it cost Elizabeth to pass over to the Catholic Church, we admire her courage for adhering to the religious truth and divine reality which were manifested to her therein. And we are likewise pleased to see that from this same adherence to the Catholic Church she experienced great peace and security", a soundness of soul that caused her to find it "natural to preserve all the good things which her membership in the fervent Episcopalian community had taught her [in New York], in so many beautiful expressions, especially of religious piety, and that she was always faithful in her esteem and affection for those from whom her Catholic profession had sadly separated her".[5] And the Holy Father finished by noting in the official presence of Episcopalian prelates and dignitaries "a motive of hope and a presage of ever better ecumenical relations".[6]

Among Elizabeth's writings there is, whether from her own thoughts or from a spiritual book she had read, a short, sensible treatment of mystery: "When we say this thing [is] a mystery, of the *thing* we say nothing, but of Ourselves we say that we do not comprehend this thing—as defect of strength in us makes some weights to be immovable, so likewise defect of understanding makes some truths to be mysterious."[7] Before she ever confronted the mystery of the Church, she stumbled upon a lesser but nonetheless obstructive mystery, something she did not comprehend because she had never considered it, the possibility that there was only one true Church, or even that any church was truly necessary. She had always taken for granted that

[4] Paul VI, *AASCO*.
[5] Ibid.
[6] Ibid.
[7] 9.6, [Instruction], n.d., in *CW*, 3a:249, brackets in published version.

"everybody would be Saved who meant well".[8] As she
explained to Father Bruté years later when he made an
attempt to convert her sister, Mary Bayley Post: "Your
letter to Sister [is] admirable, if first the big stone of darkest
ignorance and indifference was removed on the point of
FIRST NECESSITY—*that there is any true Church or false
church, right FAITH or wrong Faith.* But, blessed Soul, [nei-
ther] you, nor anyone who has not been in that ignorance
or indifference, can imagine the size and depth of it."[9]
She tried to make him see that, secure in the Church as
she was now, she had once been as adrift and heedless as
Mary Post:

> And putting myself again a moment in the place of my sis-
> ter (even with my great advantage of having been passion-
> ately attached to religion when a Protestant, which she
> is not), I imagine I read your letter and, looking up with
> vacant surprise, would say: "What does the Man mean?
> Would he say that all who believe in Our Lord are not
> safe, or even if a poor Turk or savage does not believe,
> is he to be blamed for it?... They make God a merciful
> being indeed, if he would condemn souls of his own cre-
> ation for their Parents bringing them in the world on one
> side of it or the other."[10]

Eliza Craig Sadler had also been the target of Bruté's
zeal. She was not in the least offended; rather, she praised
his kind thought of her and devotion to his duty, but her
answer was exactly what Elizabeth could have predicted:
"Truth, however, obliges me", Mrs. Sadler told Bruté, "to

[8] 3.31, Journal to Amabilia Filicchi, July 19, 1804, entry of August 28, in
CW, 1:369.
[9] 7.49, Elizabeth Seton to Rev. Simon Bruté, P.S.S., [September 1816], in
CW, 2:423.
[10] Ibid., 423–24.

assure you that I feel it impossible to subscribe to the belief that out of your Church there can be no Christians. Ever since I have been capable of reason, I have endeavored humbly to make the law of my Redeemer the rule and guide of my actions, unworthily and imperfectly, but not blindly; and I believe that *He* who sees the inmost thoughts will judge of my faith, as He promised to do by all those who believe in His Name."[11]

Elizabeth further buttressed her opinion of the fruitlessness of Bruté's attempts with the example of her brother-in-law, Dr. Wright Post:

> My Brother [Wright] Post once asked me so simply: "Sister Seton, they say you go to the Catholic Church. What is the difference?"
>
> "*It is the first church, my brother, the old church, the Apostles begun*" (answered the poor, trembling Betsy Seton, dreading always to be pushed on a subject she could only feel, but never express to these cool reasoners).
>
> "*Church of the Apostles*", said my Brother, "Why, is not every church from the Apostles?"[12]

Speak as she might of "cool reasoners", Elizabeth seemed to insist in the end that the ignorance she once shared had little to do with reason or arguments. "Forever accustomed to look only to little exterior attractions", she explained, "as the dress and quiet of the Quakers, a sweet enthusiastic preaching among the Methodists, a soft melting music of low voices among Anabaptists, or any other such nonsense. The thought of a right Faith or wrong Faith, true church or false one, never enters the mind of one among a hundred."[13]

[11] Eliza Sadler to Rev. Simon Bruté, P.S.S., November 30, 1816, Saint Elizabeth Ann Seton, 1-3-3-11:B19, APSL.

[12] 7.49, Elizabeth Seton to Rev. Simon Bruté, P.S.S., [September 1816], in *CW*, 2:424, brackets in published version.

[13] Ibid.

Amusingly enough, Bruté, for his part, failed to understand Elizabeth's attitude or exposition, for he wrote across the top of this letter: "A letter to try to convert Mrs. Post, her sister, to the Catholic faith—how useless she thought it—most curious."[14]

Certainly Elizabeth had no least thought of one true Church when she met the Filicchi in Livorno, Italy. It was her evident piety—passing acquaintances noticed. Their remarks prompted the Filicchi brothers to acquaint her with the Catholic practices almost as soon as she arrived among them. "May the good Almighty God enlighten your mind and strengthen your heart to see and follow in Religion the surest, true way to the eternal blessings", Antonio prayed.[15] Filippo informed her directly of her obligation to seek the truth. She tried to pass it off with banter: "Oh, my, sir . . . if there is but one Faith, and nobody pleases God without it, where are all the good people who die out of it?"[16] Filippo was not to be deterred: "I don't know", he answered frankly. "That depends on what light of Faith they had re[ceive]d. But I know where people will go who can know the right Faith, if they pray for it and inquire for it, and yet do neither."[17] Nothing could be blunter than that, with its affirmation of the grace God was extending her and the dire results of its rejection.

Whether from embarrassment or unease or even fright, Elizabeth tried to maintain lightness of tone: "Much as to say, Sir, you want me to pray and inquire, and be of your Faith?" . . . "Pray and inquire . . . that is all I ask you" was

[14] Ibid., 423n1.

[15] Antonio Filicchi to Elizabeth Seton, January 9, 1804, Saint Elizabeth Ann Seton, 1-3-3-10(1), APSL.

[16] 2.11, Elizabeth Seton to Rebecca Seton, January 28, 1804, entry of February 10, in CW, 1:290.

[17] Ibid., brackets in published version.

the unmoving reply.[18] It was an important conversation—
the fact that Elizabeth recorded it word for word for
Rebecca Seton attests to that—and Filippo had found his
mark: Elizabeth did set out seriously on the long, painful
road of prayer, inquiry, and discernment, however light-
heartedly she attempted to describe it for Rebecca: "So,
dearest Bec, I am laughing with God when I try to be
serious and say daily, as the good gentleman told me, in
old Mr. Pope's words: *'If I am right, O teach my heart still
in the right to stay; if I am wrong, thy grace impart to find the
better way.'* Not that I can think there is a better way than
I know—but everyone must be respected in their own."[19]

   Elizabeth's earnest and prayerful seeking was furthered
and sweetened by her immediate attraction to certain
Catholic teachings and practices, such as the day-long
availability of the churches for private prayer, the belief
in the Real Presence of Christ in the Eucharist in these
same churches, devotion to the Blessed Virgin, fasting,
and penance.[20] But the uncompromising fact of a single true Faith and its consequences did not confront
her until, at her minister Rev. John Henry Hobart's
request, she had read Thomas Newton's *Dissertation of
the Prophecies.* She had felt, perhaps, that if her inquiries
led nowhere, she could always retreat to the haven of
her native Episcopal Church. Now she realized that this
was not so. "It grieves my very Soul", she cried out to
Amabilia Filicchi, "to see that Protestants as well as your
(as I thought, hard and severe) principles see the thing so
differently; since this book so Valued by them sends all
followers of the Pope to the bottomless pit"—and she

   [18] Ibid.
   [19] Ibid. Here, Elizabeth is quoting the English poet Alexander Pope (1688–
1744).
   [20] Cf. Annabelle M. Melville, *Elizabeth Bayley Seton 1774–1821*, ed. Betty
Ann McNeil, D.C. (Hanover, Pa.: The Sheridan Press, 2009), 93–98.

finished ruefully, her eye on the first millennium and a half of Christendom—"it appears by the account made of them from the Apostles' time, that a greater part of the world must be already there, at that rate."[21]

There was no turning back, and Elizabeth pushed on bravely. When Hobart asked her, "What more would you have when you act according to your best judgment?" she answered that her judgment would be enough for this world, "but I fear in the next to meet another question".[22]

Throughout the bitterness of the struggle, which eventually frayed Elizabeth's nerves and physically reduced her almost to a skeleton, she never let go of her confidence in God. She implored Him, "Enlighten me to see the truth, unmixed with doubts and hesitations", and assured Antonio Filicchi, "I read the promises given to St. Peter and the Sixth Chapter [of St.] John every day and then ask God, can I offend Him by believing those express words?"[23]

The sense and authority of Scripture were very strong in Elizabeth. "I read my dear St. Francis [de Sales, *Introduction to the Devout Life*], and ask if it is possible that I shall dare to think differently from him, or seek heaven any other way. I have read your *England's Reformation*, and find its evidence too conclusive to admit of any reply. God will not forsake me, Antonio. I know that He will unite me to His flock; and, although now my Faith is unsettled, I am assured that He will not disappoint my hope which is fixed on His own word, that He will not despise the humble, contrite heart."[24]

How unerringly this sincere but sorely tried and confused woman penetrated the mystery of the Church's

[21] 3.31, Journal to Amabilia Filicchi, July 19, 1804, entry of August 28, in *CW*, 1:369.
[22] 3.7, Elizabeth Seton to Antonio Filicchi, August 30, 1804, entry of September 8, in *CW*, 1:319.
[23] Ibid., entry of August 30, 317–18. See Jn 6:68.
[24] Ibid., 318.

lowliness! A century and a half later, the Fathers of Vatican II were to expound these very virtues of the Church that she possessed in imitation of her Master and Head: "Just as Christ carried out the work of redemption in poverty and persecution, so the Church is called to follow the same route that it might communicate the fruits of salvation to men. Christ Jesus, 'though He was by nature God ... emptied Himself, taking the nature of a slave' (Phil 2:6), and 'being rich, became poor' (2 Cor 8:9) for our sakes. Thus, the Church, although it needs human resources to carry out its mission, is not set up to seek earthly glory, but to proclaim, even by its own example, humility and self-sacrifice."[25] The Fathers, too, were to confirm the rightness of Elizabeth's trust: "Christ was sent by the Father 'to bring good news to the poor, to heal the contrite of heart' (Lk 4:18)."[26]

Despite Elizabeth's striving for complete self-honesty and disinterestedness, the struggle to the truth was so long and bitter that Bishop Carroll warned that, even so, she "ought to consider whether the tears she sheds and the prayers she offers to heaven are purely for God's sake and arise solely from compunction for Sin, and are unmixed with any alloy of worldly respects or inordinate Solicitude for the attainment of Some worldly purpose". He continued, "A fear arises in my mind that God discovers in her some lurking imperfection and defers the final grace of her conversion, till her soul be entirely purified of its irregular attachments."[27] The bishop's fears were surely justified, for without his being fully aware of it, he seems to have sensed that this was a struggle for a great and unusual soul. Indeed,

[25] LG 8.
[26] Ibid.
[27] Archbishop John Carroll to Antonio Filicchi, January 13, 1805, Saint Elizabeth Ann Seton, 1-3-3-1(38), APSL.

Elizabeth's own accounts of her anguish of heart and mind confirmed his uneasiness, for no matter what she did to attain truth and peace, she was rebuffed again and again; her exertions brought only further confusion, distress, and darkness.

"I fell on my face before God (remember I tell you all)", Elizabeth revealed to Antonio Filicchi,

and appealed to him as my righteous Judge, if hardness of heart, or unwillingness to be taught, or any human reasons stood between me and the truth; If I would not rejoice to cast my sorrows on the Bosom of the Blessed Mary—to entreat the influence of all His Blessed Saints and angels, to pray for precious Souls even more than for myself, and account myself happy in dying for His Sacred Truth—if once my soul could know it was pleasing Him. I remembered how much these exercises had comforted and delighted me at Leghorn, and recalled all the reasons which had there convinced me of their truth—and immediately a cloud of doubts and replies raised a contest in this poor Soul, and I could only again cry out for mercy to a sinner.[28]

Although Antonio and his brother Filippo continued faithfully in writing Elizabeth long, encouraging letters, they also unwittingly added to her confusion—she was being pushed and pulled by friends on both sides—and Filippo at length gave her what was probably the best advice of all. "Avoid the labyrinth of controversies", he wrote. "They will not make you wiser."[29] Even the best advice, however, does not always work out in practice, as Elizabeth discovered:

[28] 3.8, Elizabeth Seton to Antonio Filicchi, September 19, [1804], in *CW*, 1:321.

[29] Filippo Filicchi to Elizabeth Seton, October 22, 1804, Saint Elizabeth Ann Seton, 1-3-3-10:14, APSL.

After reading the life of St. Mary Magdalen, I thought: "Come, my Soul, let us turn from all these Suggestions of one side or the other, and quietly resolve to go to that church which has at least the multitude of the wise and good on its side"; and began to consider the first steps I must take. The first step—is it not to declare I believe all that is taught by the Council of Trent?—and if I said that, would not the Searcher of hearts know my falsehood and insincerity? Could you say that you would be satisfied with his Bread and believe the cup, which He equally commanded, unnecessary? Could you believe that the Prayers and Litanies addressed to Our Blessed Lady were acceptable to God, though not commanded in Scripture?[30]

Elizabeth knew the root cause of her trouble better than anyone: "Far different is my situation from those who are uninstructed," she told Antonio, "but my hard case is to have a head turned with instruction, without the light in my Soul to direct it where to rest."[31] In the end, the long sought and prayed for light flooded Elizabeth's soul in God's gift and stilled the turmoil of controversy and doubt: "I WILL GO PEACEABLY and FIRMLY TO THE CATHOLIC CHURCH: for if Faith is so important to our Salvation, I will seek it where true Faith first began, seek it among those who received it from GOD HIMSELF", she announced resolutely to Amabilia Filicchi. "The controversies on it I am quite incapable of deciding; and as the strictest Protestant allows salvation to a good Catholic, to the Catholics I will go and

[30] 3.8, Elizabeth Seton to Antonio Filicchi, September 19, [1804], in *CW*, 1:321–22. Only since Vatican II has the Catholic Church resumed distributing Communion to the faithful under both species.

[31] 3.10, Elizabeth Seton to Antonio Filicchi, October 9, 1804, entry of October 11, in *CW*, 1:327.

try to be a good one. May God accept my intention and pity me."[32]

Elizabeth saw now clearly what Filippo meant, that faith, not conviction, was the key, that faith was all that was required. "I tell you a secret hidden almost from my own Soul, it is so delicate," she acknowledged to Simon Bruté many years later,

> *that* my hatred of opposition, troublesome inquiries, etc. brought me in the Church more than Conviction—how often I argued to my fearful, uncertain heart, at all events Catholics must be as safe as any other religion; they say none are safe but themselves—*perhaps it is true.* If not, at all events I shall be safe with them as any other—it is the Way of Suffering and the Cross for me that is another point of Security . . . there, dearest G, you read what I would have carried to the grave, only I wish you to know well, as far as I can tell you, the impossibility for a poor Protestant to see *our Meaning* without being led step by step and the Voil lifted little by little—I am cold to my bones, and hand and heart trembling while I think how I have passed through the thousand mazes—and my thousand *ifs* to Our God, yet appealing to Him the *if* was only fear to displease Him . . . but I was ALONE WITH HIM.[33]

The mazes were gone and the *ifs* forgotten on March 14, 1805, when, in the presence of Father Matthew O'Brien and Antonio Filicchi at Saint Peter's Catholic Church, Elizabeth united herself fully with "the one Church of Christ which in the Creed is professed as one, holy, catholic and

[32] 3.31, Journal to Amabilia Filicchi, July 19, 1804, entry of January 1805, in *CW*, 1:374.

[33] 7.49, Elizabeth Seton to Rev. Simon Bruté, P.S.S., [September 1816], in *CW*, 2:425.

apostolic".[34] Father John Cheverus of Boston had given her the final push. "The doubts which arise in your mind do not destroy your faith; they only disturb your mind", he had assured her. "Who in this life, my dear Madam, is perfectly free from such troubles? 'We see as through a glass in an obscure manner,' we stand like Israelites at the foot of the holy mountain, but in spite of dark clouds and the noise of thunder, we perceive some rays of the glory of the Lord, and we hear His divine Voice. I would, therefore, advise your joining the Catholic Church as soon as possible, and when doubts arise, say only: 'I believe, O Lord, help Thou my unbelief.' "[35]

While the word *Magisterium*, the Church's teaching authority, was probably unknown to Elizabeth, now, ten days after Cheverus' welcome urging, she penetrated with grace into the mystery of the Church and not only freely accepted but also proclaimed her teaching authority. "After all were gone, I was called to the little room next [to] the Altar", she wrote happily to Amabilia Filicchi, "and there PROFESSED to believe what the Council of Trent believes and teaches; laughing with my heart to my Savior, who saw that I knew not what the Council of Trent believed—only that it believed what the Church of God declared to be its belief, and consequently is now my belief."[36]

Surely, by this act Elizabeth was embracing that "one Church of Christ which in the Creed is professed as one, holy, catholic and apostolic, which our Savior, after His

[34] LG 8.

[35] Rev. John Cheverus to Elizabeth Seton, March 4, 1805, formerly in Archives, Sisters of Charity of New York (hereafter cited as AMSV), 100-115-1-12; transferred 2022-EAS-2-41 to APSL. Cheverus is quoting 1 Cor 13:12 and Mk 9:24.

[36] 3.31, Journal to Amabilia Filicchi, July 19, 1804, entry of [March 14, 1805], in *CW*, 1:375.

Resurrection, commissioned Peter to shepherd, and him and the other apostles to extend and direct with authority, which He erected for all ages as 'the pillar and mainstay of the truth.' This Church constituted and organized in the world as a society, subsists in the Catholic Church, which is governed by the successor of Peter and by the Bishops in communion with him."[37]

From the first, Elizabeth was an "*adorer* . . . of the Mystery of *the Church*, the only Ark in *the world*".[38] Once she had entered that ark, she gave it her unstinted loyalty and submission. Her respect for hierarchy, the ordered succession of superiors placed over her by God—pastor, spiritual director, ecclesiastical superior, bishop, pope—was untrammeled by self. As a new Catholic, she expressed that "the counsel and excellent directions of [Father] O'B[rien] . . . strengthen me and, being sometimes enforced by command, give a determination to my actions which is now indispensable."[39]

For the remaining years of her life, she found the same guidance and ascetical surety in the succeeding spiritual directors sent her by God, and she so taught the Sisters of Charity, her spiritual daughters. "What was the first rule of our dear Savior's life?" she asked in an instruction.[40]

You know it was to do his Father's will. Well, then, the first end I propose in our daily work is to do the will of God; secondly, to do it in the manner he wills it; and thirdly, to do it because it is his will. I know what his will is by those

[37] *LG* 8, quoting 1 Tim 3:15.
[38] 7.66, Elizabeth Seton to Rev. Simon Bruté, P.S.S., [December 26, 1816], in *CW*, 2:454.
[39] 3.25, Elizabeth Seton to Antonio Filicchi, April 22, 1805, in *CW*, 1:356, second brackets in published version.
[40] Charles I. White, *Life of Mrs. Eliza A. Seton: Foundress and First Superior of the Sisters or Daughters of Charity in the United States of America* (Baltimore, Md.: John Murphy & Co., 1859), 322.

who direct me; whatever they bid me do, if it is ever so small in itself, is the will of God for me. Then, do it in the manner he wills it, not sewing an old thing as if it was new, or a new thing as if it was old; not fretting because the oven is too hot, or in a fuss because it is too cold. You understand: not flying and driving because you are hurried, nor creeping like a snail because no one pushes you.[41]

Elizabeth had immediate joy, too, in the sacramental life of the Church. Although she was introduced to Catholic liturgy in the annual and distinctive rites of Holy Week and was completely mystified, the veil was lifted whenever she discerned the structure of "the Divine Sacrifice [the Mass]". She described it as "so commanding and yet already so familiar for all my wants and necessities. That speaks for itself, and I am All at home in it."[42] From her days of preparation as an Episcopalian, she was, of course, even more at home with the Holy Eucharist, for whose first reception as a Catholic she counted "the days and hours"; and it became, as it was intended, an instant source of strength in resisting the indignation of family and friends at her conversion.[43] "From circumstances of peculiar impressions on my mind", she told Antonio, "I have been obliged to watch it so carefully and keep so near the fountain head, that I have been three times to Communion since you left me, not to influence my Faith, but to keep Peace in my Soul, which without this heavenly resource would be agitated and discomposed by the frequent assaults which, in my immediate situation, are naturally made on my feelings."[44]

[41] Ibid.

[42] 3.31, Journal to Amabilia Filicchi, July 19, 1804, entry of April 14, 1805, in CW, 1:377.

[43] Ibid., entry of [March 20, 1805], 376.

[44] 3.25, Elizabeth Seton to Antonio Filicchi, April 22, 1805, in CW, 1:356.

Most striking of all was Elizabeth's reaching out for the Sacrament of Penance, also called the Sacrament of Reconciliation, which is not always fully appreciated by native Catholics and is sometimes of special discomfort and even fright to converts. Indeed, this sacrament played a decisive role in Elizabeth's final resolve to become a Catholic. She recalled that on the fateful Sunday in January in Saint George's Chapel, at "the bowing of my heart before the [Episcopalian] Bishop to receive his Absolution—which is given publicly and universally to all in the church—I had not the least faith in his Prayer, and looked for an Apostolic loosing from my sins, which by the books Mr. H[obart] had given me to read, I find they do not claim or admit."[45] How different her eager awaiting of the Catholic sacrament: "So delighted now to prepare for this GOOD CONFESSION which, bad as I am, I would be ready to make on the house top to insure the GOOD ABSOLUTION I hope for, after it."[46]

When Elizabeth made her first Confession on March 20, 1805, it was an act of joy and was remarkable for her instant perception of Christ in the sacrament. "IT IS DONE!" she exclaimed to Amabilia. "Easy enough: the kindest, most respectable confessor is this Mr. O['Brien], with the compassion and yet firmness in this work of Mercy which I would have expected from Our Lord Himself. Our Lord Himself I saw alone in him, both in his and my part of this Venerable Sacrament, for, oh, Amabilia, how awful those words of unloosing after a thirty years' bondage! I felt as if my chains fell, as those of St. Peter at the touch of the divine Messenger. My God, what new scenes for my Soul!"[47]

[45] 3.31, Journal to Amabilia Filicchi, July 19, 1804, entry of January 1805, in *CW*, 1:373, second brackets in published version.

[46] Ibid., entry of [March 14, 1805], 376.

[47] Ibid., brackets in published version.

The following year Elizabeth was firmly and forever established in the full strength of the Church when Bishop John Carroll came to New York and, after a week of personal instruction and spiritual direction, confirmed her on Pentecost Sunday, May 26, 1806. She told Antonio contentedly, "Mr. Tisserant could not be here and Mr. Hurley was proxy for him and added the Name of Mary to the Ann Elizabeth which present the three most endearing ideas in the World—and contain the moments of the mysteries of salvation."[48] The only sacrament proper to her and yet to be received was the Sacrament of Extreme Unction (last rites), now called the Sacrament of Anointing of the Sick. When Bruté administered the sacrament on September 24, 1820— it was repeated on January 2, 1821—he noted: "Mother so calm, so present, so recollected, and wholly trusted to her blessed Lord. Her eyes so expressive,—the look that pierces heaven, and the soul visible in it."[49]

There is no evidence that Elizabeth was rebaptized, that is, baptized conditionally, in the Catholic Church. Bishop Carroll and Bishop Cheverus both believed in the validity of Baptism as then conferred in the Episcopal Church, and in fact Carroll warned his priests against rebaptizing needlessly, citing penalties laid down by the Church for doing so.

It would be well to explore what the Church, as illuminated by the Second Vatican Council, meant to Saint Elizabeth Ann. The Dogmatic Constitution of the Church *Lumen Gentium* teaches that

> Christ, the one Mediator, established and continually sustains here on earth His holy Church, the community of faith, hope and charity, as an entity with visible delineation

[48] 4.19, Elizabeth Seton to Antonio Filicchi, May 28, 1806, in *CW*, 1:408.

[49] [Sister Loyola Law, D.C., ed.], *Mother Seton: Notes by Rev. Simon Gabriel Bruté*, entry of September 24, 1820, (Emmitsburg, Md.: Daughters of Charity, 1884), 4.

through which He communicated truth and grace to all. But, the society structured with hierarchical organs and the Mystical Body of Christ, are not to be considered as two realities, nor are the visible assembly and the spiritual community, nor the earthly Church and the Church enriched with heavenly things; rather they form one complex reality which coalesces from a divine and a human element. For this reason, by no weak analogy, it is compared to the mystery of the incarnate Word. As the assumed nature inseparably united to Him, serves the divine Word as a living organ of salvation, so, in a similar way, does the visible social structure of the Church serve the Spirit of Christ, who vivifies it, in the building up of the body.[50]

The Fathers of the Council acknowledged that "in the building up of Christ's Body various members and functions have their part to play."[51] This is ordained by God: "There is only one Spirit who, according to His own richness and the needs of the ministries, gives His different gifts for the welfare of the Church."[52] There is a primacy of gifts: "What has a special place among these gifts is the grace of the apostles to whose authority the Spirit Himself subjected even those who were endowed with charisms."[53] This grace and authority of the apostles subsist in the pope and the bishops in union with him.

The pope, bishops, and priests share the ministerial priesthood. "Though they differ from one another in essence and not only in degree, the common priesthood of the faithful and the ministerial or hierarchical priesthood are nonetheless interrelated: each of them in its own special way is a participation in the one priesthood of Christ", so teach the Fathers of Vatican II. "The ministerial priest, by the sacred

[50] LG 8.
[51] LG 7.
[52] Ibid.
[53] Ibid.

power he enjoys, teaches and rules the priestly people; acting in the person of Christ, he makes present the Eucharistic sacrifice, and offers it to God in the name of all the people. But the faithful, in virtue of their royal priesthood, join in the offering of the Eucharist. They likewise exercise that priesthood in receiving the sacraments, in prayer and thanksgiving, in the witness of a holy life, and by self-denial and active charity."[54] How well, from this definition, did Elizabeth Seton exercise her priesthood!

Even Saint Thérèse of Lisieux, now a Doctor of the Church because of her writings and spirituality, who used the word *little* to describe everything she did and was, had problems with her place and her identity in the Church. Having practically forced herself into the contemplative quiet of the cloister, she found herself besieged through her desire for divine and human service—not, be it noted, for power or influence—by a tumultuous desire for the missions and martyrdom, surely unrequitable where she was but with a "thirst for the Martyr's crown".[55] She wrote, "I opened ... the Epistles of St. Paul to seek relief in my sufferings. My eyes fell on the 12th and 13th chapters of the First Epistle to the Corinthians. I read that all cannot become Apostles, Prophets, and Doctors; that the Church is composed of different members; that the eye cannot also be the hand"—it was in vain. "The answer was clear," she confessed, "but it did not fulfill my desires, or give to me the peace I sought."[56]

But, she continued, "without being discouraged I read on, and found comfort in this counsel: 'Be zealous for the better gifts. And I show unto you a yet more excellent way.' The Apostle then explains how all perfect gifts are nothing

---

[54] LG 10.

[55] Thérèse of Lisieux, *The Story of the Soul*, trans. Thomas N. Taylor (New York: Cosimo Classics, 1912), 159.

[56] Ibid., 160.

without Love"—this made great sense to her, since love was her whole motivation—"that Charity is the most excellent way of going surely to God. At last I had found rest."[57]

"Meditating on the mystical Body of Holy Church, I could not recognise myself among any of its members as described by St. Paul," she admitted quite simply, "or was it not rather that I wished to recognise myself in all"—not certainly out of self-love but out of a sense of usefulness.[58]

> Charity provided me with the key to my vocation. I understood that since the Church is a body composed of different members, the noblest and most important of all the organs would not be wanting. I knew that the Church has a heart, that this heart burns with love, and that it is love alone which gives life to its members. I knew that if this love were extinguished, the Apostles would no longer preach the Gospel, and the Martyrs would refuse to shed their blood. I understood that love embraces all vocations[59]

—how profound and satisfying to each member of the Mystical Body with his part divinely assigned!—

> that it is all things, and that it reaches out through all the ages, and to the uttermost limits of the earth, because it is eternal.
>
> Then, beside myself with joy, I cried out: O Jesus, my Love, at last I have found my vocation. My vocation is love! Yes, I have found my place in the bosom of the Church, and this place, O my God, Thou hast Thyself given to me: in the heart of the Church, my Mother, I will be LOVE! ... Thus I shall be all things: thus will my dream be realised.[60]

[57] Ibid.
[58] Ibid.
[59] Ibid.
[60] Ibid., 160–161.

That same Church has assigned these words to be read in the divine office of Saint Thérèse's feast day, because they summarize her spirituality.

> There is a striking and humbling passage in Saint Augustine vis-à-vis Our Lady and the Church. "The Virgin Mary is both holy and blessed, and yet the Church is greater than she", he writes. "Mary is a part of the Church, a member of the Church, a holy, an eminent—the most eminent—member, but still only a member of the entire body. The body undoubtedly is greater than she, one of its members. This body has the Lord for its head, and head and body together make up the whole Christ. In other words, our head is divine—our head is God."[61]

Saint Elizabeth Ann Seton's soul was docile and lowly before the mystery of the Church. It breathed forth gratitude when her days were running down, when she expressed her heartfelt thanks to those at her bedside: "I thank God for having made me a child of His Church. When you come to this hour, you *will know* what it is to be a child of the Church."[62] The use of the word *child* is significant. She was, in her own eyes, most gladly a child, with all the trust and dependence and utter love the word implies; she believed most fully that, as Jesus warned, unless she became as a little child, she would not enter the Kingdom of heaven. It was a usual word with her. When she felt that she had acted awkwardly or even wrongfully in the first days of the Sisterhood, she assured Bishop Carroll: "You will see how good a child I am going to be. Quite a little child. And perhaps you will have often to give me

---

[61] Saint Augustine, "Sermon 72 A," 7, in *The Works of Saint Augustine*, part 3, vol. 3, trans. Edmund Hill, ed. John Rotelle (New York: New City Press, 1991), 228.

[62] [Law], *Mother Seton: Notes*, entry of January 1821, 46.

the food of little children yet, but I will do my best as I have promised you in every case."[63] On her deathbed, that great moment of farewell to her Sisters, she struggled mightily to pronounce the words that were her sacred legacy to them: "Be children of the Church, be children of the Church."[64]

Elizabeth had no difficulty in being "a sheep in the flock", which is what Father Bruté called her in praising the "reverence, tenderness, and interest she felt for her Superiors—for their holy life—for seeing them true priests". He added ruefully: "Ah! that priests felt for themselves as she felt they should be—how did she suffer even at their imperfections! At their faults how sorrowfully, yet how charitably."[65] She might naturally consider herself the center of the plans for the school and the Sisterhood she had been brought to Baltimore to found, but if she did so for a moment, she quickly corrected herself: "So much of my, or rather *the scheme* of these reverend gentlemen", she told Antonio Filicchi, "depends on your concurrence and support that I dare not form a wish."[66] When the plans were reaching maturity, she avowed further, "If I had a choice, and my will should decide in a moment, I would remain silent in His hands."[67]

Elizabeth remained just as detached in spirit when the official establishment of the community was being readied in the Archdiocese of Baltimore, the Premier See. "The constitutions proposed have been discussed by our Rev.

---

[63] 6.9, Elizabeth Seton to Archbishop John Carroll, November 2, 1809, in *CW*, 2:88.

[64] A-7.268, Account by Rev. Simon Bruté, P.S.S., of Elizabeth Seton's Last Days, January 2, 1821, in *CW*, 2:767.

[65] [Law], *Mother Seton: Notes*, 70.

[66] 5.7, Elizabeth Seton to Antonio Filicchi, August 20, 1808, in *CW*, 2:28.

[67] 5.18, Elizabeth Seton to Filippo Filicchi, February 8, 1809, in *CW*, 2:55.

Director," she informed the archbishop, "and I find he makes some observations on my Situation relative to them; but surely an Individual is not to be considered where a public good is in question; and you know I would gladly make every sacrifice you think consistent with my first and inseparable obligations as a Mother."[68] Although the director, Father John Dubois, had a temperament very different from Elizabeth's, and his meticulousness annoyed her to the point that she sometimes made innocent fun of him with the Sisters, there was never a question of flouting him, either first as director or later as superior of the community. In fact, Elizabeth told Carroll that Dubois had always been her preference for superior because "being on the spot"—he lived up the road at Mount Saint Mary's—"he sees things in a different point of view from those who are distant ... [and] he always and invariably has recommended me to refer constantly to you, which is not only in the order of Providence, but the only safety I can find for the peace of my mind."[69]

The bishop himself was, quite simply, "her spiritual father", and Elizabeth's obedience to him was unqualified. Even when she protested vehemently to him when Father Dubourg was "acting like a tyrant", then over what she rightfully considered usurpations of her community and school by the high-handed Father David, she could finish: "But if, after consideration of every circumstance, you still think things must remain as they are—whatever you dictate, I will abide by through every difficulty."[70] When Carroll

[68] 6.83, Elizabeth Seton to Archbishop John Carroll, September 5, 1811, in *CW*, 2:195–96.

[69] 6.76, Elizabeth Seton to Archbishop John Carroll, May 13, 1811, in *CW*, 2:184.

[70] 6.4, Elizabeth Seton to Archbishop John Carroll, [August 6, 1809], in *CW*, 2:78; 6.23, Elizabeth Seton to Archbishop John Carroll, January 25, 1810, in *CW*, 2:107.

lay dying at eighty years of age, Elizabeth confided to a former pupil: "My eyes are blind with writing and tears. Our Blessed Archbishop's situation, though we must give and resign him, presses hard on me as well as on thousands— harder on me than you would imagine."[71]

Although Pope Pius VII was a distant figure in a remote land, he was nonetheless an undeniable reality and rock of unity and truth. Elizabeth entered with a daughter's sorrow into his sufferings in Napoleon's prisons, making his prayer of submission to the Will of God her favorite prayer unto death: "May the most just, the most high and the most amiable will of God be in all things fulfilled, praised and exalted above all forever."[72] Her first letter to Antonio Filicchi after the emperor's final downfall began with her joy at "the glad and happy news of the Restoration of our holy Father".[73] A tender sign of filial love was in a note to Napoleon's forlorn young nephew Jerome, a pupil at Mount Saint Mary's, who had asked Mother Seton for an *Agnus Dei* "to preserve me in the vacations from the dangers that will surround me".[74] "Dear Jerome," she replied, "it is a great pleasure to me to send you the *Agnus Dei*. I wish I had one handsomely covered, but you will mind only the Virtue of the prayers our Holy Father has said over it."[75]

Elizabeth's unwavering submission to God's Will, as revealed through the Church and her ministers, was a testament to the transformative power of faith. Her profound love for God was the driving force behind her submission.

[71] 6.217, Elizabeth Seton to Ellen Wiseman, [November 27, 1815], in *CW*, 2:361.

[72] Melville, *Elizabeth Bayley Seton*, 264nk.

[73] 6.167, Elizabeth Seton to Antonio Filicchi, July 1, 1814, in *CW*, 2:276.

[74] Jerome N. Bonaparte to Elizabeth Seton, June 21 [1816], Saint Elizabeth Ann Seton, 1-3-3-4(100), APSL.

[75] 7.30, Elizabeth Seton to Jerome Bonaparte, [June 1816], in *CW*, 2:401.

Elizabeth's example reminds us that true devotion and obedience to God lead to a life of purpose and fulfillment.

To describe that lively, volatile, even passionate woman so could provoke only laughter. She once freely acknowledged that "rules, prudence, subjections, opinions, etc. [were] dreadful walls to a burning SOUL wild as mine."[76] But those walls, freely entered, never really confined her. Her soul was more like the flag of her free country, whipping in the breeze. It was essentially a free soul, for truth had made it free; while firmly lashed to the pole of standard religious rules, it moved freely in the winds of the Spirit— the ardors, the enthusiasms, the spontaneous prayers and acts of devotion. Simon Bruté understood, because his own soul was so similar, and he gave Elizabeth's the space and air it needed. He even blew upon it with his own flashing, almost at times incoherent, spiritual cries and aspirations, then watched with satisfaction as it responded into leaping, straining life.

Elizabeth's joy in Bruté's understanding was unbounded: "Blessed G., I am so in love now with the rules", she exulted, "that I see the bit of the bridle all gold, and the *reins* all of silk. You know my sincerity, since with the little attraction to your Brother's [Dubois] government, I ever eagerly seek the grace [of the] cords he entangles me with."[77]

Over all was Elizabeth's whole-souled love of the Church: "All that I possess: *my beloved Faith*" and its "*mysteries of love*".[78] She set her calendar by its feast days, reveling in their beauty and feeding on their holiness:

---

[76] 7.193, Elizabeth Seton to Rev. Simon Bruté, P.S.S., [November 1818], in *CW*, 2:594.

[77] 6.146, Elizabeth Seton to Rev. Simon Bruté, P.S.S., n.d., in *CW*, 2:259.

[78] 7.175, Elizabeth Seton to Antonio Filicchi, August 8, 1818, in *CW*, 2:573; 7.66, Elizabeth Seton to Rev. Simon Bruté, P.S.S., [December 26, 1816], in *CW*, 2:454.

"Rogation days—the full cry of His whole Church!!!"[79] she once noted ardently, and again: "I *steal* [away] to say [the] litany of saints *for intention of the Church*, this blessed Ember Day."[80] The Church has responded in kind, as Pope Paul VI declared "before the holy Catholic Church, before our other Christian brethren in the world, before the entire American people, and before all humanity. Elizabeth Ann Bayley Seton is a Saint!... The Church has exulted with admiration and joy, and has today heard her own charism of truth poured out in the exclamation that we send up to God and announce to the world: She is a Saint!"[81]

[79] 6.195, Elizabeth Seton to Rev. Simon Bruté, P.S.S., Journal 1815, entry of Sunday, in *CW*, 2:322.

[80] Ibid., entry of Friday, 325. After Vatican II, before the reform of the liturgy under Paul VI, the three days preceding Ascension Thursday were set aside as days of special prayer and were called rogation days (from the Latin *rogare*, to ask). Ember days of prayer and penance occurred four times a year.

[81] Paul VI, *AASCO*.

.

9

"The Embrace of Him Who Is Love"

Death is still the greatest mystery of life, and it *is* a part of life, the most important part, its ending, its summing up, the irrevocable record of its success or failure. It quite naturally has a fascination for the living because of its very mystery. For the same reason, it creates uneasiness ranging from wonder to terror. Faith enables the believer to penetrate the mystery in an essential way, but even faith cannot—or, in a sense, should not—dispel human apprehension.

"My grace is sufficient for you", Jesus admonished Saint Paul,[1] and indeed His grace, so lovingly and lavishly given, transforms the worst aspects of death for those who love God. It bestows its comforts in many ways. The waning of physical strength and weariness engendered by long years makes the thought of eternal rest in the Lord something to anticipate. Mother Seton felt this when she gently chided a former pupil: "I know your uneasiness for me, but that should not be ... why uneasy at the fulfillment of the merciful designs of so dear a Providence who left me to take care of my *Bec*, to bring Jos to an age to take care of herself, and our dearest Boys to enter the way of life they were to choose.... What would you have, darling? Why be anxious if your poor, tired friend goes

---

[1] 2 Cor 12:9.

to rest?—I HOPE!"[2] There is a similar thought among her notes for instructions and conferences to the Sisters: "Consider a good Death as a call to the wedding feast of the Lamb—St. Gregory says it will not be a Dinner banquet, *but a supper*, to be followed by *ETERNAL REST*."[3] These last words in capitals are also underlined three times!

Nor is it unfounded to observe that the fear of death decreases in God's servants with the deepening of their love for Him over the years. A few privileged souls who have outdistanced all others in probing God's love and responding to it *yearn* for glorious eternal union with Him. Elizabeth Seton was such a one. The saintly bishop John Cheverus knew whereof he spoke when he told her, "I envy you, running now to the embrace of Him who is love."[4] And she herself called death "this dear, dearest thief who is to come when least expected".[5]

From earliest childhood, Elizabeth's precocious piety softened the face of death for her. She recalled that at the age of four "they asked me: did I not cry when little Kitty was dead? No, because Kitty is [*sic*] gone up to heaven. I wish I could go, too, with Mama."[6] It is significant that the psalm she learned in childhood became her lifelong "favorite": "The Lord is my Shepherd, the Lord ruleth me.... Though I walk in the midst of the shadow of Death, I will fear no evil, for thou art with me."[7] It was only in more mature years, with the comprehension of sin and its punishment, that the element of fear entered her

---

[2] 7.176, Elizabeth Seton to Ellen Wiseman, August 20, 1818, in *CW*, 2:574.

[3] 9.20, Exercise of the *Presence of God*, n.d., "Meditations on Death", in *CW*, 3a:419.

[4] Bishop John Cheverus to Elizabeth Seton, August 11, 1818, AMSV, 100-115-1-17; transferred 2022-EAS-2-46 to APSL.

[5] 7.175, Elizabeth Seton to Antonio Filicchi, August 8, 1818, in *CW*, 2:573.

[6] 10.4, *Dear Remembrances*, n.d., in *CW*, 3a:510.

[7] Ibid. See Ps 23.

soul, but it was a healthy, life-giving fear, except in the first awkward days of dawning holiness, for she knew it could be banished with sorrow, absolution, penance, and trust in her loving God.

Elizabeth had this fear all her life for loved ones, for her family and friends. The most poignant expression of her constant, nagging concern is in a letter to Julia Scott describing the deathbed of Elizabeth's sister-in-law Eliza Seton Maitland. "Julia, my precious friend, this dear Eliza did not love the world", she wrote in pity.

> She had a bitter portion in it; and you would say a life passed in the slavery of poverty and secluded from those allurements which commonly endear us to the present scene would have ensured her at least a peaceful Death. Some Nights before her last, in an interval of ease, she conversed with me and observed herself that such had been her situation, but added: "How is it, that until we are just going, we never think of the necessary dispositions to meet Death?" I made some consolatory reflections to her; but, although she said but little on the subject during her Illness ... her Fears and dread continued to the last.

Then a great cry:

> Oh, Julia, Julia, Julia! "The last, last, last sad Silence." The soul departing without Hope. Its views, its interests centered in a World it is hurried from. No Father's sheltering arms, no Heavenly Home of Joy. My Julia, Julia, Julia! Eternity—a word of transport, or of Agony. Your Friend, your own, your true, your dear Friend begs you, supplicates you, in the Name of GOD—think of IT! Oh, if she should see your precious Soul torn, dragged, an unwilling Victim—what a thought of horror![8]

---

[8] 4.33, Elizabeth Seton to Julia Scott, April 10, 1807, in *CW*, 1:435.

It had long been commonplace for anyone who was sick or dying to send for Elizabeth to nurse them. Her most precious deathbed of all, her husband's, had raised this corporal work of mercy to a ministry of *charity undertaken out of love*. "When I thank God for my 'Creation and preservation,' it is with a warm [*sic,* warmth] of feeling I never could know until now—to wait on him [in] my W[illiam's] *Soul and Body*," she had written exaltedly in the lazaretto,

> to console and soothe those hours of affliction and pain, weariness and watching which, next to God, I alone could do—to strike up the cheerful notes of Hope and Christian triumph, which from his partial love he hears with the more enjoyment from me, because to me he attributes the greatest share of them—to hear him, in pronouncing the Name of his Redeemer, declare that I first taught him the sweetness of the sound—oh, if I was in the dungeon of this Lazaretto, I should bless and Praise my God for these days of retirement and abstraction from the world, which have afforded leisure and opportunity for so blessed a work.[9]

In Elizabeth's new consecrated life of service in the Church, her perception of assisting the dying as a sacred ministry reached heights that were at the same time intimate and exalted. Despite the human grief and emotional suffering she endured in the long illnesses and wrenching deaths of her beloved daughters, there was the joy of inner peace, the reward of her own ever-deepening understanding and holiness. Of Annina's last anointing she wrote with true joy: "Her desire for the Holy Oil seemed almost

---

[9] 2.7, Elizabeth Seton to Rebecca Seton, November 19, 1803, entry of December 13, in *CW*, 1:270.

to disturb her, but our dearest was so good as to hasten our wish."[10] *Our* wish. Much of the joy was in the holy union forged by the mother and eagerly embraced by the pliant child. "The Rev[eren]d Sup[erio]r [John Dubois] arrived. What a moment for her! He must wait for a book, and she kept her eyes on a crucifix when the pouring sweat and agony of pain would permit. When it came, she presented her hands the moment they were wanted [to be anointed], with such a look of joy!!! Oh, happy, happy Mother in that hour and moment!"[11] To Eliza Craig Sadler, she confided her satisfaction in seeing Annina "receive the last Sacraments with my Sentiments of them".[12]

The afternoon before Rebecca's death, the young woman told her mother, "I have been just handing my Lord my little cup, for He will come for me—it is just full."[13] She referred, of course, to the cup of suffering that Jesus had asked James and John to drink; however, there is also a truly charming echo and consequence of what Elizabeth had told the child's dying father years before: "When you awake in that world, you will find nothing could tempt you to return to this. You will see that your care over your wife and little ones was like a hand only, to hold the cup, which God himself will give if He takes you."[14] That blessed cup of his daughter, held by him and handed over to God, was now full.

"The Superior" (Dubois) came "and seeing the pitiful situation of the poor darling, kindly offered to stay, and her

[10] A-6.99a, Elizabeth Seton's Journal of Annina's Last Illness and Death, [January–March 1812], entry of February 22, in *CW*, 2:753.

[11] Ibid., first, second, and third brackets in published version.

[12] 6.97, Elizabeth Seton to Eliza Sadler, February 13, 1812, in *CW*, 2:210.

[13] 7.58, Journal of Rebecca's Illness, 1816, May 8, 1816, entry of November 2, in *CW*, 2:440.

[14] 2.7, Journal to Rebecca Seton, November 19, 1803, entry of November 24, in *CW*, 1:258.

gratitude was inexpressible",[15] Elizabeth continued in her journal:

> At last near 10 in the morning, she said, "Let me sit once more on the bed; it will be the last struggle"—Cecil[ia O'Conway] beside her Mother's arms lifting her, she sank between US. The darling head fell on the well-known heart it loved so well.[16]

Father Dubois gave final witness to the scene: "The Mother is a miracle of divine favor. Night and day by the child, her health has not appeared to suffer. She held the child in her arms without dropping a tear all the time of her agony and even eight minutes after she had died. *Mulierem fortem* [a strong woman]."[17] There can be no denying the remembrance of the *Pieta*, in soul and even physical imitation, of the mother with both her darling daughters.

The deathbeds of Mother Seton's spiritual daughters, Sisters of Charity, each attended by her, brought her a similar spiritual happiness. She wrote a reflection on the death of Sister Maria Murphy Burke, who had brooked the disapproval of her own mother in joining the Sisterhood at Emmitsburg. The young Sister was overcome with joy at the approach of her Lord in Viaticum: "What delight for poor Mother to have been, and to be still, her *Mother*—the natural one was *present*, but the spiritual one, who had all her dear little Secrets of the Soul, was the dearest."[18] Bruté rejoiced with her: "O happy

---

[15] 7.58, Journal of Rebecca's Illness, 1816, May 8, 1816, entry of October 31, in *CW*, 2:439.

[16] Ibid., entry of November 2, 440–41, brackets in published version.

[17] Annabelle M. Melville, *Elizabeth Bayley Seton 1774–1821*, ed. Betty Ann McNeil, D.C. (Hanover, Pa.: The Sheridan Press, 2009), 329. Cf. Prov 31:10–31.

[18] 11.8, "Well now our Dearest ...", in *CW*, 3b:7.

Mother! Already three of your dear daughters in heaven, not counting the first two, the tender sisters whom your example has already led there. Give, give thanks, and redouble your zeal to follow these celestial souls."[19]

Death indeed came early and frequently to the young community, and the young in years were its special victims. The lines of tombstones with the inscribed ages— eighteen, nineteen, twenty—still stand in the *little sacred woods* as evidence of those sad and difficult first years in Saint Joseph's Valley.

Elizabeth and her Sisters faced the inevitable reality with faith and love. She formed them in faith, and they followed readily and gladly along heroic paths. "*Death in desire* has many advantages", she told them.[20] "1st, it is very agreeable to God, because by it we submit ourselves to Him as His creatures and offer ourselves a voluntary victim to His power and Majesty. 2nd, it is very useful to ourselves, because it teaches us to die by degrees; it habituates us to the acts of virtue we would wish to make at Death, and to do beforehand what we would then desire to do."[21] How quickly Mother Seton got down to hard tacks! The practical always caught her attention and preference:

> 3rd, those who are not in this practice are in danger of dying like animals, because the pain of the body so weighs down the mind that it can scarcely think of anything—but when we are versed in the art of dying, whatever the pains of the Body may be, the soul will still be able to produce those acts which it has been long accustomed to form, or should it be so oppressed and stupefied as to be incapable

of any exertion, what comfort then to have done repeat-
edly and in full consciousness what its present condition
makes so difficult, or perhaps impossible.[22]

Surely, Elizabeth's mind went back over the years
to the deathbeds of family and friends and the uneasiness they had brought her: Eliza Seton Maitland's asking, "How is it, that until we are just going, we never
think of the necessary dispositions to meet Death?"[23];
friend Catherine Cooper, "Dying in the most melancholy manner, unconscious of the change she is making
of this world for the next"[24]; and, in writing to Amabilia
Filicchi about her "soul's sister", Rebecca Seton: "How
many looks of silent distress have we exchanged about
the last passage, this exchange of time for Eternity! To
be sure, her uncommon piety and innocence and sweet
confidence in God are my full consolation; but I mean to
say that a departing soul has so many trials and temptations that, for my part, I go through a sort of agony never
to be described—even while, [trying] to keep up their
hope and courage, I appear to them most cheerful."[25]
Elizabeth "could not ... help the strong comparison of
a sick and dying bed in your happy Country, where the
poor sufferer is soothed and strengthened at once by
every help of religion; where the one you call Father of
your Soul attends and watches it in the weakness and trials of parting nature with the same care you and I watch
our little infant's body in its first struggles and wants on
its entrance into life."[26]

[22] Ibid.

[23] 4.33, Elizabeth Seton to Julia Scott, April 10, 1807, in *CW*, 1:435.

[24] 1.11, Elizabeth Seton to Eliza Sadler, June 18, 1797, in *CW*, 1:15.

[25] 3.31, Journal to Amabilia Filicchi, July 19, 1804, in *CW*, 1:367.

[26] Ibid.

There was, of course, a desire for death that was wrong, Elizabeth warned her Sisters: "We often wish for Death that we may be delivered from an unhappy life, and this desire is not good. We should never wish to get rid of our life because it is an unhappy one, or full of pains and trials; on the contrary, if there was not other evil in it, we should cherish and preserve it all in our power, since the more pains and trials we have in it, the greater sacrifices we may make to God, and the more we may prove our love to him."[27] That being said, "Consider that it is a great grace not to be afraid of Death", Elizabeth assured them, "and it is a great perfection to desire it with a well-regulated desire according to God—for what virtue can the Soul possess that is not contained in the desire of Death? It possess[es] *Humility*, since it is ready to receive all the humiliations of Death, to return to dust and corruption. It possess[es] *Poverty*, since it is ready to quit all that the world contains, and *Chastity*, since it turns from all [the world's] joys and pleasures—Go over every virtue separately; you will find that the desire of Death includes them all."[28]

Elizabeth could not fail to advance the most personal and intimate motive of all for consecrated souls: "Consider Death also as the coming of the heavenly spouse, as is said in the parable of the Virgins to whom He came by surprise at Midnight—oh, how blessed His coming to those happy ones who were waiting for Him with a holy impatience."[29]

Elizabeth's own holy impatience is evident in the fervor and emphases of her writing. "Come then, O Death!" she breaks forth at one point, "that I may no more offend

[27] 9.20, Exercise of the *Presence of God*, n.d., "Meditation on the desire of Death", in *CW*, 3a:415.

[28] Ibid., first and second brackets in published version.

[29] Ibid., "Meditations on Death", 418–19.

my God, no more oppose *His Will*—come, take my Soul, deliver it from this wretched frailty which makes it fall so often, and for what is in itself nothing—Come, *I do desire* YOU, *desire you* with my whole heart."[30]

When Elizabeth's time of yearning was over, when her own turn came, she was gloriously ready. It was anticipated two years before the event with a sudden decline of her physical powers. She was indeed ready, even straining forward. "Not even little acts for obtaining fear or anxiety about this Death", she admitted blithely to Bruté, "can move that stronghold of peace, thanksgiving, and abandon of every atom of life and its belonging to Him—even William I can see but in the great Whole", she continued, surely with some amusement over past agonies for the cherished son and perhaps surprise at this newfound peace in God, however proven before—"cannot cry, even for edification and duty"—this is a spirit of mischief certainly.[31] "You laugh. What [a] life indeed! A grey-headed carpenter whistling over the plank he measures for [Sister] Ellen [Brady]'s coffin—just beyond, the ground plowing to plant *potatoes*, just beyond again, good *Jo* (I believe) making the pit to plant Ellen for her glorious Resurrection— beautiful life, the whole delight *in God*. Oh, what relish in *that word!*"[32]

That ineffable word was the source of Elizabeth's happy contentment. "Nothing in our state of clouds and Veils I can see so plainly as how the saints died of love and joy," she told Bruté, "since I so wretched and truly miserable can only read word after word of the blessed 83rd [now, Ps 84] and 41st [now, Ps 42] Psalms in unutterable

[30] Ibid., "Meditation on the desire of Death", 416.
[31] 7.156, Elizabeth Seton to Rev. Simon Bruté, P.S.S., April 21, 1818, in *CW*, 2:549.
[32] Ibid., 549–50.

feelings ever to Our God through the thousand pressings and overflowings—God—God—God—that the Supreme delight, that He is God, and to open the mouth and heart wide that He may fill it."[33]

Elizabeth's friends far and wide were alerted. Their response is positive testimony not only to her exceptional readiness but also to the proper face all God's sons and daughters should put upon what is, after all, His coming to welcome them to eternal bliss. As she put it simply to Bruté, "We talk now all day long of my Death and how it will be just like the rest of the housework."[34] And that was a fair description of the way her friends took it too, even her Protestant brother-in-law Dr. Wright Post, who wrote,

> Perhaps you have conceived your situation more critical than it really is.... It may yet please God to restore you to that usefulness which has always marked the sphere in which you moved. That this may be His Will is my most fervent prayer. But should it be otherwise, should He in His wise and mysterious Providence deem it proper to remove you from this world of care and disquietude, what shall I say, my dear Sister? Nothing. Nothing is necessary to a mind already familiarized to the prospect of a change which sooner or later must be realized, and which is so well disciplined in the way which leads to that place of blessedness where the anxieties of this life cease from troubling, and the weary are at rest.[35]

[33] 7.286, Elizabeth Seton to Rev. Simon Bruté, P.S.S., n.d., in *CW*, 2:684. Psalm 84 and Psalm 42 in the contemporary Catholic Bible were formerly numbered Psalm 83 and Psalm 41 in the King James version used by the Protestant Episcopal Church early in the nineteenth century. Both psalms are prayers of longing for God.

[34] 7.170, Elizabeth Seton to Rev. Simon Bruté, P.S.S., July 2, 1818, in *CW*, 2:567.

[35] Dr. Wright Post to Elizabeth Seton, August 11, 1818, Saint Elizabeth Ann Seton, 1-3-3-11:25, APSL.

He quite rightly, too, refused to keep the news of Elizabeth's decline from her sister, his wife.

Rev. Pierre Babade wrote in a very matter-of-fact way, foreign to his reputation for sighs and tears: "Ten years are passed; your work is consolidated. I desire nothing more for you but a happy death.... I would like very much to see you before you die, but I foresee that the Superior will not allow me to go to Emmitsburg in the present state of things.... As soon as I hear of your death I will say Mass for the repose of your dear soul.... If you find mercy, as I hope you will, do not forget above this one who has thought so much of you here below."[36] Bishop Cheverus wrote as simply, but his own sanctity is in the few words: "I do not pity you. I envy your situation, running now to the embrace of Him who is love.... You are most frequently remembered at the altar and will be so long as I shall celebrate the Holy Mysteries. Pray for me here and in heaven."[37]

Elizabeth herself told Antonio Filicchi the news in her most casual vein but with the mixture of intimate banter and serious spiritual friendship that characterizes all her letters to him. "It is rather suspected that I, your poor little sister, am about to go and meet your Filippo," she began, "but nothing of health can be certain and calculated at my age, 45. I may recover and crack nuts yet with my nose and chin, as they say; *I know not.* All I know is that we must all be ready for this dear, dearest thief who is to come when least expected. I go almost every day to Communion (as my good confessor and Superior [John Dubois] says, *through condescension to my weakness*)"—she could never resist the

[36] Rev. Pierre Babade to Elizabeth Seton, July 12, 1818, Saint Elizabeth Ann Seton, 1-3-3-1(71), APSL.

[37] Bishop John Cheverus to Elizabeth Seton, August 11, 1818, AMSV, 100-115-1-17; transferred 2022-EAS-2-46 to APSL.

native mischievousness raised in her by the solemn Father Dubois—"so if you good people are not very good over the water [Atlantic Ocean], it is no fault of my prayers; and I hope I shall not be forgotten in yours, *to which* I so well owe all that I possess: *my beloved Faith.*"[38]

The quiet ecstasy of Elizabeth's soul was reserved, of course, for her director. "Mind not my health", she chaffed Simon Bruté.[39]

> Death grins broader in the pot every morning [when she saw her reflection as she washed], and I grin at him and I show him his Master. Oh, be blessed, blessed, blessed. I see nothing in this world but blue skies and *our* altars. All the rest is so plainly not to be looked at, but all left to Him, with tears only for Sin. We talk now all day long of my Death and how it will be just like the rest of the housework. What is it else? What came in the world for? Why in it so long? But this last great Eternal end—it seems to me so simple, when I look up at the crucifix simpler still; so that I went to sleep before I made any thanksgiving but *Te Deum* and *Magnificat* after Communion....
>
> This morning, our *adored harp* pressed close on the aching breast, *we* swept every sacred chord of praise and thanksgiving. Then, weeping under the willows of that horrid Babylon whose waters are drunk so greedily while our heavenly streams pass by unheeded, the silent harp is pressed closer and closer. G[abriel], *"blessed"*, mind not my follies. I see the everlasting hills so near and the door of my Eternity so wide open that I turn too wild sometimes.[40]

[38] 7.175, Elizabeth Seton to Antonio Filicchi, August 8, 1818, in *CW*, 2:573, first brackets in published version. Filippo Filicchi had died in 1816.

[39] 7.170, Elizabeth Seton to Rev. Simon Bruté, P.S.S., July 2, 1818, in *CW*, 2:566.

[40] Ibid., 566–67; 7.208, Elizabeth Seton to Rev. Simon Bruté, P.S.S., [Spring 1819], in *CW*, 2:606.

Elizabeth's same wondrous understanding of death, the same longing, lasted the two years remaining that God ordained for her. Acknowledging the arrival of Father John Hickey's most recent letter, five months before the end, Elizabeth wrote,

> Poor, good, dying Sister Jane [Frances Gartland] was present, and I let her share the Kiss of Peace, which she did with starting tears, feeling so well her condition to be hopeless in the senseless language of this world. Oh, my father, friend, could I hear my last stage of cough and feel my last stage of pain in the tearing away [of] my prison walls, how would I bear my joy? [The] thought of *going home*, called and by *His Will*—what a transport! But they say: "Don't you fear to die?" Such a sinner must fear, but I fear much more to live and know as I do: that every evening examen finds my account but lengthened and enlarged—I don't fear Death half as much as my hateful, vile self."[41]

In one of the long night watches, Elizabeth talked with Sister Cecilia O'Conway, one of her faithful nurses, of "departed friends, present suffering compared to the suffering of Purgatory, of souls dying in misery without Sacraments".[42] Suddenly she began to cry. "I am ashamed to complain when I remember those dear ones who have gone", she sobbed. "What agonies they must have suffered;—their poor bleeding bones! That sweet, lovely Rebecca that I told you of, though not a Catholic, suffered such bitter pains with such happy dispositions."[43]

---

[41] 7.252, Elizabeth Seton to Rev. John Hickey, P.S.S., [July 2, 1820], in *CW*, 2:659, first brackets in published version.

[42] [Sister Loyola Law, D.C., ed.], *Mother Seton: Notes by Rev. Simon Gabriel Bruté*, "Different words and short conversations with dearest Mother during her illness", n.d. (Emmitsburg, Md.: Daughters of Charity, 1884), 40.

[43] Ibid.

Kissing Elizabeth's hand, Cecilia said soothingly, "O my soul's mother! Our Lord, who knows your desires, perhaps will realize your wish of suffering a long time on this bed of sickness. O may He grant you your Purgatory in this life that in death you may fly to His bosom of peace, and rest!"[44]

"My blessed GOD," protested the dying Mother, raising her eyes to heaven, "how far from that thought am I, of going straight to Heaven,—such a miserable creature as I am!"[45] It was a protest from the depths of her heart, for, Bruté had witnessed, "a soul who felt so sacredly, with such light, the holiness of her God, had no doubt of Purgatory, had no presumption that it would not be for her".[46]

It was surely fitting for this humble, loving soul to receive, even on this side of the grave, what very few others receive: a clean bill of spiritual health. "My good Mother, your poor physician of the soul does not see you much, as he does not wish to fatigue you", read the note that Bruté handed Elizabeth.[47]

He has no cause to fear, knowing that the heavenly Physician, the Beloved, the Spouse, the Only Desire of your heart, is continually present: present in the love, confidence, abandon, which He inspires, abandon the most tender and most unreserved—present in the continual acts of penance, humility, dependence and resignation to suffer everything in union with Him, with His cross— present in the peace, the tranquil joy which He imparts; in the total disengagement which He teaches; in the grace of every moment, pain or comfort which He dispenses.[48]

[44] Ibid., 40–41.
[45] Ibid., 41.
[46] Bruté, *Memoir*, Saint Elizabeth Ann Seton, 1-3-3-12(9), APSL.
[47] Rev. Simon Bruté, P.S.S., Reflection, "My dear Mother," October 2, 1820, Saint Elizabeth Ann Seton, 1-3-3-12(17), APSL.
[48] Bruté, *Memoir*, 12, Saint Elizabeth Ann Seton, 1-3-3-12(9), APSL.

After Elizabeth's death, Bruté's apostolic spirit struggled to express what would forever remain inexpressible: "Her magnanimous faith on her deathbed! My Lord, I have seen it, felt it. Express it I cannot.... I suffer immensely in not being able to do so, for it would be a source of so much Edification if it could be communicated such as I FELT IT."[49]

---

[49] Ibid., 1-3-3-12(2), APSL. Cf. [Law], *Mother Seton: Notes*, 72.

GLOSSARY OF PERSONS

Several of these persons are not mentioned in the text of this book, but their inclusion is useful for background information.

BABADE, REV. PIERRE: A Sulpician priest at Saint Mary's Seminary who befriended Elizabeth Seton; she chose him for her confessor and spiritual advisor in Baltimore.

BARIGAZZI, REV. NICÓLA: Brother of Amabilia Filicchi; the Catholic priest who presided at a family wedding while Elizabeth Seton was staying with the Filicchi in Livorno.

BAYLEY, CATHERINE CHARLTON: First wife of Dr. Richard Bayley and the mother of his older children, Mary Magdalen, Elizabeth Ann, and Catherine (Kitty) Charlton Bayley.

BAYLEY, CATHERINE (*KITTY*) CHARLTON: Elizabeth Seton's younger sister Kitty, who died at about eighteen months of age in October 1778.

BAYLEY, CHARLOTTE AMELIA BARCLAY: Stepmother of Elizabeth Seton, second wife of Dr. Richard Bayley, and the mother of his seven youngest children.

BAYLEY, DR. RICHARD: Father of Elizabeth Seton and a prominent physician dedicated to medical research.

BAYLEY, SARAH PELL: Wife of Elizabeth Seton's paternal uncle, William LeConte Bayley, of Pelham Manor, New Rochelle, where Elizabeth and her sister stayed twice when their father was in London for several years of medical studies.

BAYLEY, WILLIAM LeCONTE: Paternal uncle of Elizabeth Ann Bayley, of Pelham Manor, New Rochelle, where Elizabeth and her sister stayed twice when their father was in London for several years of medical studies.

BERNARDIN, CARDINAL JOSEPH: Archbishop of Cincinnati and president of the American National Conference of Catholic Bishops at the time of the Seton canonization, September 14, 1975.

BONAPARTE, JEROME NAPOLEON: Son of Elizabeth Patterson of Baltimore and Jerome Bonaparte, the youngest brother to Napoleon; Elizabeth Seton befriended Jerome when he attended Mount Saint Mary's College.

BRUTÉ, REV. SIMON GABRIEL: A French missionary who joined the Sulpicians in France (1808–1824) and became the spiritual director of Elizabeth Seton and chaplain to the Sisters of Charity of St. Joseph's, Emmitsburg.

CARROLL, ARCHBISHOP JOHN: A native of Maryland, the first Catholic bishop of Baltimore, the premier see in the United States, with whom Elizabeth Seton corresponded as her spiritual father, turning to him for advice and direction.

CHEVERUS, REV. JOHN: A priest from France who befriended and advised Elizabeth Seton before and after her conversion. He became the first bishop of Boston.

CLARK, SISTER MARY XAVIER: A native of Saint-Domingue and a widow who joined Mother Seton at Emmitsburg. She became her assistant and Directress of Novices.

COOPER, REV. SAMUEL SUTHERLAND: A former sea captain and convert to Catholicism who, as a significant benefactor of

Mother Seton and the Sisters of Charity, donated funds to purchase more than two hundred acres near Emmitsburg, Maryland, where Elizabeth Seton founded the Sisters of Charity of St. Joseph's.

DUBOIS, REV. JOHN: A priest from France, Dubois joined the Sulpicians in Baltimore (1808–1824); founded Mount Saint Mary's, Emmitsburg; and became the third superior of the Sisters of Charity of St. Joseph's. Dubois translated the French rule and, in consultation with Mother Seton, adapted the *Common Rules of the Daughters of Charity* to meet the needs of the Church in America. He was with Elizabeth Seton at her death.

DUBOURG, REV. WILLIAM: The Sulpician priest, founder, and president of Saint Mary's College who invited Elizabeth Seton to Baltimore, which led to the establishment of the first native apostolic community in the United States (1809). Dubourg was the first superior for a brief period.

DUPLEIX, CATHERINE (DUÉ) MANN: A devoted friend who gave Elizabeth Seton a christening dress from Ireland for Kit's Baptism in 1800.

EGAN, REV. MICHAEL DU BURGO: A student at Mount Saint Mary's while his sister, Mary Egan, was a pupil at Saint Joseph School. Their paternal uncle was Michael Egan, O.F.M., the first bishop of Philadelphia.

FARQUHAR, ELIZA (ZIDE): Daughter of Elizabeth Curzon Farquhar and a first cousin to the Seton children. Zide was nine years older than Anna Maria (Annina) Seton.

FILICCHI, AMABILIA BARIGAZZI: Wife of Antonio Filicchi of Livorno and a gracious hostess to Elizabeth Seton and her daughter Anna Maria during their stay in Tuscany until they returned to New York in the spring of 1804.

SAINT ELIZABETH ANN SETON

FILICCHI, ANTONIO: Husband of Amabilia Barigazzi and long-time friend of William Magee Seton, who previously had apprenticed at the F. & A. Filicchi Company of Livorno.

FILICCHI, FILIPPO (PHILLIPO): Older brother of Antonio Filicchi. The brothers introduced Elizabeth Seton to Catholic doctrine and devotions. Filippo lived in Pisa and challenged her to "inquire and pray" about matters of faith.

FILICCHI, MARY COWPER: Wife of Filippo Filicchi of Pisa, who befriended the Setons in Tuscany and was a native of New York City and a convert to Catholicism.

HOBART, REV. JOHN HENRY: Assistant minister, then pastor, at Trinity Church in December 1800–1803 and Elizabeth Seton's spiritual director until 1805. Hobart bitterly opposed her conversion to Roman Catholicism.

MAITLAND, ELIZA SETON: The daughter of William Francis and Anna Maria Curzon; the oldest half sister of William Magee Seton and the wife of James Maitland, whose family had business interests in Seton, Maitland & Co.

MATIGNON, REV. FRANCIS: A French priest serving in Boston and a trusted advisor of Elizabeth Seton, who foresaw that she would do much good and contribute to the growth of the Catholic faith in the United States.

MONTINI, POPE PAUL VI: Saint Paul VI canonized Saint Elizabeth Ann Seton on September 14, 1975.

NAGOT, REV. CHARLES-FRANÇOIS: The first superior of the Society of Saint-Sulpice in North America, whom Elizabeth Seton met in Baltimore.

O'CONWAY, SISTER CECILIA: The first candidate to join Elizabeth Seton in Baltimore and the first Sister of Charity in America.

O'CONWAY, MATTHIAS: A friend of Elizabeth Seton and a benefactor who was also the father of Sister Cecilia O'Conway and a parent who sent his daughters to Saint Joseph School.

POST, DR. WRIGHT: A physician who married Elizabeth Seton's sister Mary Magdalen Bayley.

POST, MARY MAGDALEN BAYLEY: Older sister of Elizabeth Seton and wife of Dr. Wright Post.

RONCALLI, POPE JOHN XXIII: Saint John XXIII presided at the beatification of Elizabeth Ann Seton on March 17, 1963.

SADLER, ELIZA (SAD) CRAIG: Devoted friend of Elizabeth Seton and a member of the Society for the Relief of Poor Widows with Small Children.

SCOTT, JULIANA (JULIA) SITGREAVES: Devoted, lifelong friend and benefactor of Elizabeth Seton.

SETON, ANNA MARIA (ANNINA): Oldest daughter of Elizabeth Ann Bayley and William Magee Seton, who was called Annina (little Ann) by the Filicchi and who died of tuberculosis at age sixteen.

SETON, CATHERINE (KIT) (JOSEPHINE) CHARLTON: Fourth child of Elizabeth Ann Bayley and William Magee Seton, who was present when her mother died. At midlife, Kit joined the Sisters of Mercy of New York and did prison ministry until her death at ninety-one.

SETON, ELIZABETH ANN (BETSY) BAYLEY: Daughter of Catherine Charlton and Richard Bayley, Elizabeth Ann Bayley Seton is the first native-born North American to be declared a saint by the Catholic Church.

SETON, REBECCA MARY: Daughter of William Francis and Anna Maria Curzon Seton and a half sister to William Magee Seton.

Rebecca became a dear friend and confidante of Elizabeth Seton. She died weeks after Elizabeth returned to New York as a widow.

SETON, REBECCA (*BEC*) MARY: Youngest child of Elizabeth Ann Bayley and William Magee Seton, who died of tuberculosis at age fourteen. Named after her paternal aunt of the same name.

SETON, RICHARD BAYLEY: Third child of Elizabeth Ann Bayley and William Magee Seton, who died at the port of Liberia at age twenty-three.

SETON, WILLIAM: Second child of Elizabeth Ann Bayley and William Magee Seton and a retired lieutenant of the U.S. Navy, who died in New York at age seventy-one.

SETON, WILLIAM FRANCIS: A native of Scotland and father of William Magee Seton, who esteemed his daughter-in-law, Elizabeth Seton, as if she were his daughter.

SETON, WILLIAM MAGEE: The firstborn of William Francis Seton and his first wife, Rebecca Curzon, and husband of Elizabeth Ann Bayley.

TESSIER, REV. JEAN M.: Superior of the Society of Saint-Sulpice in the United States, who approved the Rule of the Sisters of Charity of St. Joseph's and submitted it to Archbishop Carroll for his approval in 1812.

TISSERANT, REV. JEAN: A French itinerant priest whose counsel Elizabeth Seton valued highly in New York after she became Catholic.

WEIS, GEORGE: A resident of Baltimore who built the house in which Elizabeth Seton lived on Paca Street and who corresponded with her after she moved to Emmitsburg.

WHITE, SISTER ROSE LANDRY: A young widow who joined Elizabeth Seton in Baltimore, became her assistant, and was sent to Philadelphia to initiate the first ministry of the Sisters of Charity beyond Emmitsburg. She succeeded Elizabeth Seton as Mother of the Sisters of Charity of St. Joseph's.

WRIGHT, CARDINAL JOHN: As prefect of the Congregation for the Clergy, Cardinal Wright was the highest-ranking American at the Vatican Curia at the time of the Seton canonization, September 14, 1975.

BIBLIOGRAPHY

Many of these sources are not cited or quoted in the text of this book, but they are useful for background information.

Abelly, Louis. *The Life of the Venerable Servant of God Vincent de Paul.* Edited by John Rybolt, C.M. Translated by William Quinn, F.S.C. 3 vols. New York: New City Press, 1993. Available from DePaul University, Chicago: https://via .library.depaul.edu/abelly/.

Bechtle, Regina, S.C., and Judith Metz, S.C., eds., and Ellin M. Kelly, mss. ed. *Elizabeth Bayley Seton Collected Writings.* 3 vols. New York: New City Press, 2000–2006. Available from DePaul University, Chicago: https://via.library .depaul.edu/seton_lcd/.

Coste, Pierre, C.M., *The Life & Works of St. Vincent de Paul.* 3 vols. New York: New City Press, 1987. Available from DePaul University, Chicago: https://via.library.depaul .edu/coste_engbio/.

Cummings, Kathleen Sprows. *A Saint of Our Own.* Chapel Hill: The University of North Carolina Press, 2019.

Dirvin, Joseph I., C.M. *Mrs. Seton, Foundress of the American Sisters of Charity.* New York: Farrar, Straus, and Giroux, 1975.

Flannery, Austin, O.P., gen. ed. *Vatican Council II, the Conciliar and Post Conciliar Documents.* Collegeville, Minn.: Liturgical Press, 1975.

Flinton, Margaret, D.C. *Louise de Marillac: Social Aspect of Her Work.* Translated by Margaret Flinton, D.C. New York: New City Press, 1992.

Kelly, Ellin M., ed. *Elizabeth Seton's Two Bibles: Her Notes and Markings.* Huntington, Ind.: Our Sunday Visitor, 1977.

Kelly, Ellin M., ed. *Numerous Choirs: A Chronicle of Elizabeth Bayley Seton and Her Spiritual Daughters. Volume I: The Seton Years 1774–1821.* Evansville, Ind.: Daughters of Charity, Mater Dei Provincialate, 1981.

Kelly, Ellin M. and Annabelle Melville, eds. *Elizabeth Seton: Selected Writings.* New York: Paulist Press, 1987.

Laverty, Rose Maria, S.C. *Loom of Many Threads: The English and French Influences on the Character of Elizabeth Ann Bayley Seton.* New York: Paulist Press, 1958.

[Law, Sister Loyola, D.C. ed.], *Mother Seton: Notes by Rev. Simon Gabriel Bruté.* Emmitsburg, Md.: Daughters of Charity, 1884.

McNeil, Betty Ann, D.C. "Elizabeth Seton—Mission of Education: Faith and Willingness to Risk". *Vincentian Heritage* 17, no. 3 (1996). Available from DePaul University, Chicago: https://via.library.depaul.edu/vhj/vol17/iss3/.

McNeil, Betty Ann, D.C. "Historical Perspectives on Elizabeth Seton and Education: School Is My Chief Business". *Journal of Catholic Education* 9, no. 3 (2006).

Melville, Annabelle M. *Elizabeth Bayley Seton 1774–1821.* Edited by Betty Ann McNeil, D.C. Hanover, Pa.: The Sheridan Press, 2009. Available from DePaul University, Chicago: https://via.library.depaul.edu/seton_bio/.

Metz, Judith, S.C. "A Charity Spirituality for Educators". *Review for Religious* 67, no. 3 (2008).

Michaud, Nathaniel, ed. "Elizabeth Seton: Bridging Centuries Bridging Cultures", papers from The Seton Legacy symposium of 1996/1997, *Vincentian Heritage* 18, no. 2 (1997). Available from DePaul University, Chicago: https://via.library.depaul.edu/vhj/vol18/iss2/.

Michaud, Nathaniel, ed. "Elizabeth Seton in Dialogue with Her Time and Ours", papers from The Seton Legacy symposium of 1992, *Vincentian Heritage* 14, no. 2 (1993). Available from DePaul University, Chicago: https://via.library.depaul.edu/vhj/vol14/iss2/.

O'Donnell, Catherine. *Elizabeth Seton: American Saint.* Ithaca, N.Y.: Cornell University Press, 2018.

O'Neill, Alice Ann, S.C. "Elizabeth Bayley Seton, Teacher: A Legacy of Charity Education". *Vincentian Heritage* 29, no. 2 (2009). Available from DePaul University, Chicago: https://via.library.depaul.edu/vhj/vol29/iss2/.

Poole, Marie, D.C., trans. and ed. *Vincent de Paul: Correspondence, Conferences, Documents.* 14 vols. New York: New City Press, 1985–2014. Available from DePaul University, Chicago: https://via.library.depaul.edu/coste_en/.

Roman, José María, C.M. *St. Vincent de Paul: A Biography.* Translated by Joyce Howard, D.C. London: Melisende, 1999.

Sullivan, Louise, D.C., trans. and ed. *Spiritual Writings of Louise de Marillac.* New York: New City Press, 1991. Available from DePaul University, Chicago: https://via.library .depaul.edu/ldmlcd/.

White, Charles I. *Life of Mrs. Eliza A. Seton: Foundress and First Superior of the Sisters or Daughters of Charity in the United States of America.* Baltimore, Md.: John Murphy and Co., 1859.

INDEX

Abraham, 60

affectionate heart of Elizabeth,
36–37, 43, 53–57, 180,
196–97, 206, 209, 224, 228

America. *See also* Baltimore;
Sisters of Charity of Saint
Joseph's
arrival of Vincentians
(Congregations of the
Mission) in, 171
British colonies in, 11
Catholic Church in, 66–67
Elizabeth's relation to,
33–34
first apostolic community
in, 31
parochial school system in,
27, 32
saints from, 33–34
Sulpicians in, 17

apostolates. *See also* Daughters
of Charity of St. Vincent
de Paul
educational, 32, 67, 171, 198,
203–4
lay apostolate, 171
of saints, 59
Vincentian, 24, 197

aridity, 164–65

Assumption, 128–29

Augustine of Hippo, Saint,
246

Babade, Pierre, 75, 79, 93, 188,
191, 264, 269

Baltimore. *See also* Carroll,
John
Babade in, 269
Bonapartes of, 270
Bruté in, 214, 218
Catholic education in, 67
Cecilia in, 188, 189
Dubois in, 219, 271
Dubourg in, 16, 190
Elizabeth in, 66–70, 118,
190, 202, 247, 271
Hickey in, 223
Saint Mary's Seminary, 17,
68, 96, 190
Sulpicians in, 68, 271

baptism, 18, 28, 94, 242, 271

Barigazzi, Nicóla (brother of
Amabilia Filicchi), 109–10,
269

Bayley, Andrew Barclay (half
brother of Elizabeth), 188

Bayley, Catherine Charlton
(mother of Elizabeth), 8, 11,
41, 42, 179, 269, 273

Bayley, Catherine Charlton
(Kitty) (sister of Elizabeth),
8, 11, 41, 269

Bayley, Charlotte Amelia
Barclay (stepmother of
Elizabeth), 8, 42, 64, 269